Twisting Throttle

AMERICA

Twisting Throttle

AMERICA

MIKE HYDE

HarperCollins*Publishers*

National Library of New Zealand Cataloguing-in-Publication Data

Hyde, Mike, 1956-

Twisting throttle America : a Kiwi's hilarious trip around
America on the smell of an oily rag / Mike Hyde.

ISBN 978-1-86950-747-3

1. Hyde, Mike, 1956-—Travel—United States. 2. Motorcycle touring
—United States. 3. United States—Description and travel. II. Title.

917.304—dc 22

First published 2009
HarperCollins*Publishers (New Zealand) Limited*
P.O. Box 1, Auckland 1140

ISBN: 978 1 86950 747 3
Cover design by Alicia Freile, Tango Media
Cover images: American flag by Hudyma Natallia / Shutterstock.com;
all other photographs courtesy of Mike Hyde
Internal text design and typesetting by Springfield West
Printed by Griffin Press, Australia

70gsm Classic used by HarperCollins*Publishers* is a natural, recyclable product made
from wood grown in sustainable forests. The manufacturing processes
conform to the environmental regulations in the country of origin, Finland.

Dedication

For Joe Lloyd

My father-in-law, Joe, lives in Shropshire, England. He sent daily texts of support. He didn't have a computer but knew where I was every step of the way by plotting progress in his US road atlas. This was his sort of adventure.

Contents

Contents

Preface

THE CABIN LIGHTS are dimmed as the plane descends into Honolulu. I look out of the window and see a jumbled mass of city lights that abruptly end in darkness at what has to be the water's edge. Isn't Pearl Harbour down there somewhere? It's always the same slightly tense feeling flying into a foreign city at night.

The moment the plane comes to a rolling halt, there's a loud *ding* as the seatbelt sign goes off. The inside of the plane erupts in a jostling crush of passengers stooping low under the overhead lockers, twisting up to lift down their carry-on and then forced to remain hunched and motionless for 10 minutes as the queue inches down the aisle. For the past 14 hours we have sat penned in, so why the stampede the moment the handbrake comes on? But then this is Hawaii. Bronzed hula girls waiting to place a scented lei around our necks. The sound of ukuleles and the scent of frangipani no doubt wafting throughout the terminal just down the air bridge. Why would you want to spend a moment more than is necessary in this stuffy steel tube when tropical smoothies and Waikiki Beach are minutes away? I leap up to grab my helmet and join the jostling jostlers.

My eyes briefly meet those of a German lady in the seat over the aisle from mine. We haven't spoken, but I hate her with a passion that threatens to stop any plans I one day may have to ride around Europe. Let me complain — sorry, explain.

As the plane took off she pointed to the ceiling and said to all around her, 'Let's go, *ja!*' Thereafter, this woman completely dominated the time of the two cabin crew who had our whole cabin to service. When the plane crossed the international dateline, she pressed the crew-call button and asked what she should do with her watch. Her gluten-free meal contained gluten, naturally. A stewardess more or less filled out the *frau's* US immigration card for her, and I just knew what was going to happen when the choice of wine was presented. It is an aircraft. There is no wine cellar in the avionics bay. Thus you have a choice of white or red. 'And vot is ze vite?' 'Sauvignon Blanc, ma'am.' 'I take ze Chardonnay.' Sitting less than a metre away, I was a captive audience to this awkward traveller. As the plane touched down, she clapped as if the pilot had made some revolutionary manoeuvre.

'What's your business in the US, sir?' I crash back to reality, standing bleary-eyed and hopeful in front of an Immigration officer. He looks Hawaiian, but could be Mexican. 'I'm riding a motorcycle around 50 states in 60 days and this is state number one.' 'Oh my God — Twisting Throttle. Sir, you are most welcome in the US. It's an honour to have you. Boys, look who's coming in! Welcome to Hawaii, Mr Throttle, and here are some free smoothie vouchers.' What he actually said was 'Really? Show me your return ticket.'

And so it was that, a little frostily I thought, I was ushered into America. If you're from a friendly country you get a visa-free entry pass for 90 days. There is zero tolerance for overstayers. Be there on Day 91 and that's it for you for future entry. So I wasn't going to be able to hang around. 50 states in 60 days. Piece of cake. How it rolled off the tongue. Sitting at a computer back home, spreadsheeting the mileage, endlessly researching and mapping the must-do motorcycle routes, how manageable and straightforward it had all seemed. Suddenly, standing alone in a crowd at the baggage carousel in Honolulu, clutching my helmet and water bottle, the magnitude of the job ahead struck home.

This is a story of a motorcycle ride around a very, very large country. Two years before, I'd ridden around the outside edge of Australia. It took 35 days and I rode 17,350 kilometres. This time the journey ahead was over 32,000 kilometres and I had proportionately less time. Not only that, there would be more bends, lower speeds, higher altitudes, busier traffic, and I'd be riding on the right. I couldn't afford to overrun my deadline of 60 days. I had a haircut booked with Johnny back home. You may scoff. This guy knows how to use clippers and, despite sort of shaving your head rather than snipping anything, he gets really booked up, he's that good. I can't afford to miss the appointment. The pressure to finish the ride in time preyed heavily on me.

America. The very name, although a non-term geographically, sits in the subconscious of all long-distance motorcyclists. Perhaps it's *Easy Rider* meets *Don Quixote*, the ghosts of Route 66, or just the images of US prairies, canyons and mountain passes that my generation grew up with. If I drew up a list of the 101 places I'd like to plant my side stand in before I die, 80 of them would be in the US. I was one of those anal kids who could name all 50 states. In short, it was a natural choice of motorcycling destination after Aussie. I just wanted to go there. The other thing to declare up-front is that I suffer from the Biggest Ball of Twine Syndrome — an obsession with places that claim bizarre things, most of them roadside attractions, perfect for highway travellers like me with a fetish for inane and highly dubious claims. Therefore, if you read on you will be taken to the birthplace not of George Washington but of Captain James T Kirk. Not to the famous battlefields of the Civil War, but to the monument of Mike The Headless Chicken. Not to the grave of John F Kennedy, but to the final resting place of Colonel Sanders. *Lonely Planet* skirts around important American icons like these, so I feel I have a duty to bring them into your lives.

So I'd crated up my Suzuki 1000cc V-Strom and shipped it to Vancouver, Canada, chosen starting point for the assault on the lower 48 states. I would rent bikes in Hawaii and Alaska. After I crossed the finishing line back in Vancouver, I'd ship the bike home again. The Suzuki, veteran of the Australian ride, wouldn't have been my first pick of touring bike, but it was three very important things. Japanese, reliable, and the only bike I owned.

So it was 10.30 p.m. on a balmy evening in Honolulu, and I was mulling over the best way to get into Waikiki from the airport. The German woman had just climbed into a taxi. I pity the driver. He'll be Vietnamese and she'll want to pay him in Euros. It will be a mess. But I can't be concerned with that. I have a lot of miles to ride and the journey starts now.

Chapter 1

Hawaii

Nickname: The Aloha State

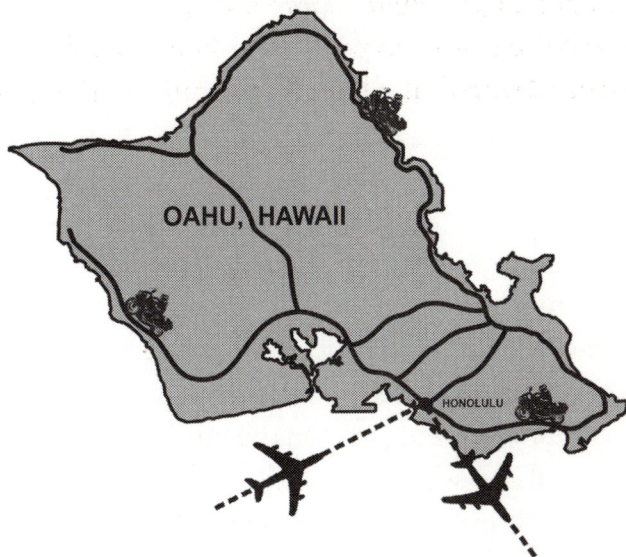

This state: 552 kilometres. Journey to date: 552 kilometres.

I'M SORRY TO START on a negative note, but I'm just a bit too old for backpacker hostels. As I'm on a limited budget, accommodation options for two nights in Honolulu — barring sleeping on the beach — led me to a hostel up an alley up a side street in Waikiki. A block towards the beach were Prada, Chanel and Louis Vuitton stores. I had the top bunk in a room with eight bunks. It was pan-gender, had a shower and a ceiling fan that wouldn't turn off.

I paid my $14 and got shown to the room. Around my bunk was a plastic curtain decorated with palm trees. By the time I made it in from the airport, found the side street, found the alley, got someone to come to open the security gate, and found the office, it was midnight. All eight bunk beds were booked and there was luggage strewn around the room. But at midnight I was the only one there. Should I climb onto my bunk, pull my curtain and go to sleep like the elderly person I felt like? Or wander back out onto the pulsating streets of Waikiki, roam around the bars, find a club, drink lots of rum, and stagger back at 4.00 a.m. with my 20-something room-mates? After all, this was Hawaii and Twisting Throttle had arrived.

I was asleep within 10 minutes and never heard them come in.

✪

Amidst snores and wheezing, I tiptoed out of the dormitory into the morning sunshine. At the excellently named Big Kahuna Motorcycles I had hired a BMW 1150R, possibly the only non-Harley on the island. It wasn't the best-kept bike, but it fired into life when I pressed the button, and I rode out into Honolulu.

The big question was which way to ride around the island of Oahu. Going counter-clockwise would put me on the seaside side of the sea, so I needed to get on the H1 freeway going east towards Diamond Head. Within minutes I was speeding *west* on the H1, going *away* from Diamond Head. I reassessed the whole Hawaii navigation thing. Frankly, how difficult can it be to find your way around an island a 20th the size of Belgium? The answer is . . . quite difficult. The way in and out of Honolulu is a maze of freeways. Once you're on the coast road, you're away, as it circumnavigates Oahu, except for the northwest corner of the island that cannot be rounded. Therefore there are two culs de sac. My mission was to ride every kilometre of road on Oahu in two days.

I pulled in at Waimanalo Beach to dip my toe in the ocean, just to be able to say I had been swimming with the sharks off Oahu. Lined up in the parking area were about 20 Harleys, with their owners fussing around each other's bikes like owners of all motorcycles do worldwide. My BMW stood out for its lack of finesse and drew a small crowd. The riders were all wearing yellow T-shirts emblazoned with *Rolling Thunder Motorcycle Club Hawaii*, reflective sunglasses, and bandanas (called 'doo-rags') on their heads. I, in turn, with a full-face helmet, looked like an astronaut. These guys spoke a sort of English sprinkled with Hawaiian phrases. Luckily, I can speak fluent Hawaiian after watching *Magnum PI* many years ago, so I could hold my own:

Rolling Thunder Leader:	Aloha, my friend, kakahiaka.
Translation to English:	*Welcome, my friend. Good morning.*
Me:	Aloha. I would like to greet you in Hawaiian. Male Ana E Pili Mai Pumehana Harley Davidson Kaua?
Translation to English:	*Hello. I would like to greet you in Hawaiian. So what are those pieces of s*** Harleys you're riding?*
Rolling Thunder Leader:	Ah, you speak fluent Hawaiian, brother. 'O wai kou inoa?
Translation to English:	*We've got a good one here, boys. What's your name?*
Me:	No Keia La, No Keia Po, A Mau Loa E Twisting Throttle Hoomau Maua Kealoha.
Translation to English:	*I am Twisting Throttle and I want to marry your sister, please.*
Rolling Thunder Leader:	Mahalo nui loa. Kipa hou mai.
Translation to English:	*Thank you very much. May you come to visit us again some day.*
Me:	Ko Aloha Makamae E Ipo.
Translation to English:	*Sweetheart, you are so precious.*
Rolling Thunder Leader:	Aloha 'oe, dickhead. Pomaika`i.
Translation to English:	*Farewell, rider. Be safe.*

Spurred on by the unexpected bonding with a local riding club, I rode away from Waimanalo Beach full of *joie de vivre* and loving Hawaii. The coast road surged around headlands with waves crashing on the jagged rocks below. To my left were enormous escarpments or cliffs, covered in a rainforesty type of tropical vegetation. I could have been riding in Colombia. I reached the town of Kailua, took a wrong turn, and ended up at the gates of a military base. Rejoining the Kamehameha Highway, I rode on to Oahu's North Shore where I was metres away from a classic palm-fringed beach with white sand, bikinis and windsurfers. Suddenly, without any warning, the heavens opened and I was drenched. It was a bizarre downpour, all over in less than five minutes. I tucked in behind a van with surfboards on the roof. It had a bumper sticker that said *You Go Your Way, I'll Go Maui.*

Just after the small settlement of Kahuku, I passed two very important road turn-offs. The first was Nudist Camp Road, but I didn't have time to ride down to investigate what the sign meant. The second was Charlie Road, leading off to the left up a hill but closed to the public. The hill is Opana Hill, and it has a history. Listen to this, it's incredibly interesting. When the Japanese attacked Pearl Harbour, a lot of the planes flew over the coast of Oahu right at this point. There was a small two-man radar station on the top of Opana Hill, and at 7.00 a.m. on the morning of 7 December 1941 Privates George Elliott and Joe Lockard were up there fiddling about with the radar machine. Suddenly the screen lit up like a Christmas tree. There were green dots pinging all over it, and they were swarming their way fast. George picked up the phone and rang their base in Honolulu at Fort Shafter. The officer on duty there was Lieutenant Kermit Tyler. He had just come on duty and it was his second day on the job. Tradition had it that when a group of American B-17 bombers was returning to base, the local radio station would broadcast Hawaiian music all night as a sort of 'welcome home, lads' thing. When Tyler had driven in to work, his car radio had been blaring out 'Hula Moon', so he'd assumed a flight of B-17s was on the way. Thus when Opana Hill radioed in a warning about lots of planes coming, he took them to be the B-17s. He radioed back Opana with the now immortal words: 'Don't worry about it.'

There was a naval hearing about the whole early-warning mess. Kermit Tyler kept his job, as he was deemed to have been ill-equipped for the post due to lack of training. 'Hula Moon' went to No. 1, and the nudist camp grew a tall hedge.

By now I was halfway around the island at Waimea, still on the coast, and hungry. There was the usual line-up of fast-food places, including a couple of local eateries called Shrimp Station and Barefoot Burgers. I was looking for somewhere to try the famous Hawaiian fish Humuhumunukunukuapua'a. Any fish that has nine 'U's in it has to be worth tasting, especially if it comes with fries and lemon. I settled on a stall that sold cold watermelon cut up into chunks the size of bricks. It was delicious. I have the stains on my T-shirt to this day.

I rode until the road ended. This was the first of two dead-ends on Oahu, stopping you from completing a full circuit of the island. I was at Dillingham Airfield looking down a dirt track which rounds the cliffs on the northwestern corner of Oahu. On my Suzuki I might have attempted it, but caution reined me in on this rented BMW road bike. The H2 freeway surged right down the middle of Oahu and I was looking out for the turn-off to Lualualei Naval Reservation and Kolekole Pass, which is a winding road over a low saddle that would put me on the leeward side of the island. The road, which bisects a naval station, was closed to the public. In fact a large part of Oahu is devoted to military installations that are off-limits. I reached Honolulu and exited the H2 on freeway H3, which crossed the narrow part of Oahu back over the north coast again.

This is where my tunnel obsession had its birthplace. There are twin tunnels called Tetsuo Harano through which the dual-laned H3 swished and spilled out high up the mountainside overlooking Kaneohe Bay. Then there was an awesome cliff-hugging twin viaduct, a concrete masterpiece of road engineering, which took the freeway down to the Hospital Rock tunnels and then to the coast. I immediately turned around and rode back across the island, this time on the Likelike Highway and the Wilson twin tunnels. Reaching Honolulu, I turned around for a third time and rode back to the north coast — this time on the Pali Highway via Pali Tunnel No. 1 there, and, needing to get back to Honolulu, Pali Tunnel No. 2 on the return leg.

I accept that this is coming across as slightly compulsive. Criss-crossing Oahu four times purely for the excitement of whooshing through mile-long road tunnels punched through the rainforest-cloaked mountainsides of the Koolau Range. Myself, I'd call it tunnel vision.

The end of my first riding day of 60 in America was drawing to a close as I wound back down into Waikiki. I followed the signs to Pearl Harbour, knowing that the visitor centre would be closed but at least wanting to glimpse the famous Arizona Memorial across the water. The car park was empty, and I parked the bike in a space closest to the harbour's edge.

At that moment a black-and-white police cruiser nosed into the car park and stopped just inside the entrance. The driver, naturally wearing sunglasses, just looked out his window at me, some 100 metres away. I carried on messing about with my camera and tripod, wondering what his concerns were. I purposely fussed about for 15 minutes just to see how long the cruiser would stay there observing. It was 15 minutes. The cop sat motionless inside his motionless car, just staring over at me. I loaded up, pretending to ignore his presence so that he wouldn't see me rattled. I rode out of the car park unnecessarily close to the cruiser, but as an innocent citizen I was a bit miffed about the attention. I lowered my tinted visor so that he wouldn't be able to see my face, just to even the score. As I passed his window, I stared at him staring at me. There was no acknowledgement from either of us, and I briefly wondered if the show of chest-puffing was that good an idea. Finally, in my mirrors I saw the police cruiser pull out of the car park and drive away. If I was on a Japanese bike in Pearl Harbour I could probably understand the antipathy, but this was a German one. Nonetheless, I resolved to be a little more circumspect with law enforcement for the rest of the trip.

My second night in the backpackers hostel was as successful as the first. At 1.00 a.m. I was alone in the dormitory, feigning sleep behind my palm-tree curtain. It felt like I was in Zombie Motel where the inmates slept during the day. And the young backpackers in my room probably did. Right now they were somewhere out there in downtown Waikiki. If I was 21, single, hormones jumping around and out for fun, I wouldn't have come to Hawaii for the tunnels.

Day Two on Oahu and I had the final dead-end to explore. That was the Farrington Highway up the leeward western coast as far as the road end at Kaena Point State Park. Riding out of Honolulu I felt I was by now a freeway pro. Day One had blown away some nervy cobwebs, and I had some more tunnels to look forward to before handing back the bike to Big Kahuna and getting to the airport.

Halfway up the Farrington, it hosed down. What I mean by hosing down is it absolutely hosed down. This was my second drenching in

Hawaii. The rain was so hard that the highway flooded in minutes and cars pulled over to wait it out. Screeching to a halt under the veranda of a fruit shop, I found myself looking at a display of Smooth Cayenne. What's that, you ask? Smooth Cayenne? Surely you know . . . *Ananas comosus*? The Bromeliad? La Piña? Dole? It's one of Hawaii's major food export crops, and I'm not referring to the macadamia nuts shipped to every duty-free shop in airports around the world. Pineapples are grown everywhere in central Oahu, up on a plateau in the middle of the island where the Dole plant is located. I'd ridden past it the day before, and briefly thought about calling in to see if they sold pineapple lumps. I caught sight of a Dole staff member at the door to the visitor centre and factory shop dressed as a giant smiley pineapple character, forcing people to have a hug and a photo, and rode on.

The incredible downpour stopped as suddenly as it had started. Traffic started moving again, and within 10 minutes the highway was bone-dry. No wonder Hawaii has the wettest place on Earth: Mt Waialiali on the neighbouring island of Kauai, where it rains 362 days of the year — and I was only 150 kilometres away from it. I hadn't packed my wet-weather gear, and I began to wonder if my research and planning were as good as I'd thought.

Riding back to Honolulu to drop off the BMW at the rental office, I was happy I had covered every arterial road on Oahu. Coming into the city on my old friend the H3 freeway, the lure of one more criss-cross through the tunnels was too great, and I carved off on the Pali Highway.

I was glad not to be spending another backpackery night. You can only feel like a grandpa so much of the time. And speaking of feeling elderly, here's another observation of Hawaii. Virtually all motorcycle riders do not wear helmets. In fact, most bikers were wearing not a lot of anything else. The standard riding apparel seemed to consist of sandals, shorts, a sleeveless vest or tank top, and reflective sunglasses. And these weren't just scooter riders beetling around the Waikiki streets. On the freeways I saw riders of very large bikes, hair streaming out behind them, looking very, very cool. In the US, helmets are compulsory in only 20 of the 50 states. Most of those are the populous eastern-seaboard states. So on 60% of America's roads you can throw away the lid and look cool. I was riding in T-shirt, jeans and boots, with no gloves, on a side of the road I wasn't used to. That was enough risk-taking for the time being. I kept the helmet fastened.

As I browsed the macadamia nuts displays in duty-free at Honolulu Airport, I looked back on this, my opening state of 50. An excellent start to the ride, but I was missing my own bike. The reunion in Vancouver was four days away, and I had some kilometres to cover before then. My flight to Anchorage, Alaska, was called for boarding. I guessed I wouldn't be riding through pineapple and sugar-cane plantations on the way to Fairbanks. I just hoped there'd be a tunnel or two.

Chapter 2

Alaska

Nickname: The Last Frontier State

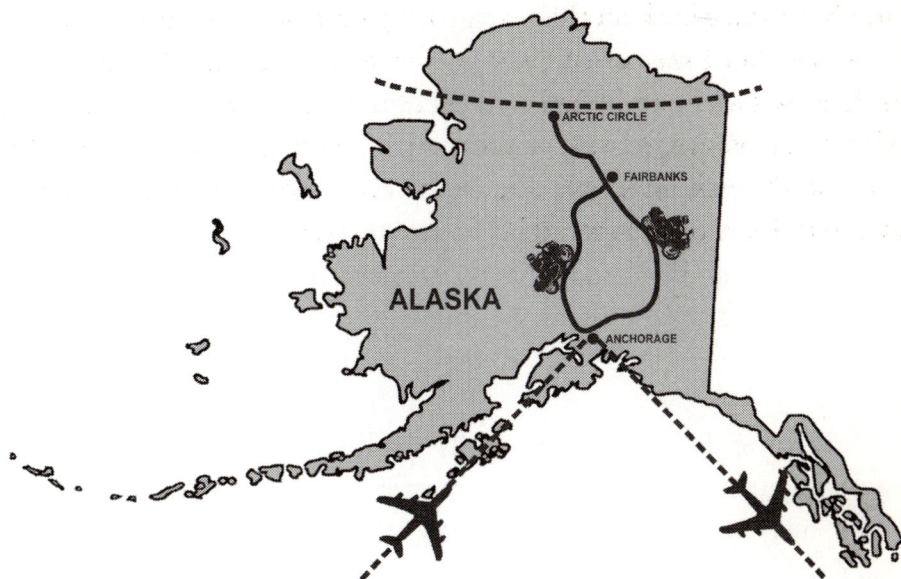

This state: 1,991 kilometres. Journey to date: 2,543 kilometres.

THE PLACE: ALASKA AIRLINES flight at 30,000 feet above the British Columbia coastline en route to Anchorage. The time: 10.00 a.m. The source of aggravation: Mason. I was sitting in the window seat, with a conversation-less couple effectively trapping me there for the five-hour flight from Seattle to Anchorage. I knew we were over some of the most spectacular scenery on Earth, but looking out the window I saw a blanket of grey cloud and my own reflection. Which meant my sole source of entertainment was Mason. To explain.

Our seats were right at the back of the plane. I don't know if this is true, but I've heard that airlines tend to place families with young children at the back to minimize disruption. That's the curse of booking on the internet: you don't find out about these things until it's too late. Mason was an American kid aged about eight or nine. He was sitting in the row behind, but on the aisle. His sister was next to him, but his mother was over the other side of the aisle with a young infant. This was Mason's main advantage. His mother was out of immediate strike range and he knew it. 'Mason, I'm having a hard time understanding your behaviour right now, honey.' I looked out at the grey blankness that was Alaska and tried to think about what lay in store for Twisting Throttle. But all I could focus on was how 'twisting' and 'throttle' were actions I'd love to use in conjunction with Mason's neck.

The moment the plane dropped out of the greyness and bumped onto the runway at Anchorage all murderous thoughts disappeared, as the four days in Alaska were about to commence. Had the kid been standing under my overhead locker I might have been tempted to let him wear my helmet, if you get my drift. But I had other preoccupations — a Kawasaki KLR650 waiting for me at Alaska Rider Rentals near the airport.

The first things I checked were the tyres. Enduro tyres fitted. Excellent. The Arctic Circle was 600 kilometres north of Anchorage, entailing a 300-kilometre return stretch on gravel and clay on the infamous Haul Road north of Fairbanks.

But there was a lot of riding to do before then, and I hit the road out of Anchorage like a madman, thinking I had 270 kilometres ahead of me, to Denali, in fading light. In fact it didn't get dark until 11.30 p.m., being so far north. The main highway to Wasilla, in the shadow of the Chugach Mountains, was fast, and I guessed I was competing with what passed for Anchorage's commuter traffic. At the Matanuska River the highway forked, and I turned north towards the Denali National Park. Even in my padded riding jacket and pants, I could feel the creeping cold. It was an incredible contrast to Hawaii just 24 hours earlier.

The highway tracked next to the Alaska Railroad and the Susitna River. At Willow it emptied out onto barren plains and began a climb up into the Denali National Park. There were a few spits of rain and absolutely no other vehicles on the road. My thoughts turned to fuel. It dawned on me that I might have a problem: the gauge showed less than half-full, and I had no idea what fuel was available on the road up to

Fairbanks. Was there even a town on the way? Alaska has the largest area of all 50 states, but with the fourth smallest number of people, making for a population density of one person per square mile. And the number of those who owned a petrol station out in the boondocks had to be few. I couldn't believe how badly I had planned for the consequences of that sobering statistic. But surely Denali National Park, which attracts tourists by the busload, had fuel?

I passed a moose-warning sign, which indicated that moose were prone to jumping out in front of vehicles. I've since found out that so far this year there had been 236 moose accidents in Alaska, with two drivers killed. I suspect that, if I rounded a bend and slammed into a moose at 120 km/h then, out of the two of us it wouldn't be me who ended up with a slight headache. I found myself scanning ahead on the sides of the road, trying to work out if I'd see a moose, deer, elk or bear if it was grazing and then suddenly bolted across my path. I concluded that it was a lottery and best not to think about it.

As the highway plugged north through interminable tundra-like scenery, I knew Mt McKinley was over there in the mist somewhere. North America's highest mountain is actually higher than Everest, if you're talking about rise distance from the plateau it sits on rather than sea level. There are the usual amazing tales of those pioneers who climbed McKinley in the early days before crampons, Kendal Mint Cake and oxygen. The one I like the best is the four men in 1910 who got to the summit carrying a bag of doughnuts and a thermos of cocoa each. I for one would have married off my sister for a hot cocoa and doughnut as I stood by the bike in the official Mt McKinley lookout, peering through the gloomy twilight into the clouds, pleading with my imagination to see something. In the end I snapped off a photo of the sign and made a mental note to buy the fridge magnet in Fairbanks.

Finally, I reached my campsite for the night at Cantwell. It was by a rushing creek, and was quite idyllic in a cold Alaskan way. On the bank of the creek was a roaring fire, and around it sat seven young men who immediately jumped up when I came in on the bike. They were a group of Jewish friends from New York who had chosen to come here as the most out-of-the-way place they could think of, for outdoor pursuits and to replenish their friendship. 'You like pasta, my friend?' I was starving and could answer only one way. 'Is the Pope a—' They didn't seem to mind the near-miss. Their pasta simmered over the fire in a billycan. It had everything in it, including chunks of what I guessed was road-kill moose. 'Eat, my friend, eat. Moshe, more pasta for the bike guy.' Shy, Aaron, Moshe, Eitan, Aron, Ariel and Noah mostly went to the same undergrad at Yeshiva University in New York. Messing about with the fellas was a heart-warming end to a cold day in Alaska and it wasn't just the fire.

The next morning when I emerged from my tent and packed up the bike, the boys were out to it. The fire was cold and the dawn was moody and sulky. It wasn't raining yet, but looked like it was just waiting for me to get on the road. I picked my way down to the creek and brushed my teeth in the frigid rushing water. The rock I was standing on gave way and my left boot went in up to my knee.

I rode north on the Kawasaki, wondering about what the day would bring. This was to be a 1,000-kilometre day up to the Arctic Circle and back to Fairbanks. The last thing I needed was sleety rain. It started to sleet and rain. I gritted my way to Nenana where I saw the bizarre sight of waters from the Tanana River flooding the deserted streets.

I started to climb a range of hills, still on the George Parks Highway to Fairbanks. The summit was shrouded in a blanket of the densest fog I have ever experienced on a bike. In second gear, I wound through the hills on a slippery, wet road in near-freezing temperatures. The assault on the Arctic Circle looked impossible, but I reminded myself that if Hillary had been so easily put off by a little bad weather he'd have spent two days sitting in Starbucks in Kathmandu. A car transporter blasted out of the mist and I was soaked in its vortex of spray. My visor was fogged up, so to be able to see I opened it a crack and let in the misty, cold sleet.

Coasting into Fairbanks I had one thing on my mind and it comprised the words 'coffee', 'hot' and 'lotsa', not necessarily in that order. Out of the grey gloom emerged a beacon of hope. It was called Carl's Grill. Ten minutes later I was wolfing down a Monsta Breakfast Combo, being a cheese melt on sourdough, bacon, eggs, hash browns and stewed coffee. I couldn't have been closer to Heaven. I fuelled up and reviewed the task ahead. The Arctic Circle was 240 kilometres north of Fairbanks. There is an unsealed road officially called the Dalton Highway, but locally known as the Haul Road due to its main purpose being for trucks to haul freight to and from the Prudhoe Bay oil fields on the shores of the Arctic Ocean, as well as being a supply road for the Trans-Alaska pipeline. The road is one of the most isolated in the US. There are no towns, and services are haphazard. The road is impassable in the wet, as it is a clay base with a gravel surface. In short, you wouldn't pop up there for a Sunday drive. It sounded fantastic.

I bargained on being able to get to the Yukon River crossing where there is a petrol pump. A fuel-up there would get me to the Arctic Circle and then back to refuel at Yukon. I went through the mental checklist of expedition essentials. Tyres: suitable. Fuel: available. Food: the Monsta Breakfast Combo should sustain me for the day. Fridge magnet: see what souvenir shops I come to.

Shortly after leaving Fairbanks, I pulled into a viewing point for the Trans-Alaska pipeline. I wasn't to know it at the time, but the pipeline was to become a close and welcoming friend throughout the day. At this viewing point, the pipeline came right up to the road and you could touch it for free. The pipeline runs 1,300 kilometres from Prudhoe Bay down to the southern Alaskan port of Valdez, and 720,000 barrels a day flow down it. Since its construction in 1977, the pipeline has suffered damage from earthquakes, permafrost, forest fires, moose rage, and the odd drunken local with too much time and nitroglycerine on his hands.

But the lady who manned the visitor viewpoint had the best story. Seven years ago a local troublemaker called Daniel Lewis fired a shotgun into a weld on the pipeline, and to his surprise out spurted a stream of bubblin' crude. Black Gold. Texas Tea. Now the first thing you know old Jed's a mill— Sorry, wrong oil story. Twenty acres of tundra were polluted by the spill of 6,000 barrels of gushing oil, and the pipeline shut down for four days during the clean-up and repair. The police started to look for the culprit and rounded up all 30 townspeople of Livengood. They finally singled out Lewis from the line-up: he was a known vandal and the townspeople were all pointing to him, but the clincher was you could only see the whites of his eyes. He got 10 years and the cellblock nickname of Slippery Dan.

The road north from Livengood was beautifully sealed, and there was not one other vehicle on it. It wound through pine forests, open tundra and as barren a landscape as you'd ever see. The surface had now dried from the morning's deluge, and the bike surged around wide, sweeping bends with a song in its twin-cylinder heart. The pipeline would appear for miles, then vanish inexplicably into the ground or around the opposite side of a hillside to the road. I found myself looking out for it, and strangely when it came into sight it gave me a slight boost of comradeship.

Eventually, after 130 kilometres on this, the Elliott Highway, I reached the end of the seal and the official start of the Dalton Highway or Haul Road. A small car was pulled up by the sign, and I chatted with the occupants as we all took photographs. It was a French couple in a rental, and they were fretting as their rental agreement banned them driving any further up the Dalton. Not only that, but they had miscalculated their fuel and were well over half a tank down from Fairbanks to where we were. I can understand only enough French to be able to get directions to a railway station, but the body language told me she was a fraction upset with him. Potentially running out of fuel in a remote part of Alaska in a small car with no cellphone coverage probably wasn't her idea of an idyllic holiday break away. All I could offer was the comfort that eventually there'd be trucks heading towards Fairbanks, and that they should just start driving back, switching off the engine on the downhill stretches and hope for the best. I would be back this way in 10 hours myself, so if they were parked roadside I'd look out for them. I rode away up the Dalton with her waving her arms at him in a fashion that suggested they'd be sleeping in separate beds that night.

The initial surface of the highway was slightly slippery, but I found that, by riding out of the tyre tracks in the centre of the road on the gravel berm, I had good traction and the extra thrill of the back wheel skewing around a bit. By now the pipeline was a comforting and constant 10 metres off to the side of the road. I could look ahead for miles and see the road undulating to the horizon across the open tundra. There were purple wildflowers, and I strained my eyes to spot some wildlife.

After almost two hours, I crested a ridge and saw below the wide Yukon River like a silver gash across the landscape. The road wound down to the bridge spanning the river at Yukon Crossing, my fuelling point. I parked up at the bridge to let two massive trucks past. They were both tankers of some kind and covered in dirt. The drivers waved and I was reminded of the protocols for who has first claim on this road. Here's what the pecking order is. Trucks. Anything else. The road is not your average tourist drive. It is a functional, no-fuss route to and from the Arctic Ocean for freight. The predominant users are big trucks hauling heavy loads and going fast. The road is not two lanes wide. Simply put: if you don't understand your place in the food chain of road users, then you are road bait. Motorcycles are dispensable on a road like this, and I adopted the well-publicized policy of acting as if you are a guest of the trucks. I can be as deferential as the next road user, so always pulled over and waved heartily as they got close. I got return waves and a slight slowing, together with the trucks' indiscernibly pulling to the right to give me room as well. It felt heart-warming, as if I had climbed a few rungs on the ladder of the road-user hierarchy.

At Yukon Crossing there is a petrol pump and a sort of café. But, bizarrely, it had no food that I could see. Fortunately, I didn't feel like eating anyway, as adrenaline was riding high. The ride was perfect in every respect. Adventurous, without being overly risky. Remote and isolated, but within calling distance of help if anything happened.

Several kilometres after Yukon, I rode across a bridge over No Name Creek. The road became noticeably harder to ride, with berms of clay and mud replacing the gravel. The solution was to throttle on and go faster. The bike found a line in the clay and I pounded along in a mesmerizing rhythm. I passed a fellow motorcyclist on a large BMW 1150GS Adventure bike, all kitted out as if he was riding around the world. He may well have been, but I never found out as the rider didn't stop. I slowed to pull over and have a chat, but the other bike continued on with just a brief wave. It was like Livingstone meeting Stanley in the jungle and pushing past him with a brief nod. On the other hand the bike was moving abnormally slowly, and it looked like the rider was struggling with the loose and boggy clay to the point he didn't want to lose momentum. This wasn't to be the last time I'd meet that bike.

✯✯

Finally, 240 kilometres after leaving Fairbanks, I reached the famous Arctic Circle sign. I had built it up in my mind to be an achievement on a par with that of Amundsen, but I found a mini-van there with Japanese teenagers taking turns to be photographed by the sign doing the peace fingers behind each other's heads. Still, it represented the northernmost point of my American ride, some 850 kilometres from Russia, and I was thrilled to dismount and take it all in while I queued for my access to the sign.

The Arctic Circle is one of five lines of latitude, or parallels, to circle the Earth. The others are the Tropics of Cancer and Capricorn, the Equator, and the Antarctic Circle. In Hawaii I had a near-miss with Cancer, as it runs between two of the islands. And as Baja, California, wasn't on my route, this parallel would have to remain unconquered territory for a while yet. Similarly, the Antarctic Circle would have to wait, but due to gradual changes in the tilt of the Earth's axis this circle of latitude is moving. The question is whether the Earth's axis is tilting faster than my cholesterol is going up. It may be a no-contest.

I took my own photo at the Arctic Circle sign using my tripod, which gave me 12 seconds to run back and pose like a polar explorer. In a shower of back-wheel-spinning gravel, I sputtered back out on to the Dalton and headed south back the way I had come. The pipeline was now on my left and I slowed my speed, wanting to enjoy this ride. It wasn't quite the midnight sun, but I was sufficiently far north for it to be light up to 11.30 p.m. Therefore I had a wonderfully extended riding day ahead of me. I fuelled up again at Yukon, noting there still wasn't any food in the café.

On the other hand it was more a truck stop, so perhaps you had to be a grizzled, polar, hat-wearing truckie to be able to order the Yukon Monsta Breakfast Combo.

Ten minutes after crossing the Yukon Bridge and climbing into the boreal forest on a plateau overlooking the Yukon basin, I saw the BMW rider pulled over in a lay-by. He was dismounting and waved at me as I passed. For the next 10 kilometres I debated whether I should have stopped to check on him. On one hand he seemed to be making very slow progress, as in the time I had been up to the Arctic Circle and back he had travelled only around 50 kilometres. But perhaps he had found the secret of getting food at Yukon and stopped there. Or had he run out of fuel or broken down? There is a code of conduct among motorcyclists that you never pass another rider who may need help. It's a matter of sorting out if they need help or have just stopped to take a photo. Racked with indecision, I turned around and rode back 10 kilometres to the clearing. He was still there. I took off my helmet and we shook hands. He was just taking a photo. He had made the trek up to Prudhoe Bay and was taking four days to do the round trip. We swapped ride notes, playing the usual subliminal game of one-upmanship as to who was doing the more epic journey, and shook hands again.

The ride back to Fairbanks was a lot shorter than I wanted it to be. I was enjoying the off-roading, and the KLR650 was the perfect machine to handle the greasy surface and patches of deep gravel. I didn't come across the French couple, now probably estranged, and wondered how they'd got on. Having had nothing to eat for 600 kilometres, I was hungry to the point of stomach cramps as I coasted downhill into Fairbanks. I found a cheap room in a hotel called the Captain Bartlett, and almost cried for joy when I saw a Denny's right next door. Within minutes, a chicken burger with double pickle, double fries and bottomless coke were consumed, and not for the first time that day I thought about Amundsen returning from his polar conquest. Hopefully his local Denny's was likewise open when he climbed off his sled.

That night I cleaned my muddy boots, riding pants and panniers in the shower at the Captain Bartlett. When I say 'night', I mean the smudgy greyness that existed between midnight and 3.00 a.m. Consider being a resident of Fairbanks. On 21 June the sun is up for 21 hours with 24 hours of usable daylight. Golf clubs never close. On 21 December the sun is up for two hours with five hours of usable daylight. You might as well not bother teeing off.

The next morning I rode away from the Captain Bartlett before the chambermaid could see the bathroom and fetch the manager. I rode into downtown Fairbanks and parked the bike in the triangular space created between the last parking space in a row of angle-parking spaces and the kerb. When I came out of the souvenir shop, magnet in hand, I found a piece of paper wedged under my seat. Thinking it was a bill from the Bartlett, I found it was a parking ticket for $40. A handy sticker on it said that if I didn't pay in five days the fine would double. The bike rental company had my credit card details, so fleeing Alaska wasn't an option. I couldn't believe the injustice. But if I complained directly to the mayor of Fairbanks, my parking ticket would be the least of her worries. Her name is Terry Strle. See, you don't know how to pronounce it either!

A short ride south from Fairbanks is North Pole. That's the town of North Pole, not the striped barber-pole 2,700 kilometres to the north. The town's biggest attraction is Santa Claus House. Its address is the corner of St Nicholas Drive and Rudolph Way. Outside, funnily enough, is the world's largest fibreglass statue of Santa. All the emergency services vehicles in town are either red or green, and candy canes adorn the lampposts. Santa Claus House runs its own website and online shopping portal. Their trademark product is the Original Letter from Santa for $7.50, or you can splash out another $2.50 for the Original Letter and Deed combo. But what I like most about this online shopping site is how you can buy variations of Santa's letter. For example, there's one for the 'difficult child', one for 'baby's first Christmas', and one for a 'not-so-good' adult. But my favourite version is the letter to a 'non-believer'. This must have been a tough one for Santa to write, wishing Merry Christmas to a kid who knows you don't exist. Anyway, what parent would put Santa under that sort of pressure by ordering one of these online? Probably a not-so-good one.

North Pole's post office receives thousands of letters a year from people wanting the town's postmark on their Christmas cards to family and friends. But as I climbed off the bike in the car park of Santa Claus House, I thought about the hundreds of thousands of kids' letters to Santa which end up here. Half a million letters arrive in December from all around the world. But the number is dropping as kids fire off emails to Santa instead. Websites have mushroomed, offering blogs to Santa and the elves. Some Santa sites have spam filters to block out persistent children who operate on the more-emails-more-presents theory. But the big unknown is: if I write to Santa at North Pole, will he reply? I was about to be able to put the question to the big guy himself. I went in.

Santa Claus House is an amazing emporium of everything Christmas. I picked my way, helmet in hand, through displays of lights, tinsel, decorations and snowy pine cones to the grotto. There he was. Astride a throne and alongside a diminutive Mrs Claus was the most authentic non-mall-like Santa I'd seen. He had a white mane of a beard and spectacles. I queued with several small children and finally got summoned by Santa, who looked suspicious. 'Howdy,' I said. 'And what's your name, young fella?' 'Twisting Throttle.' 'And what do you want for Christmas?' 'How about a new TPS for a Suzuki V-Strom?' Mrs Claus looked up at her husband. 'TPS?' He humoured her. 'Yes, dear: TPS. Throttle Position Sensor. It's a sensor that reads throttle position and sends that data as a varying voltage to the engine's computer for fuel-injector pulse width. You got the 04 or 05?' '04,' I replied. 'Right. You don't need a new TPS for Christmas, young man. Just loosen the hold-down screws and rotate the old TPS, thus changing its position relative to the primary throttle plates and therefore the voltage output.' 'What about a PlayStation then?' I could have chatted to Santa all day. I wanted to see what more he knew about fuel injection, but there was a line-up of kids and angry-looking mothers. I had used up my quota of Santa-time. 'Merry Christmas, young Throttle. Set the TPS to 1.125 volts at idle and see how you go.'

I rode away from Santa Claus House in North Pole thrilled with my encounter. I found out that the 500,000 letters to Santa are sent to the local high school, whose students try their best to reply. So if you're reading this, and you are a believer, please think twice before taking up Santa's time writing to him. He needs to bone-up on suspension, as I want to ask him, by email of course, how to add a pre-load spacer to the rear shock.

★★★

I was shaken out of my yuletide musings by two F16s screaming overhead. By the time the noise penetrated my helmet, the jets were specks on the horizon, wheeling around to make another pass over nearby Eielson Air Force Base. I now know that these F16s were part of the 18th Aggressor Squadron of the 354th Fighter Wing based at Eielson. Each plane costs $70 million. It can fly at 2,400 km/h, and in 60 seconds can climb 15 kilometres into the sky. All I could think, as I watched the two F16s scream low over the air-force base, was whether their TPS was adjusted correctly.

By this time I was riding in the company of a North Pole from North Pole called Rikki Homchick who had made contact with me after reading *Twisting Throttle Australia*. We reached Delta Junction where the highway splits. Highway 2 heads southeast to Canada, and Highway 4, otherwise known as the Richardson Highway, continues southwest back to Anchorage. But Delta represented a more significant destination, and I refer of course to that august eating establishment: Buffalo Bill's. Rikki was a platinum customer of Bill's and this was going to be his treat. Inside the restaurant is a huge buffalo head on the wall. It made you want to go back outside and see if the rest of the buffalo is hanging out the other side of the wall. I hung my helmet on its horn and we sat down. The menu in this diner was outstanding. There was all manner of grilled and fried food for this motorcycling culinary connoisseur, and I had a hard job choosing what sort of meat to have in my burger. In the end I decided to make this meal-stop an educational research one. Many of you will be wondering about the difference between buffalo and bison. Are they in fact the same animal? The answer is a resounding 'no'. There are clear differences, and here's what they are. Bison comes with a pickle, lettuce, melted cheese, and shoestring fries. With buffalo you get red onion, no cheese, and curly fries. It's good to be able to clear that up. By the time I left Alaska, I also wanted to be able to understand the difference between elk and caribou.

The buffalo and bison burgers at Delta weighed heavily within me for a long time. Adding to my sense of lethargy was the fact I was stationary in a long line of traffic at a road-construction site, having farewelled Rikki who turned back for home at North Pole. Here's the thing about American roadworks. It's not just a mile or so of road maintenance involving a few men in fluoro vests leaning on shovels and a digger or two. Almost without exception, their road-construction zones are like war zones with cones. The first notable feature is that you don't get to drive through these zones on your own. You have to follow a dedicated pilot vehicle which has a sign on the back saying: *Pilot Vehicle: Follow Me*. This vehicle, usually a pick-up, goes back and forth through the construction with a gaggle of cars behind it like a motorized pied piper. If the pilot vehicle goes into the opposite lane, then so do you. It knows the way. If it slows to 15 km/h, then so do you. If the driver knocks off for his tea break, then all you other drivers grab a mug and have a cuppa, too. The lesson in all this is that you have to observe the rules. If you get too impatient and step outside them, you incur the wrath of the construction-zone workers; and as they're the ones at the controls of large machinery that can pick up rocks, it doesn't pay to mess with them. I was to see the outcome of driver impatience later in my ride.

After clearing the construction, I rode into . . . into . . . well, nothing. I say 'nothing' because there almost isn't a way to describe the open, barren plateau between Delta and Paxson, in which I was a mere speck. It was inhospitable, yet exciting. Every so often there were fir trees in massive plantations. The Delta River looked frigid, and a low band of mist hid the far-off mountaintops. There were spectacular rainbows all over the place, and showers came and went. The odd thing was I didn't seem to be getting wet. It was like riding in Scandinavia — and I say that without having ridden in Scandinavia. The road was undulating and fast, and I notched up the speed taking silly risks on some of the corners. I recognized the devil-may-care signs creeping into my riding and buttoned off. Several small squirrels darted across the road, and I passed through an area with hundreds of miniature lakes. A stunning glacier in the near-distance plunged down a mountainside, and the ever-present Trans-Alaska pipeline came and went. We were both heading south. The pipeline to Valdez oil terminal, and Twisting Throttle to somewhere hopefully soon to call home for the night. I had no camping gear on the Alaskan leg of my journey, so I had to throw budget concerns to the wind and look for cheap accommodation.

I reached a town called Glennallen almost spent. It was nine o'clock and getting dusky. I saw a hotel called the Caribou Inn, and went in. Standing in front of me at reception were two Dutch guys who owned the Harleys outside. The receptionist explained she had two rooms left. One was in the main wing for $143 and the other was in the annex for $9. One had sheets, its own bathroom, little chocolates on the pillow, and cable TV. The other had a rubbish bin, a mattress, the communal shower down the hall, and a light with no bulb. I prayed the Harley boys would take the little chocolates. 'How many cable channels?' they asked. 'Fourteen.' 'We'll take it.' I could have kissed them. A $143 hit on my budget would have seen me pushing the bike back to Anchorage. I unloaded my gear onto the mattress in the annex and went to switch on the light. That's right: no bulb.

The menu posted outside the restaurant was enticing. They had caribou burgers. Call it poor metabolism, but I couldn't bring myself to eat buffalo, bison and caribou in one day. I just wasn't that carnivorous. I briefly considered the elk *pâté* and halibut chowder, but after the splurge on lunch at Delta I had no money left in the day's kitty. I went to bed in my cold, dark annex room at the Caribou Inn, cursing those Harley riders and wondering if they had eaten their chocolates.

My last day in Alaska dawned at 4.00 a.m. Without curtains the light streamed in, and I woke with a stiff neck and groaning stomach. I wondered if the restaurant did moose sausages. It was another bleakish day, but I found it strangely exhilarating despite the conditions. I rode out of Glennallen on Highway 1 pointing towards Anchorage.

Every so often I'd pass a sign as part of the Adopt A Highway programme. I wasn't to know it then, but that concept was all over the US. Here's how it works. Any individual or organization can sponsor a 2-mile section of highway. It costs nothing, but your job is to pick up litter at least three times a year within your adopted stretch of road. From both sides. The local authority in return provides you with safety vests, rubbish bags, and a roadside sign acknowledging your adoption. The agreement lasts three years. I had seen signs all along the Alaskan roads I had ridden and was warmed by the community spirit. I hadn't seen anyone actually picking up litter, but then again I hadn't seen any litter either. There are rules about who can pick up litter under this scheme. In some of the more remote areas you need to able to out-run animals, for example.

I sped past an Adopt A Highway sign that turned my head. It was sponsored by Raven Wolf Java Joint. Tell me that doesn't sound like a drug dealer in a cabin in the woods somewhere. Raven Wolf? Who or what is that? Within minutes I had my answer, as well as being introduced to another American cultural custom — that of the coffee kiosk. Off the road, in a lay-by in a grove of trees, sat a small hut decorated with Native Indian-looking bits and pieces, from kites to wooden eagles on sticks. This was the coffee — java to be specific — dispensing establishment belonging to Mrs R Wolf. These small kiosks, of which I was to come across hundreds in my trip around America, simply dole out cups of hot filtered coffee to drive-ups. You don't actually go in, as the kiosks are about as roomy as a dog kennel. You pull up at a sliding window and get your coffee-to-go. Don't ask for any muffins or caribou burgers, as the menu is what the proprietors call single-itemed. Coffee.

I dismounted next to a beaver carved out of a log and sidled up to the window. It slowly opened. A silver-haired lady stuck her head out. 'Morning.' 'Morning.' I took her to be Raven Wolf in person. She looked a bit Native Indian-ish, possibly Eskimo-ish, and I had a thousand questions about what she was doing here in this little coffee hut. 'Coffee?' 'Yes, please. Sounds good.' As she stared at me, her eyes became yellow and piercing. A far-off howl like a coyote made my blood run cold. Suddenly the old woman raised her head and let out an evil screech. She lifted her hand to point at me, and I could see that it was a gnarled talon with the claws of an eagle. 'You. Stranger,' the bird woman rasped, her lips protruding like a beak. 'I am the raven wolf. Many come to seek the raven yet find the wolf.' I turned to flee back to the bike, but the wooden animal carvings had come to life. Advancing slowly towards me were rodents and foxes. Another howl of death came from behind the cabin, this time a lot closer. 'Tell me, old woman, what is it you want from me?' '$4.50 for the coffee. Help yourself to sweetener.' I was jolted out of my dark thoughts and reached for my wallet. In fact, Mrs W was sweetness herself and made a living from selling coffee to travellers and hoping to upsell her carvings. Her pride and joy was a life-size bear. At times like this I'm glad I'm on a bike.

The final episode in this interesting roadside stop was that, as I was fussing around the bike, I kicked over my coffee. Raven was looking at me expectantly from the window of her hut but didn't see the spill, as it was on the far side of the bike. For the next 10 minutes I sat on my seat and pretended to sip from the empty cup, throwing her appreciative nods and thumbs-up signs. She seemed pleased. But I still didn't buy the wooden bear.

For the next two hours I rode through absolutely spectacular Alaskan terrain. The Matanuska Glacier came within 2 kilometres of the road. Anchorage residents drive up to the Matanuska for a day trip, it is that accessible. At the glacier lookout I met a couple touring on a Harley. They were from Fairbanks and had been planning the 1,200-kilometre round trip for years. It was taking them a week, which meant an average riding distance of 180 kilometres a day. I couldn't imagine how you'd ride either that slowly or take so many breaks. They asked me how far I was riding. I said I had been on the road three days from Fairbanks, omitting the Arctic Circle deviation. That lie was two things: vaguely true, and preserving their dream. The remaining 31,000 kilometres needn't be mentioned. They looked pleased and rode with me for 5 kilometres before pulling over at a rest area.

I was rapidly nearing Anchorage when a sudden downpour sent me careening into a café's car park for cover. As it was time for my daily meal, I shucked off my wet jacket and went in. The diner had the usual grill menu, but it wasn't the food that made this a wonderfully entertaining lunchtime distraction. Two odd things happened.

First, two young men at a nearby table became obsessed with the definition of a combo. They had ordered a BBQ bacon cheeseburger combo, but were frantic about whether it included fries. They carried on a conversation from their table with the counter girl, who couldn't find the words to convince them they had in fact ordered, and were shortly to receive, a combo including fries. Admittedly, the menu board above the counter was a bit ambiguous on that score. For $7.25, you could get a BBQ bacon cheeseburger combo. For $8.25, you could get a BBQ bacon cheeseburger *with fries*. So therefore — and this was both their point and that of the rest of us in the diner drawn into the debate — if the fries component was $1, then what formed the cheaper combo? If you got fries with the combo anyway, then why charge an extra $1 for the second option? Everyone in the diner waited with bated breath for what would happen. Had the boys paid $1 unnecessarily, or would the combo be the burger plus something other than fries? Time ticked slowly by. We all studied the table menu cards with heads down, but secretly our eyes were on the door from the kitchen waiting for the answer to the combo conundrum. The door opened and a girl came out carrying a tray. Thank God. There were fries on the plates and she gave the boys a $1 refund. The atmosphere noticeably lightened, but I steered away from any combo meal, that was for sure.

And then another bizarre event took place in this diner. An older couple walked in, went up to the counter and placed an order for some ribs. The odd thing was that the man kept completing his sentences with 'and that completes'. After giving the girl his order, he concluded 'and that completes our order'. The couple sat down at the table next to mine, and the man drank a glass of water, chatting to his wife. Then he said 'and that completes a good glass of water'. I put this down to linguistic coincidence until he looked out the window and remarked 'and that completes the rain shower by the looks'. I could have sat in this diner all day. What entertainment might the dinner traffic bring? I had finished my burger before their ribs came out, and I was itching to wait around to hear the inevitable 'and that completes a wonderful meal of ribs'. I rode way from that diner slightly unfulfilled, but smiling.

I returned the rented KLR650 to Alaska Rider Rentals undamaged and with an additional nearly 2,000 kilometres on the clock. I had trouble navigating manually to the hire company out near the airport, as street names in Anchorage are numbers and letters. For example, riding down 36th Ave I'd pass G Street and then H Street. Then into 40th Ave and across A Street and B Street. It was like playing battleships with myself. But I finally arrived at the depot, sinking a destroyer on the way, thus ending a brilliant ride around state #2.

I had seven hours to kill at Anchorage airport, before my flight down to Vancouver, and $2.80 to spend on dinner. I made the Starbucks muffin last an hour by eating one raisin every five minutes. It gave me something to do at 2.00 a.m. in the nearly deserted terminal.

And that completes . . . Chapter 2.

Chapter 3

Washington

Nickname: The Evergreen State

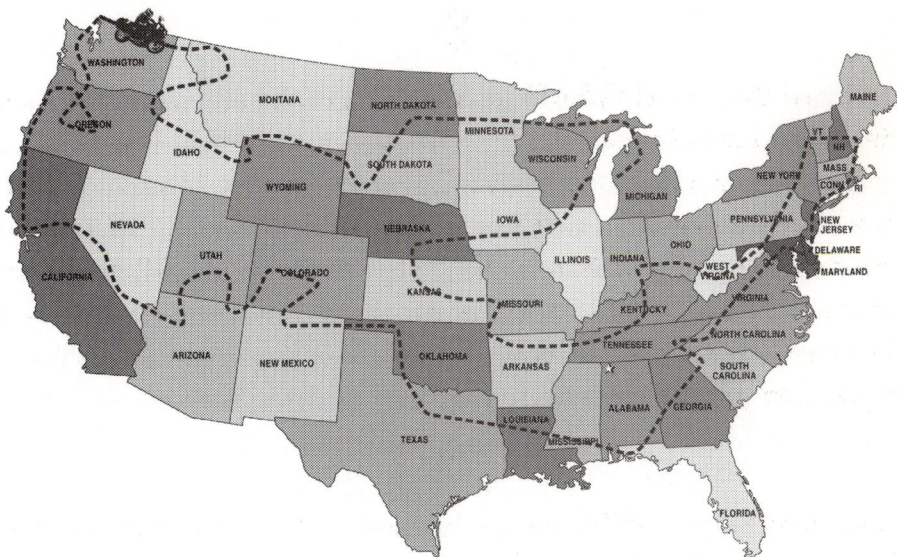

This state: 970 kilometres. Journey to date: 3,513 kilometres.

T HE PLANE TOUCHED DOWN at Vancouver after a seven-hour flight via Seattle. I should have been feeling the type of grottiness you feel after intermittent sleep throughout a flight, but I couldn't have been more hyped if I was on steroids. After all, this was the day of the reunion of Twisting Throttle and his machine. The Suzuki 1000 V-Strom — the same bike on which I had ridden around Australia — was waiting somewhere near the airport in a crate. It had been at sea for a month and in a freight yard for three weeks. It was in all probability very grumpy. I suspected that when I hooked up the battery and pressed the electric start button it would pout. If that happened, I would be forced to have words. Most bikes don't know the pleasure of a new clutch, rear shock, front and rear tyres, chain, two sprockets, heated grips, oil filter, air filter, brake pads, spark plugs, headlight bulb, and front fork preload, and being cleaned within an inch of its life all in one service. Therefore I felt I had a right to demand co-operation.

But I knew I was suffering pre-ride jitters. The bike's suitability for a trip like this was beyond question, and we rode well as a team. In the 50,000 kilometres we have done together before America, there'd never been a puncture or cross word between us. The bike has done everything I asked, and in turn I have not overloaded the alternator, stalled it or smoked the brakes. It has been a relationship built on respect and frequent oil changes. Basking in this heart-warming glow I found myself watching the forklift guy bring out the crate from deep within the bowels of the freight warehouse. I was in the company of a mate from Vancouver, Keith Evans, who was kindly acting as my ground handler, similar to Steve Darwen in Sydney two years before. I'd be staying with Keith at the start and finish of the ride. Keith's advantage was that he could be bought off with a good red wine. His house was 3 kilometres from the US border and he rode a BMW. He offered to escort me to the border. I knew what that meant, as the same thing had happened when Steve had offered an escort out of Sydney — he'd finally waved me off near the Queensland border. I secretly hoped Keith and his wife, Pat, would ride further than the border. It would be good to have company for the opening salvo in Washington.

⁎⁎⁎

I unpacked the Suzuki in the freight yard and loaded the panniers. I had three pieces of luggage. In the top box were all the tools I needed to change a tyre roadside, from spare tubes to tyre irons. It also contained charging and USB cables for the laptop, cellphone, GPS, digital camera and hair dryer. The left-hand pannier was my admin centre. In it was a heavily padded laptop computer, a road atlas, a litre of oil for my Scottoiler chain-oiling device, and an empty bag for fridge magnets. The right-hand pannier contained my clothes and ablutionary aids such as toothbrush and towel, which neatly doubled as wheel-rim cleaning aids. I carried two pairs of socks, two pairs of undies, two T-shirts, one pair of jeans, hot-weather gloves and a pair of sneakers. Yes, it sounds excessive, but I was to be on the road for eight weeks. My camping arsenal was in a canvas bag strapped to the rear seat. In there was a tent and footprint, a sleeping bag, my pillow (embarrassingly called a 'cuddle buddy'), a camp stretcher, and a case with six copies of *Twisting Throttle Australia*. My plan was to effect entry into places, otherwise off-limits to tourists, such as the White House and Pentagon, by offering a signed copy of the book if I could hand it to the President personally. I might even decide not to charge him for it.

On the front of the bike I installed some handy toys to make life a little easier on the road. Here's what my electronic companions would be for the next two months.

The handiest little fella was SPOT, a small orange device about the size of a cellphone. 'SPOT' stands for Satellite Personal Tracker. When switched on, it emits a signal to any overhead satellite, which then plots my position on a Google map displayed on my website. Every 10 minutes. Therefore, my riding progress would show up as a snail trail across America in real time. There was also a button on SPOT sombrely labelled 911. If I pressed that button in an emergency, the next sound I would hear would be the whirring blades of a medevac helicopter. For $99 a year, I subscribe to the SPOT service for this emergency callout and the tracking. SPOT operates on two AA batteries and is waterproof. So long as the two little LCD lights were blinking in unison, it was happily communicating with satellites. I wondered if the Pentagon had such fine technology. I made a mental note to show SPOT to them when I called in.

On my Australian ride I had a GPS and a separate iPod with 492 songs loaded. I came back from that ride and immediately deleted the 491 I had grown to hate. For America, I had upgraded to a GPS that also played music. I had to preselect the type of human voice that would give me navigational directions through my helmet speakers. As I had for Australia, I opted for British female. My other options ranged from Czech male to — and this is political correctness gone mad — Italian transgender. I chose British female, as she might have to sing along with the inbuilt MP3 player. I installed a 4Gb card in the GPS, on which were stored 657 songs. My music selection — roundly derided by readers of my Australian book — I'm sorry to say still included John Denver, Roger

Whittaker and The Sweet. I honestly tried to make an effort, but age and musical ignorance beat me. Anyway, I challenge any of you to sing along to Snoop Dogg on a motorbike.

Also mounted up in the cockpit were a charger for my digital camera batteries, hard-wired to the battery, my camera bag cable-tied to my windscreen, and of course my portable coffee-maker.

The bike was ready. My helmet was on. The front wheel was on the starting line. I turned the key and the dashboard lights glowed. My thumb hovered nervously over the start switch. Seconds later, the Suzuki roared into life without even a stutter from the battery. I kicked it into first and idled out the freight yard's gate into Vancouver traffic. The ride around the lower 48 had begun. It was truly a special moment.

Three bikes wound their way towards the US border in light drizzle. Keith and Pat Evans, riding their BMWs, were leading. I was happy to ride sweep and adjust to the rustiness of the loaded-up Suzuki after the comparatively lighter rental bikes in Hawaii and Alaska. It was like driving a semi after a mini-van.

The road out of Vancouver tracked metres from the actual US border. And here's the odd thing: the border was merely a shallow ditch that, frankly, I could have ridden across as easily as your front lawn. We were parallel to it on the Canadian side. I could have thrown a stone onto the equivalent road on the US side, it was that close. I wondered about all the controls down on the Mexican border — namely, fences, no-man's land and anti-illegal immigrant squads in 4WDs — and contrasted that with this shallow ditch. And speaking of border anomalies, here's another one. In Vancouver there is a small peninsula called Point Roberts that is US territory but cut off from the US as it is joined to Canada. Therefore the 1,300 residents of this suburban 12-square-kilometre US enclave can reach their homes only by travelling through Canada. It is part of the US because it lies south of the 49th parallel, the official latitude defining the US–Canadian border around this part of British Columbia. So if you're a Point Roberts, therefore US, citizen and you want to go 10-pin bowling, you need to take your passport as it's an international trip for you. There's a petrol station in Point Roberts creaming it, as it can sell gasoline at US prices, which are cheaper than those in Canada.

Border crossings were still top of mind as we reached the town of Sumas and queued to leave Canada. I had to get my bike's carnet, a sort of vehicular passport, stamped by Canadian Customs as evidence of exporting the bike out of the country. Getting Customs to do this is often hit-and-miss, as many decide to put discretionary bureaucratic hurdles in the way. Jump ahead to Chapter 41 and you'll see what I mean. I was slightly apprehensive as I lined up at the Sumas Customs counter, but not so much that I didn't have a $20 note ready. I knew how these border posts worked in foreign countries. 'Yeah?' 'Morning. Got my bike's carnet here for stamping out of Canada.' 'What's a carnet, chief?' 'Like a passport. That's the bike out there. All I need is a stamp.' 'Where?' 'Out there in the car park by that tree.' 'No, where do you want the stamp?' 'Right there'll do.' The sound of a stamp thudding down on my carnet. 'Next.' And so I crossed into the United States with the minimum of red tape, $20 note intact for lunch, and whistling a merry tune.

We rode south by the Nooksack River in light drizzle. I settled into the bike's rhythm and started to relax. For the first time I thought about the job ahead. This was state #3 of 50, and I had 30,000 kilometres in front of me in which to stay upright, safe and sane. It's one thing to sit in front of a computer and endlessly research roads and routes, quite another to be riding on the wrong side of the road actually doing it. The feeling was exhilarating. Small towns called Marblemount, Rockport and Concrete seemed to suggest a certain geological theme prevailing. We were heading into the North Cascades National Park on Route 20. In Marblemount, I had an elk burger at the Buffalo Run Inn. It tasted like buffalo. Still under drizzly skies, the road wound up to the lakes of Diablo and Ross, and thereafter to the summits of Rainy and then Washington Passes.

The view as I rounded the bend on the downhill after Washington Pass was breathtaking. I pulled over onto the shoulder and reached for my camera. I kicked down the side stand and made to dismount. The side stand sunk into the spongy clay of the shoulder and the bike started to topple. A fraction before it passed the point of no return, I stretched my leg out and held the 300-kilogram bike steady at an angle. It was a clash of wills. It wanted to lie down, and I wanted to stay up. Man will always triumph over machine, and by twisting the front wheel down the slope I managed to get it upright. These were the Cascades, which is a good description of how the sweat was moving down my back. But despite the near-miss, I found myself blinking at the view as the highway curved back on itself in a perfect 180-degree U-bend backdropped by massive forest-covered granite peaks.

The other thing that was blinking was my fuel light. I had ridden at pace through Newhalem, the last petrol station before Winthrop, some 50 kilometres east of where I was now. I doubted my reserve tank would get me there. Thus I free-wheeled, engine off, for 20 kilometres as Route 20 descended through the Okanogan National Forest towards unleaded salvation. I made a note to be more sensible about refuelling. I had assumed that America, the land of the automobile, would have fuel places every few miles. I laugh now to think of that. In fact, being cautious about fuelling became a major preoccupation, with good cause, throughout the 50-state ride.

Popping out the other side of the North Cascades produced two new experiences: other bikes on the road, and deer-warning signs. In Alaska, I can remember passing only six other bikes in nearly 2,000 kilometres. Here in Washington, I was passing that many between gear changes. In the small town of Winthrop, the main street was clogged with motorcycles. It was also my introduction to the psychological game of TWO: two-wheeled one-upmanship, otherwise known as 'bet my bike looks better than yours'. It's hard to dress up a Japanese road/adventure bike like mine. The most bling I carried was a chrome chain guard, now covered in oil spray from the Scottoiler. Yet strolling up the main street of Winthrop I passed hundreds of parked Harleys, BMW tourers and Honda Goldwings absolutely decorated to the n-th degree. Coffee-cup holders, stars-and-stripes fluttering from the rear seat, chrome studs all over the leatherwork — and that was just the riders: you should have seen their bikes. I wasn't to know it here in Winthrop, but the game of TWO would be played out all over the country whenever groups of bikers formed up. On the surface, it was mutual admiration for the other guy's machine if it had way more useless decoration than yours. Under the surface, it was rampant jealousy bordering on bling rage. I would constantly feel like the ugly sister at the ball.

I started to pass deer-warning signs, with added notices saying things like *High kill zone next 13 miles*. According to deercrash.com, I was in one of the top 10 states for deer fatalities. In 2008, there were 1.5 million reported accidents of cars hitting deer across the US. Two hundred people have been killed in those accidents, and the deer were not so thrilled about it either. It is possible to mount a deer whistle on your vehicle. Everyone apart from deerwhistles.com thinks these Handy Bambis are a waste of time, as deer, like humans, can't hear ultrasonic sounds. In fact, some university tests show deer whistles can cause more problems than they solve.

Deer #1:   Say, what's that whistling noise?
Deer #2:   Dunno. Let's step out onto the highway to see. Ooh look, it's
            coming from that logging tru—

There were also warning signs for bighorn sheep. Then more deer signs. I wondered if it would be safer riding through the fields instead.

Still with Keith and Pat, I rode through Omak, Tonasket and Oroville, heading back to the Canadian border. The night was to be spent at the most hospitable home of their friends, Bob and Iris Stubbs in Osoyoos, a whisker inside British Columbia. Bob heard about my near-drop at Washington Pass and fashioned a square of plywood attached to a cord to act as a side-stand plate for those pesky soft shoulders. This piece of wood was to become one of my most useful accessories. Before turning in for the night, I checked that the bike was OK and introduced Woody to the other pieces of on-board bling.

The next morning saw an azure blue sky and a dry road heading east along the border. This was no ordinary road. It was the Crowsnest Highway, and after a breathtaking switchback out of Osoyoos it climbed Anarchist Mountain. Descending the mountain to the small border crossing at Midway was simply fun. Wide, sweeping corners and beautifully constructed passes through the British Columbian woodland made me fast-forward the MP3 player to Ingrid Kertesi singing 'Ave Maria'. I couldn't have been more laid-back if I was flat-lining.

Minutes later I moved forward to Officer Cooper, singing another tune. Coops was the border guard manning Midway border post where we lined up waiting for processing. At the front was a 4WD towing a huge caravan. It had a dog on board. The dog's papers weren't in order. These were US citizens trying to get back home. Coops rejected their protestations, which became a little heated. Even I know you don't argue with officialdom. Didn't these naïve people know about $20 notes folded up in your passport? Officer Cooper kept their passports while the driver was forced to do a humiliating eight-point turn and drive back into Canada, ruing the day he didn't get his canine carnet stamped. Tough but fair.

Keith and Pat breezed through on their BC plates. My foreign plate raised Coop's eyebrows. 'Morning.' 'Morning.' 'Passport, please.' 'Here you go, officer.' 'Thank you, Mr . . . ah . . . Mr Throttle. Here, you can have this $20 note back. What's your business in the United States?' 'I'm riding through 50 states in 60 days and this is my second day in the lower 48.' 'Fine. Are you carrying any drugs or medicines?' 'Just cholesterol pills.' 'Are they prescription?' 'Yes.' 'Are they sealed in dispensing canisters?' 'Yes.' 'What's your cholesterol?' '5.7.' 'Hah. Mine's 5. That's the Suzy with the TL motor?' 'Yeah, and fully adjusted TLS.' From that moment we bonded, and I got my carnet stamped easily. If I'd had a dog in my top box, he'd have got through as well.

Back in the US again, it started to rain as we rode through Republic, across the Kettle River range, summiting Sherman Pass and down into Kettle Falls. The Falls represented two things. My riding companions' departure back to Vancouver, and Keith's worst joke so far. A young Cheyenne girl goes into a store and buys some budget no-name-brand toilet paper. 'Why's it called no-name?' she asks the storekeeper. 'Well, if you got a better name for it I'd be glad to hear it.' Two days later, she returns to the store. 'I've got a better name for that toilet paper of yours.' 'What's that, kid?' 'John Wayne toilet paper.' 'Why John Wayne?' 'Cos it's rough, tough and doesn't take shit from Indians.' With that, the two Vancouverians rode off. I'd see them again on Day 60 back on the other side of Washington. There was a lot of riding to do in the meantime.

I rode out towards Spokane alongside the massive Columbia River. This 2000-kilometre-long river is the largest in the Pacific Northwest and the fourth largest in the US. I will admit here, in Chapter 3, that I have an obsession for large bridges and dams. That will become obvious as you read on. I say this because I was presently thundering down Highway 25 towards Grand Coulee Dam a mere 100 kilometres away down the Columbia. The Grand Coulee is the fourth largest hydroelectricity-producing dam in the world, the largest concrete structure in the US, and taller than the Great Pyramid at Giza. With the concrete in that dam you could build a four-foot-wide pavement twice around the equator. I love statistics like that. In short, the Grand Coulee Dam was worth the detour. And I missed it.

At a blip of a place called Hunters, I pulled into a shabby-looking gas station. It was closed, but two men leaning against a pick-up truck pointed to the back of my bike. I looked down and embarrassingly noticed my pannier lid gaping open with a pair of underpants hanging out. I slammed the lid shut, waved nonchalantly to the men as if this was nothing, and put on an extra show of machismo by over-revving as I careened off in a shower of gravel. Several minutes later I realized I had turned up the wrong road, but ego would not allow me to turn around and ride past the men again. What a curse it is to be a male sometimes. So not only had I missed out on the Grand Coulee, but half my underwear inventory had blown out somewhere on the banks of the Columbia River. I wondered how the turbines downstream would handle the alien object.

I reached the settlement of Loon Lake and gassed up. I saw a sign to Gifford Ferrry. Whoever had the job of prrroof-reading at the rrroad-sign factory wasn't on song the day they made that one. Shortly after that, I reached the home of John and Lissie Holman at Medical Lake, near Spokane. They had invited me to stay the night, and served up BBQ chicken and cold beer. I asked to stay for three more nights, but they quickly made excuses. It may have been that pair of underpants hanging off my rear number plate.

Day Three was to be a quick sprint across the Idaho panhandle as I made a beeline for Glacier National Park in Montana, my first test of real riding. I rode briefly through Spokane commuter traffic on the I-90 as I crossed into Idaho at Post Falls. The meandering road alongside Lake Coeur d'Alene was fast, empty and simply beautiful riding. The interstate was as smooth as glass and swooped through the forest as I looked for the off-ramp to Kingston.

This raises the interesting question of how I chose the route each day. Back home planning the ride from my desk involved some mapping software, a cup of coffee and my road atlas. I read many motorcycling books about must-do roads and plotted them in the mapping program on my computer. Assuming the squiggly lines in the road atlas meant nice twisty roads, I entered those as well. I searched high and low on the internet for logs of local motorcyclists who had reported wonderful riding routes in their backyard. These likewise went into the mapping. Finally, after weeks of this, I sat back and looked at my computer screen. The map of America was covered in squiggles. I joined up as many as possible, providing the general direction was onwards to the neighbouring state. The end result was a tortuous route map around America that looked impossible. In the scenic states — such as Montana, Wyoming, Colorado and Utah — it looked like a worm trail, as almost every highway was designated a 'scenic byway' by that state's roading authority. I chose to upload this theoretical route into my GPS and see what happened on the day. And the day was now.

At Kingston, I stopped for breakfast and fuel. The bike drank 91 unleaded, the rider drank Mountain Dew. I dragged out the road atlas and traced a line between where I was and Glacier National Park. There were endless possibilities, so I adopted a policy which ended up serving me well for the whole trip: look for the light yellow lines, meaning back roads. I would enter in the start and finish points into the GPS as well as certain via points, and let it think it had calculated the route all by itself, whereas in reality I had forced it in a particular direction using these via points. It was all about preserving the GPS's ego. I have often wondered whether this rather ad-hoc route decision-making was the best way to go. But parking up on the roadside, getting out the atlas and knowing you have hundreds of choices literally at your fingertips is such an adventurous feeling I would not do it any other way.

The back road I decided on was labelled Thompson Pass, and it crossed into Montana at 1,500 metres. I had no idea of the state of the road, or even if it was sealed all the way. But with a full tank, a clear, sunny morning, squirrels scampering in the trees, and Bachman-Turner Overdrive's 'Free Wheelin'' crooning into my helmet, I was primed for adventure and the unknown. I rode off into the forest on top of the world.

Chapter 4

Montana

Nickname: The Treasure State

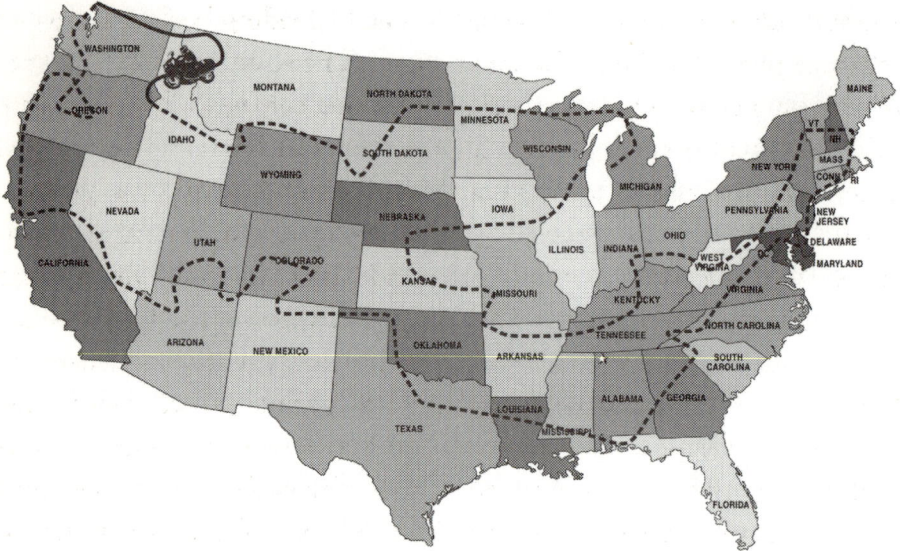

This state: 943 kilometres. Journey to date: 4,456 kilometres.

Montana. Land of Shining Mountains. Big Sky Country. The Last Best Place. Montana has more official nicknames than any other state. I suppose that's because it's hard to know where to start pinning a description on it. It's the fourth largest state in size, but has the third lowest population density. That means there's a whole lot of Montana out there with no people. I was only 10 minutes into Montana and already I could feel the remoteness.

The road up to Thompson Pass was a magic ride. Massive fir trees lined the twisting road that curved around craggy bluffs. I could imagine there had been a nuclear disaster and I was the last person on Earth. There was nothing to indicate any sign of human habitation: no houses, cars, planes in the sky, or road signs. Just me, the bike, and the highway carving through this endless forest under a big, blue sky. It was totally mesmerizing.

I reached the settlement of Plains down on the plains and felt the familiar pangs of hunger. I fuelled up and examined the culinary offerings inside the petrol station. Petrol station grub? I can sense the note of disgust in the way you're holding this book, so it's time to explain the whole food-and-fuel scene. I think of it as saving time by feeding both the beasts at the same place. Dual fuel. Crude and food. The science of GAStronomy. When you go in to pay for your gas, you are confronted by a range of food displays that is hard to resist. First, I don't rush to sit down in a café or restaurant by myself among couples and families, with only the sauce bottle label to read for something to do. And then there's the downtime factor. I'm trained to eat on the run, or ride. I like to scoff and off. These petrol stations know this, and they make it easy to choose your food and get out. By the time I've walked back to the bike, I've usually finished my paper-bag meal. Fried chicken, hot dogs, doughnuts, wings, cheese melts and bacon bagels. Washed down with a fizzy lemon or something a bit healthier to drink, such as a flavoured milk, this highway fare is delicious. It's cheap, sitting in warmers everywhere, and pairs of tongs are waiting for discerning customers like me to help themselves. I know that sort of diet must stop soon, but please cut me some slack for this the first week.

And so it was I lay on the grass in a park in Plains by a railway line shovelling down some greasy fried chicken, curly fries, onion rings and a Sprite. A line of Harleys rumbled down the main street, saw the parked Suzuki and each rider waved. It was uplifting.

From Plains, I turned onto Route 28 and headed for Kalispell and Flathead Lake. A quarter of the way there, near Lonepine, I saw some smoke drifts up ahead. As I got nearer, the smoke thickened and became unpleasant. There seemed to be a forest fire some miles away in the hills, and this thick, white smoke was sitting like a blanket right over the valley in which I was riding. I pulled over to think about what to do. There was no other traffic in either direction. There were no fire-warning signs, or any sort of indication whether it would be a good idea to go on or turn back. What if the fire had just flared up and the authorities didn't know about it? And where actually was the fire? Just up the road? And how far off the road? Was I riding towards flames gusting over the road, or was it just a lot of smoke with nothing to worry about except a bronchial attack?

In an unusual bout of indecision, I sat on the bike for a few minutes gazing into the swirling smoke. It was acrid to the nostril, and my eyes weren't too happy with it either. I simply didn't know what to do. What would have helped is for an open-topped convertible with a gaily laughing family and their dog to have driven past, tooting loudly and having a singsong. That would have put my mind at rest. Then a defiant mood swept over me. It was a man-or-mouse decision and Twisting Throttle eats cheese for nobody. I kicked the bike into first and sped off into the haze.

It lasted for about 8 kilometres and I saw no actual fire. As I descended into Elmo, at Flathead Lake, several fire-rescue vehicles raced the other way. It was then that I noticed the brown pick-up.

Flathead Lake was big, like an inland sea. Highway 93 curved up its western shore to Kalispell, 35 kilometres away. I was doing perhaps 105 km/h, a touch over the speed limit of 100. Over the last kilometre or two I had gained on a brown-coloured Chevy pick-up truck. I overtook it on a straight stretch and continued enjoying the lake views. In my mirrors I saw the pick-up noticeably pick up the pace, and it soon sat just a few feet behind me, the driver invisible in the glare of the sun on his windscreen. I assumed he was called Gomer and didn't like being passed. Game on. For the next 10 kilometres in sparse traffic, the pick-up tailed me. I was iffy about out-running him, as I had seen two state troopers sitting roadside since passing Elmo.

The futility of tailgating a bike lies in the mismatch of not only outright speed when it comes to a drag-off, but also in manoeuvrability in traffic. We soon came upon a line of cars caught behind a slow delivery van with a fibreglass dog on its roof. An overtaking lane could be seen about 500 metres ahead. I was sorry to say goodbye to Chevy Chase, but it was time to put him in his place. At the back of this queue. While the line of cars pulled out one by one in the overtaking lane, I stayed behind them, reducing speed and blocking the pick-up. As the lane was reaching its end I swerved into the slow lane, roared up behind the delivery van, passing the line of cars on the inside, and executed a Rossi-like piece of overtaking that put me in front of the lot. The pick-up was at the rear of the whole mêlée, and I last saw him in my mirrors, a speck in the distance, trapped behind Mr Dogwash. I couldn't be positive, but I'm sure he was signalling me out his window with one raised finger, probably humbly acknowledging who took line honours in that encounter.

It was a nice distraction, but I soon forgot about the duel as the distant peaks of Glacier National Park appeared on the horizon as I reached Whitefish. My route in Montana was more or less one big loop, crossing back into Idaho near Missoula. The reason for the loop was Glacier. Or, more specifically, the Going To The Sun Road. Even the name evokes adventure. As well as bridges and dams, I have an obsession for challenging roads. The Going To The Sun Road traversing Glacier National Park was to be an excellent introduction. RVs and trailers are banned, and there are virtually no guardrails as avalanches wipe them away. Built in 1933, it's open only in the summer as it takes 10 weeks to snowplough. Remember that road from the opening credits of *The Shining*? Jack Nicholson driving his VW up the mountain road towards that haunted hotel? That's the easy side of the Going To The Sun. The Sunday-drive bit. The challenging section is the climb up to Logan Pass from the western end. Heaven's Peak, Bird Woman Falls, Weeping Wall, Haystack Butte, Rising Sun. Even the names of the features on the way up sound epic.

At West Glacier I paid my national park entrance fee of $12 and rode in. For miles the road tracked along the shore of Lake McDonald, with only glimpses through the trees towards the huge granite mountains ahead. And then, abruptly, the road started to climb in a series of switchbacks, clearing the tree line and plunging me into a staggering mountain landscape. Vista upon vista of massive, craggy cliff faces and sheer rock walls were almost too hard to take in. The drop-off a few feet to my right at the road edge was hair-raising. The few cars I came up behind were crawling up in first gear. None of the drivers were looking at the view. Much of the road was one-lane, and the cars were hugging the rock wall away from the precipitous drop. I had to wait for pull-over points to overtake. Waterfalls cascaded over green, mossy cliffs, and the whole landscape looked primeval. I was stopping in the middle of the roadway frequently to take photos. At one point I came up behind a water tanker spraying water over a dusty unpaved section. Luckily a small road tunnel caused the tanker to pull over and I got past.

The narrow road wound its way to the summit of Logan Pass. As I pulled over to absorb the view, I heard a loud whining coming from somewhere down by my front forks. I also noticed my temperature gauge several bars higher than normal. The first wave of dread that I may have a cooling problem swept over me. I quickly shut the bike down and considered what could be happening. A holed radiator? My cooling-fan bearing blown? I racked my memory for when I had last topped up the radiator with water. Surely I had done that as part of the pre-trip service? But I hadn't checked the coolant level in Vancouver. Maybe there was a slow leak? But could a stone have bypassed the radiator guard? Highly unlikely. Think about this. Doesn't the fan switch itself on when the thermostat detects that the engine is getting hot? In other words, it kicks in at low speed or high revving. Or is the fan actually on all the time like a car? How could I not know that basic fact about my bike? And what was that high-pitched whining? Doesn't that mean a bearing is failing? So if the temperature gauge is high, then the engine's not being cooled. Ergo, the fan is broken. Therefore, I have to let air cool the motor and get the broken fan fixed. Thank God I'm at the top of Logan Pass and not the bottom. Parked there at the top of the Going To The Sun Road, in the fading twilight, squatting beside my front end, peering into the engine cavity, I thought about those rich, sponsored motorcyclists who ride around the world with support crews tailing them. This brief rage of envy soon passed.

I switched on the bike again and heard the high-pitched whining. I saw my temperature bars start to climb again. I poked a stick gently up into the fan's blades and it didn't get chopped off. The fan was clearly not working. I rushed to mount up and sped off down Logan Pass. The flow of cool evening air soon brought the gauge level down, and I wondered if I could ride all the way around America avoiding towns and traffic lights. As night was rapidly approaching, I began to think about where to stay. A camping-ground sign soon appeared and I slowed. Thus my lesson about how camping grounds work in the US commenced. It cost me $20 and I'm happy to share it with you for free.

There are two primary types of camping grounds. The first are the highly organized camping parks with pools, and ice-cream-eating contests for the kids, where the toilets flush, there is Wi-Fi and the staff wear yellow shirts. The organization administering these is called KOA or Kampgrounds Of America. The other sort is the more do-it-yourself variety, often in state forest parks. These operate on an honesty system where you pay a fee, usually around $20. The toilets are smelly and there's no ice-cream, and bears are very fond of them. They are also hugely popular in summer vacation time. But the trick is you have to know the system.

You drive in and tootle around the looping camp-area access road until you find a vacant site. You can't just pitch your tent under a tree and claim it as your own. You have to pitch in a labelled site that comprises a pull-over area for your car, a wooden picnic table and a rusty steel campfire ring. This prevents campgrounds becoming overcrowded and looking like Woodstock. Once you've located an empty site, you stake your claim by throwing down your camping gear, return to the entrance, put your $20 into an envelope marked with your site number, detach a receipt, and drop your payment down the metal tube. You display the receipt in a small stake poked into the ground by your site. Sometime in the evening a park ranger comes around and checks for receipts to make sure you're not a bad-debtor camper. A key element in this time-honoured process is finding your site *before* paying.

Here at the Rising Sun campground at St Mary Lake in Glacier National Park I did it the other way around, and that's how I lost $20. I dropped the money down the tube and rode slowly around the access road, fan whining, looking for an empty site. The place was bristling with scouts and families, roaring campfires, roasting damper, games of Frisbee, and one or two RVs and the associated clinking of Chardonnay glasses. But not a spare site to be found. Heads were turning at the high-pitched whining, so I took all this on the chin as an expensive lesson in understanding the camping system. At the entrance to the area was a huge sign warning of bear attacks with some do's and don'ts. It put me off pulling off into the woods down the road and setting up camp.

I rode on to the small town of St Mary. I found a KOA, where, sure enough, the staff in the office wore yellow shirts. 'Good evening, sir. We were just about to close. Good to see you. Welcome to KOA St Mary. How may we serve you today?' I was taken aback at the customer service ethic considering this was merely a campground, and wondered if I had walked into Macy's by mistake. It was like checking into a hotel. The difference was that I was in Row C over by the fir trees wing. I paid $25 and got a map of the KOA site, with the kindly lady circling the hut where the $4 all-you-can-eat-pancakes would be the next morning. I rode the whining bike over to Row C, which was deserted, and found site C18 next to three bushes and a rubbish bin. By the light of the distant toilet block I pitched my tent, unfolded my camp stretcher, unrolled my sleeping bag, glugged down the last of my water and, aware of the local bear menace, hung some raw meat on a hook just inside my tent. OK, I made that last one up. I hung it just outside my tent. What actually happened was that I lay down, in full riding gear, and that's the last thing I remember.

I was up, de-pitched and 10 kilometres down the road before the KOA staff even thought about the all-you-can-eat-pancakes. It was an early start all right at 6.00 a.m., but I wanted to get to Missoula before the Suzuki dealership there closed. I had no idea if the cooling-fan problem would see me stopping every hour, so better to be on the safe side. Highway 89 to Choteau was a beauty. Arrow-straight across the Blackfeet Indian Reservation plateau, the highway gave me panoramic views of East Glacier. If I thought the peaks of West Glacier the day before were craggy, these ones in the close distance were craggier.

As I rounded a bend, a large black bear ambled across the road about 50 metres in front of me. Scampering across behind mum were two bear cubs. The trio paused briefly at the sound of the bike and shambled away into the scrub and were lost to sight. This would be my only bear-sighting in America, and I recalled the handy instructional brochures that were available at KOA, with no shortage of advice on what to do if confronted by a bear. Here's the gist.

First, establish what type of bear it is, because this has a — and I'm sorry about this — bearing on what you do next.

Is the bear black? It is? Then it's a Black Bear you're dealing with. Don't climb a tree, as Black Bears are excellent climbers. Don't play dead, as you might as well just give him a knife, fork and serviette and he can get on with his meal. If you're in a group and you all run away, make sure you're not the slowest. The only thing you can do if a Black Bear attacks is fight back. The literature says to rain blows on the bear's eyes and snout. You may have to put down the gun, knife and bear-repellent first to keep your hands free.

Is it a Grizzly Bear? Maybe, but how do you tell? Well, it will be brown, furry, and looking down at you rather than the other way around; there will be a lot of saliva dripping from its fangs; but the clincher to identifying it as a Grizzly will be the way it is slashing at you with its claws. Don't try to out-run it unless you're an Olympic sprinter. The best thing to do is roll up in the foetal position and play dead. If you're lucky, it will pat you around a bit and then wander off bored. Stay in the foetal position until (a) you're certain the bear has not just popped away to fetch some garnish and (b) your heart rate has calmed down. Two days should do it. The brochures say you should then locate two things. A park ranger to tell them about a wild bear on the loose, and some fresh underwear. Finally, the helpful advice says that if you have a rifle you should use it. You reckon?

But the funny thing that occurred to me as I sped along the open, empty highway, excited about the bear sighting, was how many open-range cattle were grazing around the place. Do bears and cattle coexist? I would have thought that they'd be a beef buffet. If I was a bear hungry for food, why would I risk dragging off a sleeping camper when there were dumb cows aplenty out on the grassland?

Still mulling over those bear facts, I reached Choteau and turned onto Route 287 to Augusta. Immediately I felt a stab of pain on my neck. It could only be one thing. I slammed on the brakes and careened onto the verge, ripping my helmet off. With padded gloves I flicked off the bee and tried to see the back of my neck in the bike's mirror. Stupidly, I rubbed the soreness and ended up mashing the sting into my skin. Bee-stings don't normally worry me, but this one was making me light-headed. I took off my gloves, and with my fingertips gingerly felt around for any little barb that I could yank out. I think I felt one and picked at it frantically. After a while the pain ebbed away and it was just red and itchy.

I was riding fast and avoiding towns. The air rushing through to the engine was cooling it nicely, rendering the broken fan redundant. I started to climb up a long, slow incline that took me into rolling wooded hills, and within an hour I'd crossed the Continental Divide as I summited Rogers Pass. These were the Rockies. Under a big, blue sky, the mountains glistened. I saw several deer far off the road and a lone eagle circling, but I had the road to myself. I just stopped myself in time from fast-forwarding the MP3 player to John Denver — it was that intoxicating.

I pulled over in Lincoln. It was midday and I was ravenous. At this early stage in the trip I was lapsing into the regime of eating one meal a day at lunchtime after the morning's food-less riding. It wasn't that I wasn't hungry in the morning. It was just the preoccupation with keeping up the pace and getting a good opening mileage under my belt before the day presented too many distractions.

Over the road was a diner called Moose Saloon. I went in and my eyes adjusted to the dim light. This was my first diner experience and I felt at a loss, because I didn't know the system in America. Do you wait for someone to show you to a table? Do you just sit down and hope they see you? Do you ring a bell? 'Hey, honey. How're ya doin'?' The waitress who popped up out of nowhere was of mature years and had a pencil behind one ear. 'Table fer one?' 'Yes, please,' I said. She led me to the sad-singles section, which was right underneath a moose's head.

Herewith is the diner process if you are a single. Sit down and be given the menu and a glass of water. In no more than three minutes, the waitress will be back to take your order. It is imperative you know what you want by that first visit. If you dawdle trying to decide on your meal choice, you will miss the cut. Place your order assertively and unambiguously. Diner pros will tell the waitress what they want in such a fashion that she does not have to ask any supporting questions, such as 'How do you want your eggs?' 'Will that be on rye or wholemeal?' 'Decaf or filter?' Here is an example of a diner pro at work.

Waitress: Ready to order, honey?
Diner pro: Sure am, Nancy. Give me a Reubens on rye, toasted, slaw on the side, pepperjack cheese, Thousand Island and a decaf. Say, how's Earl these days?

And this was my attempt.

Waitress: Ready to order, honey?
Me: Not sure if I'll have the Reubens or the Flapjack . . .
Waitress: I'll come back.
Me: No, wait: I'll take the Reubens, please.
Waitress: Rye or wholemeal? Toasted or fresh? Any sides? What dressing? Which cheese? Filter or decaf? Black or Grizzly?
Me: How's Earl these days?

It was a mess, but the eventual Reubens grilled pastrami sandwich was delicious. More importantly, I had learned a crucial lesson in diner etiquette. But the induction wasn't over. The final part of the process was how to pay. Like you, I've seen those movies where the customer calls out 'Check!' and is given the bill at their table. They then throw down a note and walk out. A few questions. Do diners really trust you to leave their premises like that? The moment you go outside, do they sprint over to see that you've left money? What if the low-life at the next table reaches over and pockets your $10 bill? What if you want a receipt for tax purposes?

The waitress sauntered over to refill my coffee. 'Just the check, please,' I said, with an air of authority. It worked. She came back with a little note ripped from her pad: *Reubens $7.45*. So what bill do I fish out of my wallet? It has to be $10 surely. But that means I'm leaving a $2.55 tip, representing 34% of the meal. Was her service that good? I wanted to leave the usual 10% tip, but at an embarrassingly paltry 74 cents I thought I'd round it up to a dollar. So the vexatious issue was how did I pay $8.45 and get change for my $10 when she'd disappeared back to the kitchen? Standing there in the Moose Saloon in Montana fretting about overpaying for my sandwich, I knew I had to sort out this problem for future diner visits. The answer was to stock up my wallet with $1 bills, thus minimizing loss through over-generosity. Nancy the waitress won that day. She got a 34% tip from the dark-clothed, silent motorcycling stranger. I could see her at home that night telling Earl about her amazing luck.

The sun was high in the afternoon sky as I rode into Missoula. I punched into the GPS the address of the bike shop, and followed its instructions out into the suburbs.

'Yessir? What can we do fer you?' 'I've got a DL1000 V-Strom outside. The cooling fan's not going on and it's overheating. Been a problem since Glacier. Can you take a look?' The mechanic wheeled the bike into the workshop. 'I'll try to jump-start the fan.' I watched as he put what looked like a voltmeter up into the dark recess by the front forks. 'Yep, fan's blown all right,' he announced. 'We can get a new fan from Suzuki overnight. Cost you $400. Sir?' I came to with some smelling salts. '$400? I wasn't thinking of hiring a limo to go down to Texas to collect it.' In fact what I said was: 'Phew, that's quite a bit, isn't it? Well, if it's blown, it's blown. Can you fit it tomorrow?' 'Well, there's the thing. Workshop's a bit stacked up this week and we're expecting a baby any day now.' 'OK, I'll deliver the baby if you can fit my fan.' What I really said was: 'Can you order the fan and I'll pick it up in two days from . . . from . . .' I checked my road atlas. 'Hailey, Idaho?' 'Sure.'

I rode away from Missoula not completely convinced of this whole fan thing. I was getting sick of pulling over every 15 minutes to let the bike cool down whenever I saw the temperature gauge max out. I decided to call it a day as the evening dusk fell over Missoula. For the second night in a row, I camped at a KOA kampground in amongst RVs, caravans and tents the size of my house back home. I heard an announcement over the Tannoy that there was an all-you-can-eat ice-cream event taking place in the recreation block at 9.00 p.m. The cost was $2.50. I laughed derisively as I zipped up my tent ready for sleep. I hoped Nancy was enjoying my ice-cream money.

Chapter 5

Idaho

Nickname: The Spud State

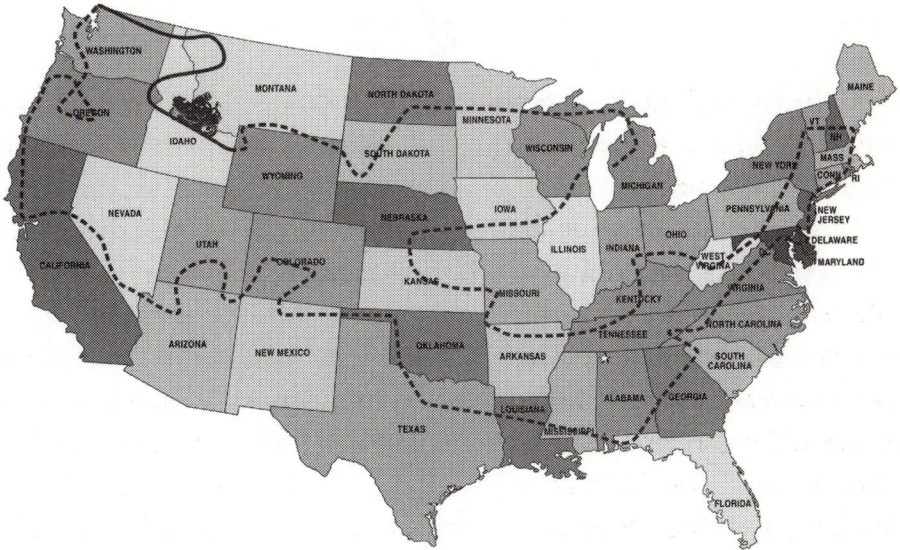

This state: 1,873 kilometres. Journey to date: 6,329 kilometres.

I KNEW IT WOULD HAPPEN. I just didn't expect it to have been so early in the trip. I was so meticulous in my packing up each morning that I can't imagine what went so wrong. Looking back it may have been a terrible lapse of concentration, maybe travel fatigue or possibly just an act of God. Whatever, I stood stock-still trying to take it in. Surely the journey would not end here, in a lay-by high in the wooded hills just over the state line in Idaho? Deer looked up from their roadside foraging with expressions of sympathy. Several rabbits gathered at the edge of the clearing to see what would happen next. The word had gone out through the forest that Twisting Throttle was in trouble. I couldn't believe my bad judgement. A moment's inattention and now disaster.

I stood looking down at the rear of my bike. That morning I'd strapped on the two bungee cords tying on my camping gear. Now there was one. Somewhere between Missoula and this place, the Lolo Pass, one of my bungees had flown off. I had ridden on with a key member of my support crew abandoned on the highway. Sure I could buy another one in Kooskia, down the road. And one bungee is probably all you need to hold a tent on board. It was on a deeper plane than the mere loss of a $10 rubber cord with two plastic hooks. My gear ensemble is a close-knit team. A tight unit. A family. To lose one of the staff was bad for morale. A precursor to the metaphoric wheels coming off the wagon. If I couldn't keep the support crew together at this early stage, how could I expect the whole machine to finish the ride intact? I was more than mildly affected at the loss of the bungee. It was a sad thing to have happened, and I didn't like the thought of riding on leaving a man down in enemy territory. But what could I do? Go back? A hundred kilometres? And what if it had flicked off with such force that it was off the road? I re-secured the camping gear with the remaining bungee — the widow — making a commitment to my team that I would be a more responsible leader in the future. We rode away from the Lolo Pass clearing a unit stronger for our sad loss.

The memory of a lost bungee cord soon faded on the downhill coast along the Lochsa River on the staggeringly beautiful Highway 12. I tucked in behind a small MG convertible that was only 2 metres behind a huge RV. The small soft-topped car was so insanely close to the giant motor home that I wondered what the driver was thinking. As it rounded a bend I discovered the car was actually being towed by the RV and there was no one in it. Over the other side of the river was a collection of shabby-looking motel units with a sign *Hot Tubs and Cold Beer*. The RV turned off to cross the bridge over the river. Was it the tub or the beer that appealed?

The Lolo highway was captivating. The road curved in slow, lazy arcs for miles, tracking the slow, lazy river, which sparkled in the warm morning sunshine. Green meadows stretched to the edge of the woods on the far bank. Several fishermen flicked their fly rods in pools. The bike rode itself. I merely hung on to stay upright. Leaning left. Leaning right. I started cutting corners, trying to keep as straight a line as possible through the endless curves. It was a risky game, but I was alone on the road and didn't care. The Lolo had lulled me into a state of euphoria where I felt bullet-proof. The MP3 player was going through its own soporific patch of Enya, and I just about fell off the bike we were such a laid-back duo. And then I hit the deer.

When I say I 'hit' the deer, what I mean is I didn't hit the deer. But should have. I rounded yet another sweeping bend at speed to find a young buck stationary on the road, looking at me bearing down on him. I only had time to register the deer in my sights, utter the first syllable of a common stress-related one-syllable word of exclamation, and twitch my foot towards the brake. In a flash the deer bolted. It bounded across the road in a single leap, and vanished into the woods. How I missed the animal still mystifies me. I was less than a second away from carnage, and was still instinctively braking hard 50 metres on. Shaking, I rode on analysing all the 'what ifs'. What if I'd been riding 5 km/h faster? What if I'd swerved and gone the same way as the deer? What if the deer had just stayed put and I'd slammed into it? There was no answer. It was a sobering lesson from the school of when your number's up, your number's up. I'd sat the exam in the University of Que Sera Sera and fluked a 51% pass. Come around a corner, see a deer on the road. Roll the dice. Spin the roulette wheel. Black 13? No? It is not your time: you ride tomorrow.

Still sweaty-palmed from my first close deer-strike, I rolled into Lewiston on the Washington state line. The bike was overheating as I ambled through downtown looking for the road to Clarkston and the Snake River south into Oregon. Suddenly the bars on the temperature gauge climbed to the maximum five: I had less than a minute to pull off the road. I careened into the first driveway I saw and braked to a halt. A car followed me in and pulled up behind me, trapping me in the driveway.

It was then that I noted it was a McDonald's Drive Thru. The car in front of me was placing its order and moving forward to the cashier. I had to kill the engine to stop the overheating: any moment it was going to seize. 'Welcome to McDonald's. How may we serve you today?'

I dismounted and pushed the bike forward to the window. 'Milkshake, please. Banana?' 'Banana shake. $2.25, sir.' I had no idea what to do with the shake. Why oh why didn't I order a burger and just rest it on the tank? I accepted the milkshake, already attracting looks from kids peering out the back window of the car in front. I wedged the shake in the mess of cables behind my handlebars, hoping it would stay upright, and pushed the bike into the car park under a tree. I ripped off my helmet and sat down in an unnecessary state of stress. The midday sun was frying me in my padded riding gear, and so I changed into hot-weather riding apparel, namely jeans and a T-shirt, taking sips from the shake.

I reviewed progress in Idaho so far. Lost bungee cord, near-miss with a deer, pushing the bike through a McDonald's Drive Thru. I've had less eventful mornings.

The temperature soared as I rode into Oregon, temporarily, along Highway 3 tracking the Snake River through the Wallowa-Whitman National Forest. The road plunged into a canyon in an amazing series of switchbacks and 180-degree bends with precipitous drop-offs. There were no guardrails and I kept my eyes firmly on the road. My antennae were on full deer-alert. I crossed Rattlesnake Summit and started the steep descent into the Grande River valley. Sweat was dripping off me in my helmet. I hadn't had any liquid for three hours, unless you can call a McDonald's shake liquid. I wondered about dehydration. In Australia, I'd ridden with a Camelbak backpack containing 3 litres of water and a tube permanently in my mouth. I hadn't even thought about water intake on this ride, thinking it was an outbacky issue and I wouldn't need it. But in the dry heat of the Joseph Canyon I cursed my assumptions and vowed to always carry a water bottle.

The day was drawing to a close as the sun set slowly in the west. I rode to Hells Canyon Overlook on a twisting, isolated, narrow road through the forest. Hells Canyon — 2,500 metres deep — is America's deepest river gorge, carved out by the Snake River. Several deer were grazing by the roadside, and so my right foot was permanently resting on the rear-brake lever. I wondered whether I'd ridden too far this day. It was dusk,

I had no idea where I could camp, and my stomach was cramping with hunger. When I fuelled up in Enterprise, I glugged down 2 litres of cold water. I was so bloated I couldn't force down any food, enticing though the fried-food warmer at the Texaco gas station was.

But there was one last thing I had to do: make a side trip to Half.com. 'What th—?' you ask. There's a small town just over the Oregon border called Halfway, population 350. In 1999, an auction website business named Half.com was founded by an entrepreneur, and as an advertising gimmick offered the town of Halfway, in return for changing its name, $100,000, some computers for the local school and a prize at the County Fair. A company man in a suit drove to Halfway for a meeting with Mayor Dick Crow. The townspeople of Halfway had a meeting and said make that $100,000, some computers for the school, a prize at the County Fair and get Starbucks to come to town and you've got a deal. The American media went mad over the first US dot-com city in history. The school got their Windows 3.1 computers, and Elroy Spankle won the County Fair prize for best marrow. But just as Halfway, sorry Half.com, was mulling over whether next year's contract could get them some keyboards so they could get 'that super web thing running', the company Half.com was bought by eBay for $300 million. So ended Halfway's 15 minutes of fame. And I'll be honest with you: Halfway was not worth the round trip of 40 kilometres off my route.

It was dark by the time I pulled into a camping area by the Snake River at Oxbow, right on the Idaho–Oregon border and the official start of Hells Canyon. I pitched my tent in the light of a full moon, and swatted away flies as I gazed out over the twinkling ripples on Oxbow Lake. An RV was parked by the lake's shore. It had a portable satellite dish the size of a wardrobe set up on the grass. I suppose after an hour of watching ripples on a moonlit lake even professional campers need 70 channels to fall back on. Hungry and tired, I simply lay down in my tent and fell asleep, once again fully clothed.

The next morning I had one thought only. Eggs. And bacon. And sausage. And maybe tomato. Definitely bottomless coffee. I reached silly speeds curving up from the Snake River valley floor into the hills of Idaho. My goal was to reach the next diner in the next town. And reach it I did. The town was Cambridge, the diner was Lucky's. Being a diner pro, I knew the routine. Walk in, letting the door slam so they knew there was a customer. Nod civilly to the locals up on stools at the servery. Flop down at a table by the window so I could keep an eye on the bike.

Within a minute I had a glass of water, a filter coffee and the menu. Within two minutes the waitress was back. 'What'll it be, hon?' 'Lucky's Big Breakfast, please. Bacon, not ham. Side of toast. Sourdough bread.' 'How you want your eggs, hon?' Damn. Damn. Damn. I was not quite the pro yet. I should have anticipated the egg question. I felt like a tourist. 'Over easy, please.' 'Sure thing, hon. Be right out.' I studied my road atlas to give me something to do. Then my breakfast arrived and it was utterly delicious. I ate it like a maniac and saved the last half-slice of toast to wipe the plate bone-clean of remaining egg-yolk residue. It was nectar from Heaven.

And being a diner pro I knew the next move. 'More coffee, hon?' 'Nah. Just the check, please.' The bill was $6.30. I didn't want to fall into the trap of leaving a 60% tip, so I walked up to the counter to pay. I handed over $10 and she gave me $3.30 change. Erm, shouldn't that have been $3.70 change? Thus I learned my next lesson about America: sales tax. No price is what it seems. Each state has its own rules about applying sales tax, so displayed prices exclude any taxes. So unless you are a local or an accountant, you have no idea what your tax might be. Some sales taxes are exempt on crucial products, like food or fridge magnets. Idaho is one of 14 states that lobs a tax on food. If I had eaten breakfast back in Oxbow, Oregon, there wouldn't have been any tax. But then they may not have had sourdough toast, so you have to weigh up cost–benefit. I came to expect some small amount to be added onto everything. But I had to be careful, as most of my cash was in $10 notes. An average diner breakfast or lunch was around $8, especially if the pancakes were extra, so by the time tax was added and in the euphoria of mopping up the divine egg yolk, when I'd get really generous with a tip, I would often have to cough up some coins on top of my $10.

Lightly burping, I rode away from Lucky's a contented traveller. I was riding the Payette River Scenic Byway and crooning to Steve Miller. I passed a sign in a front yard that said *God Blesses Obedient Nations*, and wondered if I came from one. The Payette River Scenic Byway became the Wildlife Canyon Scenic Byway, which became the Ponderosa Pine Scenic Byway. The road swooped up through woodland, rounding bluffs overlooking the idyllic Payette River. Families were rafting down the river, bobbing over medium-sized rapids. I pulled over to take a photo at a lookout over the Boise Mountains.

Up roared a Harley. The leather-tasselled rider dismounted and lifted off his helmet. I quickly changed Steve Miller to ACDC. We shook hands. This was Carlito from Sacramento, and he was taking the long way home from a work conference in San Diego. He was a debt collector and I wondered what type of conference it was. 'I do mainly domestic repossessions,' he explained. We both had the same type of GPS. Carlito cursed his Garmin as it had locked up on him several days ago. 'F***'n' piece of f***'n' s***!' His main problem was he couldn't play his Steve Miller MP3s. 'No problem, mate. Hand it over.' I whipped out a small allen key, removed the GPS battery, counted to five, replaced the battery and rebooted it. The GPS burst into life. Carlito was rapt. 'Cheers, dude. F***'n' A1. You ever have any debtor problems in Sacramento, here's my card. Better f*** off. Have a good ride, dude.' With that, he roared off in a shower of gravel. It was an excellent display. I looked at his card. It was blank except for *Carlito B. Repossessions. No bulls****.*

I rode for the next two hours in the shadow of the majestic Sawtooth Mountains. Bizarrely, I kept seeing shapes in the rock faces that looked like the Madonna. At some time in my trip I hoped to find a piece of rock, a sliver of bark or even some sourdough toast that resembled the Virgin Mary, and then sell it on eBay to help cover expenses. Seeing her in a mountain range was not financially helpful, but I still got a buzz. I struck road construction at Sun Valley ski area, and immediately the bike started overheating again. It reminded me that my new cooling fan was waiting for me an hour down the road in Hailey at the home of friends Curtis and Mary Ann Crowdson.

When I arrived, Curtis asked if I liked barbecued salmon and cold beer. I would have married his sister if he'd made that a condition. Mary Ann suggested I might want to have a shower, looking at me with an expression that meant it wasn't a question. I took my boots off for the first time in two days and Curtis's sister said no to my marriage proposal.

The next morning, we rode to a small town called Arco, past the Craters of the Moon National Monument. The Apollo space programme used the area to train astronauts in collecting rock samples in a moon-like environment. Then in 1969, when they got to the real moon, they discovered it was nothing like the Idaho Craters of the Moon. Still it was a weird area of lava and basalt rock formations to ride through.

Our main goal was rapidly approaching in Arco: Pickles Diner, famous for their Big Pickles Breakfast. I was determined to act like a real diner pro, especially in front of my American friend. Eggs, over easy. Eggs, over easy. Eggs, over easy. Get it right. The waitress ambled over. 'Ready to order, boys?' 'Sure. Big Pickles Breakfast for me. Sausage links. Hash browns. Sourdough toast. And eggs easy over. Please.' 'What he means is *over easy*, Dolores. Gimme the same. How's Jesse these days?' I felt like Grasshopper.

We parted at Arco, and I rode out into the Idaho desert with the Grand Tetons in the distance. I tucked in behind an RV with the slogan on the back *Life is an adventure — take your Attitude*. It didn't make sense. What does taking your attitude mean? Take it where? Surely if life was an adventure, wouldn't you be better to lose your attitude rather than take it with you? If you are afflicted with an attitude but want your life to be an adventure, aren't you disadvantaged? I rode behind this RV as we toiled across the hot, barren landscape, trying to figure out the catchphrase. In the end I got sick of the mental turmoil and pulled out to overtake. It was then I saw that the make of the RV was called Attitude. Oh well. It filled in 20 minutes of desert riding.

My overnight stop near the state line with Wyoming was in Driggs. Desperate for a cold beer after a hot day in the saddle, I ordered a Bitch Creek Beer, brewed by a local company. I wish I hadn't. Overlooking Driggs was the back side of the Grand Tetons — that spectacularly shaped line of mountains that you see on chocolate-box lids. The following day's ride would be a beauty. Tetons and Yellowstone. I had to get an early night, but I was wide awake. I had to get anaesthetized. I ordered another Bitch Creek.

Chapter 6

Wyoming

Nickname: The Cowboy State

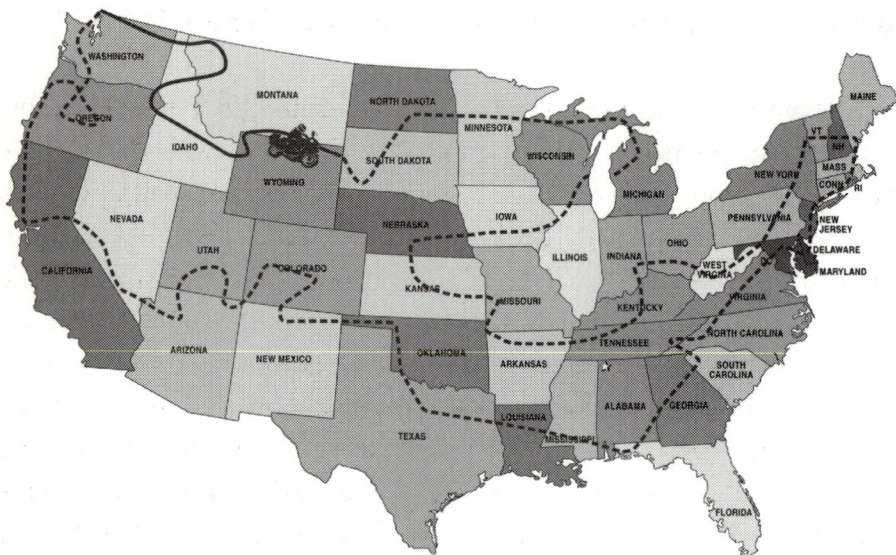

This state: 1,568 kilometres. Journey to date: 7,897 kilometres.

I'LL LIST SOME TECHNICAL WORDS and see if you can figure out what they relate to. Here goes then. Preplay. Jetting. Gazer. Cone splashing. Waning. End play. Dagwood. No? Then you're not a geyser buff, because these are all very common geyser terms, especially if you are a geyser-gazer. I have not made that up. A geyser-gazer is the official name for geeks who gaze at geysers, and several surrounded me as I gazed at Old Faithful in Yellowstone National Park. The Dagwood? That was the sandwich I'd had before wandering over to watch the geyser erupt.

To most tourists, Old Faithful is simply a plume of boiling water that shoots up into the sky every hour and fills in the time nicely between drinks. To the serious geyser-gazer, it all starts with the period of preplay before the eruption. That's those little bursts of steam that you think could turn into the big one. After preplay, you get small jetting and some cone splashing, which gets those dumb tourists starting to click off pictures wondering if that's all Old Faithful is. But this is just the geyser messing with you, because suddenly we're into the eruption proper. It spurts up, then wanes. Up, then wanes. Then comes the end play as it dies down, known as 'terminal waning'. A bit more cone splashing, and then *blub*. You've waited an hour for this and wonder if you'd have been better going straight to your hotel and logging onto the Old Faithful Live WebCam instead.

The only thing worse is meandering over to the viewing platform just as the performance is on its final wane. But that's why it's called Old Faithful. Because you can predict when it will next erupt almost to the minute. There are only three geysers in the world that have this stunning predictability, and they're all called Old Faithful. How, you ask? Bear with me here. You take the time of the first real surge of boiling water when it shooshes up into the sky. Let's call that the geyser 'rise'. Then you take the time at the point of the last little sputter of cone splashing. Let's call that when the geyser 'dies'. If dies minus rise equals two minutes, then you know without a shadow of a doubt that Old Faithful will erupt again in 57 minutes' time. If dies minus rise equals 5 minutes, then Old Faithful will need a bigger rest and won't erupt again for 1.5 hours. This formula is completely accurate, true and is used by park rangers to announce when Old F is ready to blow. Thus visitors can spend more time in the bar, rather than sitting about out in the sun gazing at the preplay.

The reason you've had to read a full page about this interesting geyser phenomenon is because I was quite taken with it. Not so much the whole boiling-water thing, rather the uncanny set-your-watch sort of predictability that I didn't think occurred with Mother Nature. If I were she, I'd just blow skywards whenever I wanted and so what if tourists on the surface had to hang around. After all, this was Yellowstone National Park. Half the world's geothermal features are in Yellowstone: 9,000 square kilometres of grizzlies, lakes, wolves, grassland, bison, petrified forests, elk, earthquakes and Yogi Bear.

I had arrived at the south entrance after a grand old meander through the Grand Teton National Park, which is almost attached to Yellowstone. The Tetons are the mountain range you gape at after riding through the town of Jackson. And Jackson is the sort of rich tourist town that you gape at when you see some of the cars being driven around. They may well be driven by a celebrity, because many movie stars have holiday homes in Jackson. I sent a postcard home to Mum from the post office and signed it *love from Michael, Jackson*. I know, I'd been on the road a while, but she liked it.

✦

The Tetons are best viewed as reflected in the beautiful Jenny Lake. I ended up following a huge, white tour bus through the woods on a narrow one-way road leading up to the car park at the lake. There was a particular spot where it was obvious the best photos were to be had. The craggy peaks were mirrored in the calm, blue, sparkling lake, framed by beech trees. The bus emptied out 24 elderly Japanese couples and 24 digital cameras, with what was probably an instruction to get the photo and get back. Meantime I had parked the bike, ripped off my helmet and dashed to the scenic lookout, camera at the ready. The problem was how to get my photo taken. I have learned, as a sad solo tourist, that the trick is to offer to snap someone else's picture with their camera and inevitably they reciprocate.

The scrum reached the lookout at the same time as I did, and started clicking. Him of her, her of him. I approached the first couple at the head of the orderly queue and gestured that I would be happy to take their joint photo. They nodded appreciatively and handed me their camera. It was no bigger than a credit card. They shuffled together in front of the mountain vista and looked stern. I took their photo. A second later there was a tug on my arm as the second couple in line handed me their camera. But the weird thing was that the first couple stayed put. Also the second couple did not make a move to muscle them out of the way. I had no choice but to take a photo of couple one with couple two's camera. Then couple one handed me their camera for a second time while couple two joined them. I took the photo with one hand while holding the spare camera in the other. Then couple two gestured to couple one's camera in my spare hand and smiled. I completed the series by taking a photo on couple one's camera of the foursome. They collected their cameras from me, said 'sank you', and beetled off up the path. A tug on my arm. Couple three holding out their camera . . . I rode away from Jenny Lake with two things: carpal tunnel and no photo.

But 40 years ago at this very spot another tourist like me, probably riding a Norton Sportster, hit pay-dirt with their photography. Linda Baker had her 8mm cine-camera out when she heard a bang. Looking up, she saw a fireball streaking across the afternoon sky. She got it on a grainy yet clear film, and put it away for 30 years knowing that one day YouTube would be invented. The fireball was in fact a meteor that 'grazed' the Earth, entering the atmosphere and spending 100 seconds scaring the living tetons out of everyone from Utah to Alberta before bouncing back out into space. If it had not come in at such a grazing angle, it would have hit with an impact similar to Hiroshima. Linda's husband, Lyall, who was busy taking photos for Japanese tourists at the time, articulated what everyone was thinking as they gazed at the sight. 'What the f*—?' Since then there have been four meteoroids, called 'bolides', which have collided with the Earth but have grazed off in an Armageddonish game of celestial billiards.

I reached the ranger booth at Yellowstone's south entrance. The entry fee for a bike was $12. The speed limit throughout the park is 70 km/h, and virtually everyone sticks to it except bolides. It's not the place to drive through if you're in a hurry. There were a huge number of bikes on the road and we all gave up waving to each other after a time. The road into Yellowstone looped around the park for 150 kilometres, and at the low speed I knew I'd be camping somewhere within it that night. After stopping at Old Faithful, buying the fridge magnet and changing into hot-weather riding gear, I carried on through Yellowstone towards Mammoth Hot Springs. Rounding a bend I braked to a halt behind a line of cars all stopped in the middle of the road. The occupants were clustered on the roadside, looking down a bank into the woods. This really annoyed me, and I was disgusted at the herd mentality of tourists in general. If there were two people looking at something it became a queue, a magnet for others to see what was going on, a flock of sheep blindly following the mob. I got off the bike and joined the group. We all peered down the bank into what was sparse undergrowth by a stream. I turned to the guy next to me: 'What's down there?' 'Nothing. It's right here', and he pointed to a fallen log not 3 metres away from where we were standing. Suddenly I saw it. A massive elk with massive antlers was basking in the sun on the other side of the log, its antlers looking like branches of the log. It was such incredible camouflage that I hadn't even seen it.

The light was fading as I coasted downhill from Mt Washburn into the settlement of Canyon Village. I pitched my tent in the trees and did some maintenance on the bike — chain-lubing, oil-checking, cable-tightening, tyre-pressure-measuring. My helmet was perched on the mirrors and I had America, Crosby Stills and Nash, and Fleetwood Mac sounding out through the helmet speakers into the dark forest. My dinner was a tin of peaches bought at a petrol station. I opened it with a screwdriver and tyre iron. The syrup splashed all down my T-shirt. Several young elk came to the edge of the clearing to watch the show. Darkness descended on the lonely campsite like a curtain being pulled. I sat astride the bike, boots up on the windscreen, slurping down peaches and listening to James Blunt. I don't remember crawling into my sleeping bag, but that night I had the best sleep of the trip.

By 6.30 the next morning, I was accelerating through the gears on an empty road across a wide prairie. I say 'prairie' because it had two things I thought were a bit prairie-ish: bison and no trees. Or perhaps they were buffalo. Whatever, there were hundreds of them. It was quite a sight and I pulled over on a crest in the road to take it in. Herds of these bison were dots in the far distance, clumps of them were gathered around — and in — a watering hole, but the interesting ones were 2 metres away from me on the road just ambling past. They weren't even on the correct side of the dotted line. I could see the whites, or actually reds, of their small eyes in those massive heads. The odd bison gave a harrumphing sort of cough, but most just strolled casually past, one so close to the bike that it grazed my mirror. I could have patted it. I wondered if some prehistoric sixth sense caused them to know I had eaten a bison burger in Alaska.

Now the reason you were attracted to my book when you first saw it on the shelf and started thumbing through it was clearly that you expected it to be a voyage of educational discovery through America. So, conscious of that responsibility to readers, I now offer two highly interesting facts about the smelly, shaggy, horned creature I was engaging with in Yellowstone. First, it is wrong to call it a buffalo. Buffalo are found in Africa and Asia, wallowing in mud holes. They're different animals, albeit both in the Bovidae family. I learned this from the internet, so it must be right. Secondly, the plural of bison is not 'bisons'; it is 'bison'. Therefore, they have more in common with sheep and fish than you'd think.

But back to the bison/buffalo thing: listen to this. Before the bow and arrow were invented by Native Indians, they'd hunt and kill bison by driving them over cliffs called 'buffalo jumps'. Their legs would break (the bison's not the Indians') and they'd be killed. There's a famous place just north of the Canadian border in Alberta called Head-Smashed-In-Buffalo-Jump that is a tourist attraction for those wanting to learn about this macabre hunting technique. Up there, the local Blackfoot Indians would stampede the bison towards the 10-metre-high cliff and over they'd go. The place got its name from an unfortunate accident wherein a young Blackfoot thought he'd watch all this from the foot of the buffalo jump not the top. As he gazed up at the cliff, he could hear the crescendo of hoof beats and saw a swirling cloud of dust, as hundreds of bison thought they were lemmings and galloped to certain death towards the cliff edge. The last two things that went through the young Blackfoot's head were 'Oh s***' and a hoof. Hence the name Head-Smashed-In-Buffalo-Jump.

Leaving the bison shambling down the road, I rode on towards the eastern exit of Yellowstone Park, alongside the stunning Yellowstone Lake which is fed by the beautiful Yellowstone River. An otter frolicked in the shallows, and gusts of steam wafted up from geothermal activity on the shoreline. I rode up Sylvan Pass without having passed a single vehicle for over an hour. Oddly, none of the trees had any foliage on them — they were just bare trunks and branches. These were lodgepole pines that had been burned in the great fire of 1988 when Yellowstone was brought to its knees by the biggest forest fire to sweep through it.

I passed by the ranger station at the East Entrance with a cheery wave to Ranger Bob. I was now thundering down the Buffalo Bill Scenic Highway heading for Cody, the rodeo capital of the world. But surely that should have been Bison Bill? This whole bison/buffalo issue simply was not going away. I rode along the Shoshone River and reached Cody at lunchtime. With just a can of peaches and an Old Faithful dagwood between me and starvation, I pootled up Main Street looking at dining options. Cody — named after William 'Buffalo Bill' Cody — has a certain theme. In one block I passed Lasso Lodge, Cowboy's Rest, The Ranch, Pardner's, Chuck Wagon Grill, Vera's Vittles, and Bubba's BBQ. I suspected I wouldn't be eating salad for lunch. I chose Bubba's, mainly because I couldn't be bothered doing a U-turn. I went in. It was branded like a real saloon, complete with fake wagon-wheels, a fibreglass horse and a sign that said *Howdy Pardner. Please Wait To Be Seated*. I loved it immediately.

What to order? I wanted to get into the swing of things, having just ridden into town, saddled my steed to the hitching rail outside and spat on the floor. I looked at the menu. What would Clint Eastwood pick? I ordered a Sloppy Bubba: barbecue pork and beef on a Bubba's bun with Bubba's fries, Bubba's coleslaw and a non-Bubba's Pepsi. But my gastronomic decision-making was as bad as always. When my Sloppy Bubba arrived, I realized it wasn't called sloppy for nothing. The plate was covered in a stewy mash of meat bits in sauce. Underneath was the bun, which was soaked in sauce. I scoffed the fries, picked at the coleslaw, stirred the stew for a while and drank the Pepsi. 'How's yer meal, darlin?' The waitress watched while I forked some stew into my mouth. 'Fantastic,' I gushed and she looked pleased. I left a $2 tip, hoping it would mollify Bubba out there in the kitchen when he saw his Sloppy Mess come back untouched.

I would have liked to flesh out the Buffalo Bill story a bit more since I was a bit of a cowboy fan as a kid. Which kid wasn't in the '60s? Here I was in the cradle of the West, and all I had to show for it was some Bubba's BBQ sauce on my moustache. I pulled over at the entrance to the Buffalo Bill Historical Centre and read the sign. Bill Cody got his nickname 'Buffalo' from killing 4,280 bison in 18 months when he had the contract to supply meat to the Kansas Pacific Railroad workers in 1867. I thought about the maths. Say he worked a six-day week with no annual leave: that's 10 bison killed each day. If he worked a 10-hour day: that's one per hour. If his job was to merely ride up alongside a herd of bison and pick them off with his rifle, it sounds do-able. But what was his job description? If he worked alone, he'd have to shoot and process surely, and did that include skinning, gutting, filleting and shrink-wrapping the bison? And when the bison herd saw him galloping towards them day after day, would they stay still — especially when they'd have noted their numbers going down by 10 after each of his visits?

I would have liked to linger at Bison Bill's Buffalo Base, but I had an afternoon of joy ahead of me so needed to get cracking. I refer to the two famous motorcycling avenues of ecstasy in this region: the Chief Joseph Scenic Byway and the Beartooth Highway. I was on the cusp of entering serious Indian country, and wondered if I'd learn a little more meaningful information than I'd gleaned about the Pale Faces so far. I kicked the bike into gear and accelerated out onto the Chief Joseph. Immediately, I liked the guy. Any Indian chief who lent his name to such a spectacular auto route had my compliments. But back in 1877, the scenery was the last thing on the chief's mind as he trekked along this route. He was leading a band of Nez Perce Indians, mostly women, children and elders, fleeing the US cavalry and trying to get to Canada. The chief's real name was Hinmuuttu Yalatlat, but everyone found 'Joseph' easier. At one point on the flight for freedom, he passed a pile of bison carcasses. 'Mornin', Bill.' 'Mornin', Joe.' 'Still shootin' bison, I see?' 'Yep. Got me a new customer. Guy called Bubba down in Cody.'

The byway wound up to Dead Indian Pass at 2,500 metres. The view took my breath away. The road could be seen winding down into the valley in a series of switchbacks you would normally expect to see in the Swiss Alps. While this was the Shoshone National Forest, in America the word 'forest' doesn't necessarily mean there are any trees. I reached the bridge spanning Sunlight Creek. Looking over the parapet I had an attack of vertigo: how on earth Chief Joseph got across I couldn't imagine, as the deep, steep-sided canyon ran for miles.

The road eventually intersected with the Beartooth Highway. This was the main event. The Beartooth is classed as an All-American Road, a title not awarded lightly. The road has to be so utterly scenic that it possesses features not able to be seen elsewhere in the US and is a tourist destination in its own right. While there are 99 scenic byways, such as the Chief Joseph, there are only 27 All-American Roads. The Beartooth has been called 'the most beautiful drive in America', but the catch is that you can only get all the way over in summer. The Beartooth Pass, at 3,300 metres, is mostly blocked by snow. Over two hours I marvelled at the zigzags, switchbacks, high rocky plateaux, shimmering mountain tarns and sheer ravines backgrounded by the craggy peaks of the Beartooth Mountains. In fact, by the time I tapped down through the gears to fuel up at Red Lodge, my hands were sweaty inside the gloves due to the absolute rush of the afternoon's riding. The only pity was that I was alone. The Chief Joseph and Beartooth needed sharing.

In need of fuel myself, I ordered a buffalo burger and milkshake at a roadside caravan in Red Lodge. Officially I was back in Montana, having crossed the state line up on the Beartooth somewhere. Dusk was painting the hills a strange shade of ochre as I rode through undulating farmland towards Wyoming again. A deer bounded across the road in front of the bike but, apart from a brief foot-twitch by the brake lever, it didn't worry me. What did worry me was the lack of suitable camping places. The countryside was open grassland and farmland. I made for the Bighorn River 25 kilometres ahead, knowing there'd be at least some riverbank trees under which to pitch a tent. I rode down a narrow clay track by the wide, slow river and found a clearing. I raised my visor — and instantly a swarm of small flies landed on my face. I decided to ride back 10 kilometres to Lovell.

This small town didn't offer anything in the way of a campground, so I searched for the cheapest-looking mom-and-pop motel. The trick is to get off Main Street, as the budget establishments are always located a street or two off the main drag. I found a suitable target and opened the door signposted *Office*. Imagine my surprise when I ended up standing in the lounge of a house, with a family seated at their dining table. They stopped eating and looked up. The mom put down her knife and fork, wiped her mouth with a napkin and welcomed me to the motel. I asked what a room would cost for a single. She said $86, which, had I been eating at the table, would have made me choke on my corn fritter. There is a negotiating technique that has worked for me a few times on other trips. 'What if I didn't use the sheets and slept in my sleeping bag on top of the bed?' '$86,' she replied. I had to find some way of getting out of there without anyone losing face, considering the family were watching and listening. She was on my wavelength. 'You could try the Lovell campground. It's free. Just go down Oregon, take a right on 3rd, then a left on Quebec. It's on the left before you get to the railroad.'

She was using the word 'campground' metaphorically. What I found was some waste ground between the railway line and a small creek. But it was free and no one else was there. I unloaded the bike in the light of a semi-full moon, pitched the tent, and wandered down to the creek to see if the water was teeth-brushing quality. A thousand frogs were in full chorus. In the distance I hear the horn of an approaching freight train. Every few seconds the horn sounded, getting louder and louder. The frogs didn't bat an eyelid. In fact I'm not sure they have eyelids to bat. Suddenly the train was blasting past, only 20 metres away. Lovell campground had all the makings of a long night.

The next morning I ate elk jerky. To explain. After crossing the Bighorn River I found myself winding up into the Bighorn Pass on the Bighorn Scenic Byway in the Bighorn National Forest near the Bighorn Canyon on Bighorn Lake, heading for Little Bighorn. There was no civilization between Lovell and Dayton, and I was as hungry as a Bighorn sheep. I rounded a sweeping bend up on the plateau and spied a caravan down in the valley with a huge yellow sign saying *Buffalo & Elk Jerky. Free Taste. Rest Room.* Wondering if the caravan also offered coffee, or perhaps — and I accept I may have been fantasizing — all-day breakfasts, I pulled in.

A man in a wheelchair greeted me. His name was Joe, he was disabled from being born with spinal cancer, and he knew his jerky or possibly that should be 'jerkies'. I looked around for the advertised rest room. Joe pointed over to some rocks. 'Wanna try some sweet-pepper elk?' he enthused, and held out a sliver of dried meat. I popped it in my mouth. It tasted salty, but frankly he could have been giving me road kill for all I knew. 'Awesome, Joe. Gimme a packet. How much?' '$12.95.' My day's meal budget was thus spent. I rode away from Joe's jerky joint feeling two things. Good about supporting his enterprise on that lonely hilltop, and wanting to throw up. I finally threw out the jerky packet in Dayton when I stopped at a diner for some real food.

To visit Little Bighorn Battlefield Monument meant another foray up into Montana and going considerably out of my way. Why did I feel the need? I'm not sure. Looking back it was probably a desire to find out some more about the whole White Man versus Indian conflict that so pervaded this area of America. It almost seemed sacrilegious not to at least try to understand the nature of the problems of the time, and Custer's Last Stand somewhat epitomized all I knew about the era. A fast ride up the I-90 interstate for 85 kilometres saw me pull up at the entrance to Little Bighorn. 'Discount $5 for motorcycles,' said the Indian attendant. A good start. The Monument is on the Crow Indian Reservation. I idled the bike up to the main lookout over Last Stand Hill. That's where they have markers, like mini tombstones, all over the grassy hillside, exactly where the soldiers dropped. I was there by myself, leaning over the wrought-iron fence and gazing down at the somewhat unkempt hillside of carnage as I tried to imagine how it played out.

In the visitor centre was a huge mural of Custer's Last Stand, showing the soldiers crouched behind piles of dead horses, firing point-blank at the Indians overwhelming them. In the middle of all this is General Custer, standing tall, brandishing his sabre, knowing he has minutes to live and wondering where his scalp and watch will end up. In the populist depictions of this final battle, Custer comes out as a hero. Reality, as always, was different. But looking over this bleached and deserted hilltop, blissful in my ignorance of what history says about the Native American conflict, I felt very, very satisfied that I had been there to see it.

But time was ticking on and I had to fuel up. The petrol station was next to Sitting Bull Subway (*Our foot-long special: kids get a free arrowhead*). As I was filling the bike, a man sauntered over. He was wearing a 10-gallon hat. 'Howdy. You ridin' far?' 'Yep. Heading for Gillette tonight.' 'Nice run along the 212. Turn off on the 59 after Broadus. Clint's the name. From Arkansaw.' 'Nice to meet you. You visiting the Little Bighorn?' I struck a raw nerve. 'F***in' injuns.' Up until now I never thought anyone actually used the word 'injun' except in *Rin Tin Tin*. 'Five years ago this place was free to the American people. Injuns took it over and now you gotta pay. F***in' rip-off injuns. Should be for the people. That's the f***in' Crow for you. This is my wife, Kathy.' 'Nice to meet you,' I said. 'We were just talking about the Bighorn Monument.' 'F***in' injuns chargin' to get in,' she grunted, obviously on Clint's side of the debate. The two anti-injun Arkansaw visitors wished me a safe ride and went back to their RV.

The ride across the Northern Cheyenne Indian Reservation was hot, dry, hard work. At a small settlement called Lame Deer, I stopped and bought a litre bottle of water to rehydrate. Outside the shop an Indian-looking man strode up to me and said, 'Can you help me out with a dollar?' 'Why?' was all I could think of asking. 'My car's run out of gas.' 'How's a dollar going to help then?' 'OK, make it $10.' He had me there in a nice counter-manoeuvre. I could have used Clint to help me out. In the end I just ignored him and rode off. I passed Chief Dull Knife College and Charging Horse Casino. The Adopt A Highway signs were back, and I noted adoptees were Jonathan Walks Last, Chief Standing Elk and someone called AA Weaselbear.

Just before Broadus I came up to a huge road-construction zone. I was in a line of slow-moving traffic hemmed in behind the *Pilot Vehicle. Follow Me* pick-up, and at 50 km/h my bike soon overheated. Each side of me were massive earth-moving machines creating dust storms. In short, there was no way I could pull over to let the engine cool, so I desperately minimized the revs in a vain attempt to get the temperature down. Shortly the gauge reached maximum and I could almost hear the water in the radiator boiling. At a halfway point through the roadworks stood a *Stop/Slow* lady in a fluoro vest. I prayed she would turn her sign to *Stop*; it stayed on *Slow*. I pulled over anyway. 'Bike's overheating. Can I stop here for 10 minutes?' 'No problem, friend. Just get off the roadway onto that there grass bit an' wait for the next pilot car.' 'Thanks a lot.' 'Sure thing. Say, can you help me out with a dollar?'

I was very happy to reach Gillette after crossing back into Wyoming for the third time. Gillette was where I had the bike booked into the local Suzuki dealer to have the new cooling fan fitted in the morning. I got a site at the Crazy Woman Campground in the middle of town. As I walked into the office, a lady came out from a caravan to deal with me. I was itching to ask — or to at least detect some sort of clue — if this was the crazy woman herself.

As I pitched my tent, my neighbour wandered over with a small Pomeranian dog called Lily who sniffed around my back wheel. I had one eye on Lily cocking her leg on my tyre and the other on the man's wife. Why? It'd been a long time on the road . . . No wait, that's not it. It was what she looked like. She emerged from the RV wearing a long, flowing kaftan-type robe completely covered in oranges. He introduced her as Orchid. On her head was a lime-green plastic shower-cap. She said hello and asked if my bike was 'one of those Harvey Donaldsons'. I knew in an instant why I prefer bush camping.

The next morning I was shaking the hand of the mechanic at Thunder Basin Motorsports. In turn he was shaking his head at me: the old fan was not broken. It was the radiator-fan switch, also known as a sending unit — which senses the temperature of the water and turns the fan on and off accordingly — that had died. The dealer in Missoula, Montana, had mistakenly identified the fan as the problem and I had bought a new one unnecessarily for $400. A new radiator switch cost $22. And Custer thought *he* was screwed.

I tried not to look on my loss of $378 in terms of diner breakfasts, fuel refills or $10 donations to local down-and-outs. However, it was a wonderfully enlightening feeling to thunder along the windy interstate to Moorcroft, knowing that I could once again go through towns, stop at traffic lights, and keep the bike idling while taking photos without worrying about the bike overheating.

My last stop in Wyoming was at Devils Tower. If you remember the movie *Close Encounters of the Third Kind*, you'll have seen Devils Tower, that 1,500-metre-high volcanic cone that looks like an upturned thimble. Devils Tower — or, as the Lakota Indians call it, Bear's Butte — is sacred to the local native tribes, who ban climbing as it desecrates the spirit of the land. 400,000 people, probably from Arkansaw, disagree and scale the vertical walls of this tower each year. For Twisting Throttle it was a take-the-photo-buy-the-fridge-magnet visit. I had more pressing places to desecrate.

Chapter 7

South Dakota

Nickname: The Sunshine State

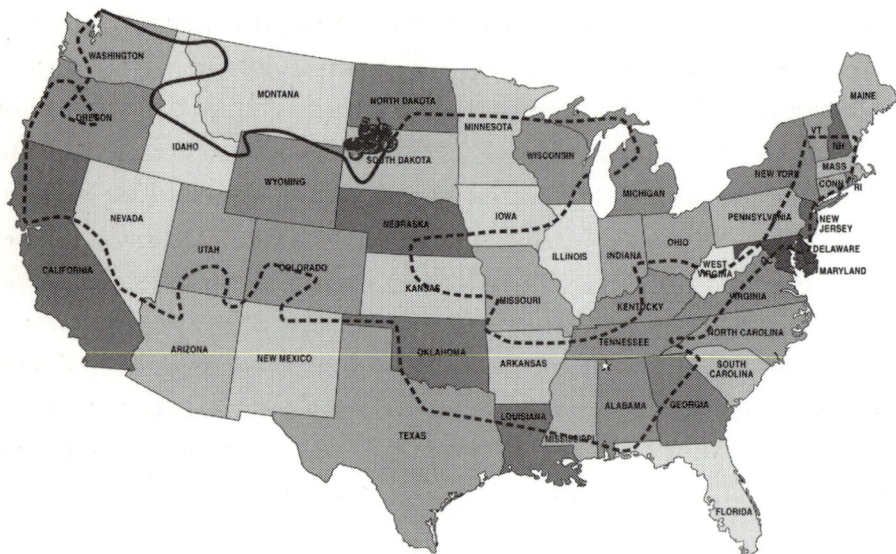

This state: 945 kilometres. Journey to date: 8,842 kilometres.

Here's a question. If a town has a population of 15, what do they all do? The reason for asking is that I had just cantered past the town sign for Aladdin, on the Wyoming–South Dakota state line. On town signs in this part of America they state the population. I wondered why. Either some sign company is onto a good thing, replacing signs every year, or the population doesn't change much.

But riding through Aladdin, population 15, the odd thing was that there was quite a bit there. A lot more infrastructure than you'd imagine 15 people could justify. For example, there was a general store, a community hall, a diner, a cemetery, a trailer park, a bar, a ranch, a post office, an antiques museum and about eight houses on the main highway that I could see. The town has its own website and two actual side streets. So, assuming the townsfolk are not 15 single people living by themselves, let's say there are (a) two proper families with kids, (b) several couples with kids flown the coop (and there's not a lot in Aladdin to keep them there, as opposed to, say, New York), (c) one or two widowed pensioners who can't bring themselves to retire in nearby Belle Fourche, and (d) Reverend White. That's seven to eight family groups making up the population of Aladdin. But I saw a lot more houses than that, and then there's the question of how they spread themselves around the businesses. Is the rancher's wife also the curator of the town museum? With mail arriving for a maximum 15 people, is the post office run off its feet? When the Perkins sisters go away for their holidays, who takes over the diner, cleans the community hall and tends the cemetery? And assuming some residents live in the trailer park, who occupies all those houses? It was something to think about in the 14 seconds that it took me to ride through Aladdin, and even now I'm none the wiser about these small specks of places in the US where the number of people living there seems a lot lower than you'd expect the town's infrastructure needs to run it. And my last thought on the subject as I sped over the state line into South Dakota was: what did Reverend White do? There wasn't a church.

I fuelled up in Belle Fourche and set about my day's quest: to find the geographic centre of the US. When the US was just the 48 contiguous states, the centre was located in Kansas. In 1959, Alaska and Hawaii were made states, and so the centre-marker post had a big relocation on its hands, much to the annoyance of the people in Lebanon, Kansas, who, overnight, had a shop full of useless fridge magnets and key-rings. But Lebanon's loss was Belle Fourche's gain, as they were the nearest town to the new geographic centre of America. There was one small flaw. The exact centre-point was in a field way off the road, and the farmer, Old Man Wilkins, wasn't happy with tourists trudging through his corn to get a photo next to the post. So the townspeople of Belle Fourche erected a new centre-marker post, some 20 kilometres south in the actual town and, surprisingly, right next door to their visitor centre, a diner and a souvenir shop. Tourists wouldn't know any different, could have a smoothie and a muffin after taking the photo, and buy a souvenir postcard, even though the name of Lebanon was crossed out in felt-pen.

But that somehow seemed a sham as I sat on the bike looking over to the small park where the post was surrounded by flags of all the states. Anyway I wasn't in the mood for a smoothie. I wanted to go 20 kilometres north, walk across the field, and stand at the precise exact uncompromising centre of the 50 states. That'll be the day Twisting Throttle panders to tourist convenience. I popped across the road to buy a key-ring and then rode north. And couldn't find the centre of the US. I entered the co-ordinates into my GPS and it took me to the junction of the 111 and the 168. It was just an intersection out on the South Dakotan plains with grassland stretching from horizon to horizon, a lone eagle circling high in the blue sky, and grasshoppers jumping on and off my windscreen. Which way do I start walking? You'd have expected a sign or a stile at least. Old Man Wilkins must really not like tourists.

I resolved to go through Lebanon, Kansas, as I rode back south towards Sturgis, feeling slightly duped by the whole centre-of-the-universe thing. I saw signs to Thunder Butte, Slim Buttes, Mud Butte, and the excellent Bear Butte. As I sped along the remote open highway over undulating prairie-like plains, I felt light taps on my boots as if stones were flicking up from the road surface. I thought nothing more of it until suddenly a small dart hit me in the nose through my open visor. It was like being poked with a syringe. I braked to a halt, jumped off the bike, and ripped off my helmet. In the bike's mirror I could see a small brown grasshopper embedded in the bridge of my nose, face first. I flicked him off and rubbed the little welt it had caused. Then I saw the carnage. The whole of the bottom of the bike was splattered with grasshopper carcasses. It was as if I had ridden through a plague of locusts all hovering two feet off the road surface. Bizarrely, apart from the taps on my boots I'd had no idea this was taking place below me. The grasshoppers were wedged in every possible nook and cranny, from the bash plate to the oil cooler to the cylinders. It would take some washing out at the next fuel stop.

I reached the town of Sturgis for no other reason than to be able to say I reached the town of Sturgis. This was exactly 10 days after the famous annual Bike Week, the largest bike rally in the world, where up to 500,000 motorcycles vie for the 500 parking spaces in town. On a Japanese bike I would have been a novelty. For six days the residents of Sturgis, an otherwise sleepy town near the wooded Black Hills of South Dakota, enjoy half a million Harley Davidsons tooling around. Entertainment ranges from KISS live in concert to the Sturgis Biker Babes. The saloons are standing-room only, and the streets are lying-room only. The most popular T-shirt sold is *I Rode to Sturgis*, being a dig at the increasing number of white-collar Harley riders who trailer their bikes to within 20 miles of the rally, unload, change into their leathers and stars-and-stripes bandanas before cruising into town like wild hogs.

I fuelled up, washed off the dead grasshoppers, treated myself to a day-old burger from the gas station's warmer, and headed up into the Black Hills. It was a warm, dusky evening, and I should have had a biker babe riding pillion behind me. Instead I fast-forwarded the MP3 player to Meat Loaf. I rode into Deadwood, and thus commenced a half-hour period where events did not go too well. Let me explain.

Deadwood is a very touristy place playing on its Wild West history, claiming to be the place where Wild Bill Hickok was murdered by Jack McCall, and where he was laid to rest along with Calamity Jane and Potato Creek Johnny. I counted at least three Wild Bill characters on horseback clip-clopping around downtown Deadwood waving to the kids. Hickok was killed at Saloon No. 10, playing poker.

I parked the bike over the road from the saloon, which was still standing but now serving nachos and oysters, and gazed across at it. I wondered how Wild Bill's final moments had played out. Apparently McCall shot him in the back of the head, enraged that Hickok condescendingly offered to pay for his breakfast after relieving him of all his money in poker. Hickok's hand at the time he slumped over the table was a pair of aces and a pair of eights, now known in poker circles as 'dead man's hand'. That morning, Wild Bill Hickok forgot two important rules. Never sit with your back to the door when holding a dead man's hand, and never offend a fellow gunfighter by recommending the nachos.

But the Hickok–McCall incident had a further impact on me as I circled the streets of downtown Deadwood looking for the road south to Custer. I now know, but didn't that evening, that Deadwood re-enacts the Hickok killing and subsequent capture of McCall as street theatre every evening in summer. I rode up a side street, assuming it to be a shortcut to the 385 South, and took a left through some orange cones I thought were just roadworks cones but were in fact to stop traffic. In the street I was now in were hundreds of people sitting and standing on the kerbside. Facing me at the other end, legs askance, stood a Wild West gunfighter in the middle of the cobbled street. He fired a revolver into the air and the gunshot sounded like a whip crack. I had ridden into the middle of the nightly street theatre, and had an audience of hundreds of tourists wondering if the motorbike was part of the show.

Fractions of a second ticked by in what seemed like minutes as it dawned on me where I was. I couldn't carry on riding up past Wild Bill, but the street was so narrow a U-turn in one go would be impossible. Some of the closer spectators realized what had happened and were starting to clap me. A marshal in a cowboy hat and fluoro vest pointed back the way I had entered the street. I manoeuvred the bike in a five-point U-turn, praying I wouldn't drop it, and just before riding away cocked my fingers at the gunfighter and loosed off a pretend shot. He fired a shot back at me, the spectators cheered, and the marshal gave me a thumbs-up as I disappeared back through the cones into welcoming oblivion. It would be true to say that I've had less stressful moments on this trip. Frankly, I have never eaten nachos since.

★★

It was a race against the encroaching darkness as I worked my way through the Black Hills National Forest towards Custer. My antennae were on full alert for deer, such was the time of day. I pulled into a lookout overlooking the Crazy Horse Memorial. The sun was minutes away from calling it a day, and the huge shape carved out of the rock face just a mile away was basked in a beautiful orange glow. I couldn't have timed the arrival at this important part of the region's heritage any better.

Crazy Horse Memorial is on-track to becoming the world's largest sculpture. But it may never be finished, as progress is so slow. Back in 1948 a carver who worked on Mt Rushmore, Korczak Ziolkowski, got a letter from the local Lakota Indian chief, Henry Standing Bear. Mr Bear's letter complained that Mt Rushmore was getting all the attention whereas 'the red man had great heroes, too'. Ziolkowski dusted off his chisel set and got to work on Thunderhead Mountain, only 13 kilometres away from Mt Rushmore. The end vision is for a mountain carving depicting the warrior Crazy Horse sitting on his galloping horse, pointing forward.

Ziolkowski refused all offers of financial help from the government, thinking that the project would be polluted by federal involvement. When he died in 1982, his parting words to his wife were: 'You must continue to work on the mountain, but go slowly so you do it right.' Mrs Ziolkowski sighed, cashed in her train ticket to Chicago, unpacked her bags and resigned herself to more calluses and bronchial problems. Seven of the Ziolkowski's 10 children now work on the mountain carving.

I pitched camp near the town of Custer, once again in the darkness with only the moon's eerie light filtering through the fir trees to illuminate the idyllic camping spot. By now I could go through the setting-up-camp motions blindfolded. Again I had nothing to eat, and with a quarter of the ride completed I still hadn't got into a food routine that meant I ate more than one actual meal a day. The last thought that went through my mind as I lay on my stretcher listening to the night sounds of the Black Hills was: what was Wild Bill Hickok's fifth card?

I stood at the railing and gazed up at Mt Rushmore. Was it larger or smaller than I expected? I wasn't sure. It was 7.30 a.m. and I'd beaten the crowds. I'll bet you can't name the four presidents whose faces are carved in the mountain. I got the two obvious ones, Washington and Lincoln. The other two escaped me, revealing an abysmal lack of local knowledge. I put that right by buying a fridge magnet and discovering the other two are Clinton and Obama. Unlike Crazy Horse this memorial was completed quickly, over 14 years, with plenty of government funding, and sculptor Gutzon Borglum's children didn't have to give up their PlayStations for hammer drills. By the time I left Mt Rushmore Visitor Centre, the tour buses were lining up at the entrance station and the sound of clicking shutters could be heard above the bike's idling engine.

The sightseeing was almost over and I was about to launch into a phase of riding hard to put on the miles. Stopping on the roadside I pulled out the road atlas, tracing a line directly from where I was now — the entrance to Badlands National Park — directly up to the Great Lakes. I had two days to cross South Dakota, North Dakota and Minnesota, and reach Lake Superior to avoid falling behind my theoretical schedule. I'd lost a day by being too touristy in this scenic Northwest, by going too slowly, not speed-wise but in my route. Laid over the map, my progress was all over the place, trying to connect as many predetermined riding routes as I could in the name of 'seeing it all'. I hoped I hadn't fallen into lazy riding mode, as I needed to put in some high-mileage days to stay on-track. I also knew that the famed Midwest southerly crosswinds would be interesting. In short, it was time to stop blethering around and get down to business.

The Badlands was an odd area of arid, windswept rock formations, ravines, gullies and canyons, which I was fleeced $10 by the local ranger in a kiosk to ride through. It was nice in a stark, surreal sort of way, but I was quite glad to reach the top of the plateau and point the bike's nose northwards towards Canada. But first I had to fill the tanks of both rider and machine. I headed for a town called Wall. And here is the strange thing. Around 15 kilometres out of Wall, I started seeing signs in the fields, barely visible to traffic passing them. And they were all about Wall Drug. 'Drive Slow. Wall Drug.' 'Free Iced Water At Wall Drug.' 'Try Our 5¢ Coffees At Wall Drug.' 'Wall Warmly Welcomes You. Sign Sponsored By Wall Drug.' 'Not Far Now. Wall Drug.' 'Only 5 Minutes To Our Famous BBQ Ribs At Wall Drug.' There were no fewer than 30 of these billboards. I guessed that Wall Drug meant a drug store in Wall. But was a drug store in a town with 800 citizens likely to be that big?

Here's what I now know about Wall Drug. Yes, it is a drug store, but it's more like a sprawling shopping mall, cowboy-themed and containing restaurants, department stores, shops and sideshows. It is a famed tourist attraction, mostly because of its incredible self-promotion by plastering South Dakota with billboards, like the 30 or so I had ridden past in the 15 kilometres from the Badlands. Thanks to its reputation for free iced water, 5-cent coffees, and billboards proclaiming how far it is to get there, Wall Drug enjoys worldwide promotion. For example, at the US base at the South Pole, there's a sign that says *Free Iced Water Here. Wall Drug.* The US troops in Afghanistan put up a sign outside their foxhole saying *7,000 miles to Wall Drug.* Personally, I hate this sort of overt marketing PR and resent being taken as a dumb tourist who would fall for this puerile self-promotion. I quickly finished my BBQ ribs and free iced water, and downed my second 5-cent coffee before buying a key-ring and a magnet. I rode away from Wall Drug determined not to spend one more minute in its clutches.

And then there was the wind. They called the wind 'Mariah'; I called it something else. It blew directly from the south, so, as long as I was riding due north I could almost switch off the bike's motor and still travel at 120 km/h. But my track was northeast and the pattern of the roads in north South Dakota was grid-like. This meant I had to ride in stretches of 50 kilometres first due east, then due north, then due east again. After I'd finished an easterly segment, I was spent. The wind gusted so strongly that I was permanently at an angle, and fighting to ride straight as the gusts slammed the bike over to the other side of the road. Torrid, it was.

All afternoon I slowly worked my way in this zigzag fashion towards the North Dakota state line. I passed through Pierre and enjoyed a moment gazing at the slow-moving Missouri River. This was where *Dances with Wolves* was filmed. I spent the next half-hour riding across the dry, windswept prairie shouting out 'Tetanka!' Looking back, I believe it was the combination of heat and battle fatigue from combating the crosswinds. Towns were non-existent and I felt exposed and alone, like a speck on a huge plateau of grassy nothingness. Occasionally silos would appear on the horizon, and I passed the odd pick-up truck with a friendly wave to the Stetson-hatted driver. There was a sign on a derelict building:

Varmint Hunters Association. Exactly what varmints they hunted out there was beyond me. Possibly moles, field mice or snakes, I'm not sure.

I was getting a fraction concerned about accommodation for the night. It had been four hours of wind warfare since Wall, and I was still an hour away from North Dakota. For morale purposes I wanted to get across the state line to pretend that I had less distance to travel the next day. But where to camp out in this wide, open grassland desert? Small farming settlements of Selby, Mound City and Herreld offered nothing, and tumbleweeds all but rolled along their deserted main streets.

Just across the border in North Dakota a gust of wind slammed into the bike, and my camera battery-charger, velcroed onto a small shelf inside the windscreen, flew off onto the road. I found the charger intact, but my spare camera batteries were gone, scattered somewhere over the last 100 metres.

I found a patch of waste ground in a small town called Strasburg. I think it was their town park. It looked perfect. I hid the bike in some trees and pitched the tent in a billowing wind. I had some two-day-old jalapeño kettle chips and half a bottle of warm water. It was heaven. I lay down on the ground inside the tent, not even bothering with the stretcher. The next day would be the charge towards the Great Lakes. You know where the Great Lakes are? 900 kilometres from Wall Drug, of course.

Chapter 8

North Dakota

Nickname: The Roughrider State

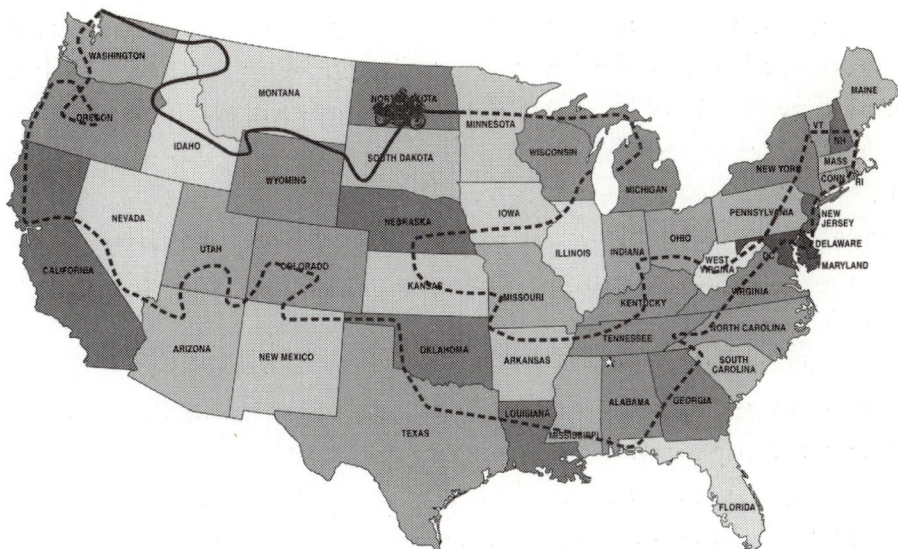

This state: 397 kilometres. Journey to date: 9,239 kilometres.

G OD, NORTH DAKOTA. In one side. Out the other. Flat. Relentlessly flat. Corn. Long, featureless highway. Sun in my eyes. Hard to concentrate. Perspiration. Mind drifting. Reciting over and over 'The Rime of the Ancient Motorcyclist':

> *Hour after hour, hour after hour*
> *He rode, nor breath nor motion*
> *As idle as a pointless blip*
> *Upon a pointless ocean*
> *Sweating, sweating, everywhere*
> *And both his boots did stink*
> *Corn, corn, everywhere*
> *Would drive a man to drink . . .*

Chapter 9

Minnesota–Wisconsin

Nicknames: The Gopher State–The Badger State

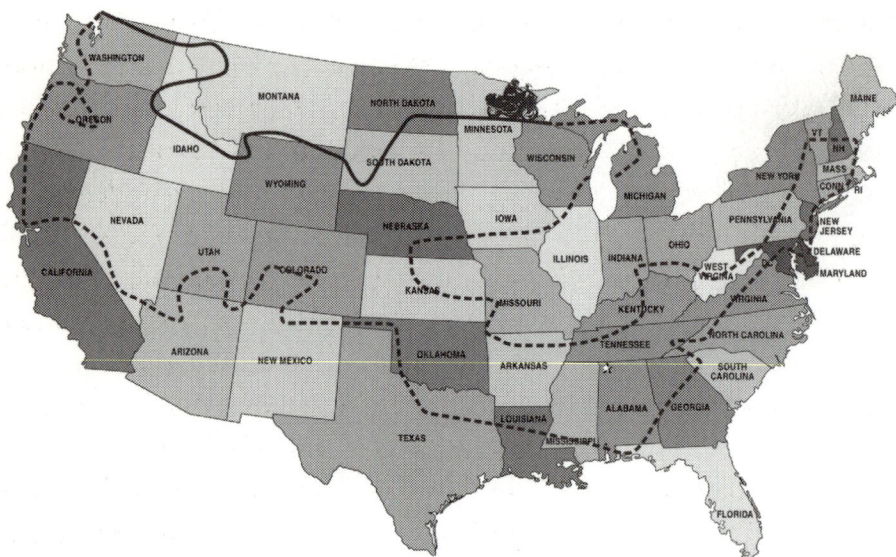

These states: 646 kilometres. Journey to date: 9,885 kilometres.

SORRY ABOUT THAT LAST CHAPTER. I wasn't myself. But I swear I have nothing to say about my 397 kilometres in North Dakota. It was flat, uneventful and very, very boring. Any state that has the motto 'Strength from the soil' is not exactly going to be a rural Disneyland. For half of my North Dakota experience, I rode along America's longest straight stretch of road, between Streeter and Hickson. It runs arrow-straight for 197 kilometres. I will never complain about the Nullarbor again. North Dakota is the 19th largest state in land area, but is 48th out of 50 states for number of people. And I saw none of them.

I crossed the state line into Minnesota determined to seek out something of cultural interest or historical significance, rather than just doing another North Dakota. They may not be sexy states like California or Florida, but the 12 states of the Midwest accounted for a quarter of my route, so I needed to drop down a gear and not just blast through. The heritage icon I selected to seek out in Minnesota was of course the World's Largest Loon. Granted, it wasn't up there with Mt Rushmore, but, leaning back in the saddle gazing up at the huge, painted-concrete loon in a small lakeside park in Vergas, I could appreciate the artistry.

But here's the interesting thing. Every state has an official state bird. Most of them sort of fit with the state, such as Arizona's Cactus Wren, New Mexico's Roadrunner, Mississippi's Mockingbird, or Pennsylvania's Ruffed Grouse. You wonder if Minnesota is in fact happy with the Common Loon depicting it. And the same with state flowers. Colorado's Rocky Mountain Columbine, Georgia's Cherokee Rose, Iowa's Wild Prairie Rose or Ohio's Scarlet Carnation. Minnesota's state flower? The Pink and White Lady's Slipper. Don't get me onto official state fish. The point here is that Minnesota — Land of 10,000 Lakes — has no pretensions to be anything other than a whole lot of nothing outside the twin cities Minneapolis–St Paul where 60% of its population live. And it was across part of this nothing that I was riding when I shot a little boy.

It was his fault. He threw a stone at me. I was idling through a small town called Moose Lake. Two little kids, a boy and girl, were playing in their unfenced garden very near the roadside. The little girl saw the bike coming and started waving. As I waved back, the little boy picked up a decent-sized stone and threw it point-blank at the bike. It bounced off my rear pannier. I braked to a halt and made a pistol shape with my hand, firing off a pretend bullet at the little boy. They both scampered around the corner of their house. The last I saw of the two rascals was the boy machine-gunning me as I rode away down the road. I wondered what the official state weapon of Minnesota was.

I felt like I'd been riding for a month. The day was turning out to be a long one in the saddle. My average speed was fast, the roads I picked were empty, and — apart from stone-throwing street urchins at Moose Lake — Minnesota was welcoming. As I rode through Wadena, I saw a billboard for the local bank: *Your bankers are your neighbours.*

In Barnum I fuelled up with 87 octane. A sticker on the pump said

Unleaded Plus contains XVP2000 detergent additive + 10% ethanol. In other words, I was expecting my bike to run on corn. The Midwest, with all its corn, is big on a blend of gasoline and 10% ethanol, the resulting fuel known as 'gasohol'. With the pressure to use renewable fuels, the move is on to push gasohol. The problem is that research shows it takes way more energy to grow the corn, convert it to ethanol and blend it with the gasoline, than the gasohol produces to run a car. The same research reports that one person could be fed for a year on the same amount of corn it takes to produce ethanol for one tank-fill of a decent-sized 4WD truck. Therefore, using gasohol enhances global warming, destroys forests and inflates food prices. Supporters of biofuel production said, 'Yeah, but what else you going to do with so much corn?' 'Feed the people' came the answer. And the people said, 'You joking? We're sick of corn.' So the food–fuel debate still rages in the US. As I topped off my tank, I hoped my fuel injectors could cope with the corn additive.

Almost at the Wisconsin state line, I had ridden 750 kilometres across North Dakota and Minnesota and I was . . . was . . . What's that expression meaning very, very tired and starts with F? Yes, fatigued, that's what I was. I didn't have the inclination to ride the I-35 into Duluth and navigate out of a city. I set the GPS to take me cross-country on back roads, zigzagging towards Lake Superior. The likeliest-looking camping place I could see in my atlas was Amnicom Falls State Forest Park. The GPS didn't recognize the name, so I decided to 'go manual'. That involved actually reading road signs and asking locals which way to go.

The light was fading quickly as I crossed into Wisconsin on a back road so back that it almost wasn't a road. Grass was growing through the paved road surface. I lost my bearings and simply ended up riding anywhere that looked like it led somewhere. I kept on heading northeast, knowing that eventually I would bump into Lake Superior. My reasoning was that it is the largest lake in the world, covers more area than South Carolina, and there is enough volume in it to cover North and South America in a foot of water. In other words, it must be out there somewhere and there was a good chance I would reach it with or without a GPS. I popped out of the maze of side roads onto Route 2, which runs all the way to Michigan, at Wentworth. It was virtually dark.

I saw an old man walking his dog, and pulled level with him. 'Excuse me, sir. Can you tell me which way to Amnicom Falls Park?' 'Eh?' 'Amnicom Falls. Which way?' 'Back down 2. Back towards Superior. Go west. Stay on the 2.' 'Are you sure? I thought it was down that way towards Ashland.' 'That's right. Go east. Towards Ashland. Get to the top of the big hill and take a left to Port Wing.' 'Thanks. How far's the big hill from here?' 'If you get to Maple, you've gone too far. That a Honda you're ridin'?' 'Yes, it is. Thanks, got to get going. Have a good evening.' 'Take care, fella.'

He'd made it up. There was no big hill eastwards. There were no signs to Port Wing. I realized this some 10 kilometres up Route 2 when I got to Maple. I turned around and rode fast back to Wentworth. The old man was still walking his dog. He waved cheerily as he saw me ride past him going the other way. It occurred to me that I was heading back to North Dakota, when I saw a turn-off to Amnicom Falls. The forest park offered excellent camping, though once again it was pitch-black. This time I kept the bike's headlights burning, which lit up the forest glade like a fairground. Perhaps it was the corn.

🛡️

The morning dawned murky grey with a few spots of rain. My hygiene, after so many nights in a tent, was questionable to the extent that when I chatted to myself I turned my head. I would need to check into a motel for a night very, very soon. What about one more night under canvas, then the treat? I pulled into a gas station in Cornucopia to top up. Pulling off my riding gloves, I placed them on my top box and put on my warmer, padded gloves. It was shaping up to be a cold-weather-gear day. Finishing the last of my Cheezels, I rode out into the forest park eager to see my first glimpse of the Great Lakes. Perhaps it was because I was focused on looking out for Lake Superior through the trees that I didn't notice the truck behind me. And that was when the duel commenced. Here's what happened.

The road, Route 13, tracked along the shore of Lake Superior, but the lake was hidden by trees. The road surface was damp from the morning lake mist. My speed was bang-on the limit of 105 km/h. I glanced in my mirror to see an 18-wheeler articulated freight truck close in on me and pull out to overtake. As he passed and I wrestled the bike in its compression wave, the truck's speed would have been no less than 120 km/h, at least 25 km/h over the heavy-vehicle speed limit. But then, just after pulling in front of me, he buttoned off his speed to 95 km/h, his lawful speed limit, and I had to brake hard to keep from ramming him. I pulled out alongside to re-overtake him and got as far as his front cab. Instantly the truck accelerated back up to 120 km/h, preventing me from getting past at my overtaking speed. On this long stretch of straight forest road we were side-by-side thundering along Route 13. It's just that he wasn't the one on the wrong side of the road. On the other hand, only one of us hadn't yet reached top gear and was astride a machine that had an official top speed of 230 km/h.

When I got in front of him, my speed was 140 km/h and still the truck stayed on my tail. There were no air horns, flipping birds or gunshots. It was a drag race pure and simple. He had 16 more wheels and four more gears. But I could get to 100 km/h in 4.4 seconds — and let's not forget my XVP2000 detergent additive + 10% ethanol. Rounding the next sweeping bend, the truck was still right up my date. There was a slight air of menace about the whole situation, and I decided to just out-sprint him and hope he didn't call in a few favours from the state troopers on his radio. Into view came a steep hill and my salvation. I bled off speed gradually until we both hit the bottom of the hill at 110 km/h. In an impulsive act of skilled yet stupid riding, I tapped the foot brake with my boot to light up the brake light and at the same time rolled the throttle. The bike surged forward up the hill, but it was too late for the truck. On seeing my brake light he crashed down two gears and lost momentum. The last I saw of the 18-wheeler's lights was crawling up the incline as I crested the brow and took line honours. Even Rossi wouldn't finish a MotoGP race with the amount of sweat I had on my face after that brush. I coasted into Bayfield in need of two hols. Gaso and alco.

I gave the bike its ethanol fix for the morning and went in to a small café to recover my composure, parking the bike out of sight behind it.

After half an hour I'd finished my eggs on toast and made to gather up my helmet and leave. 'Hey, you. Biker boy.' I looked up and silhouetted in the doorway was a 6'6" man mountain wearing leather boots, denims and a trucker's cap. Behind him, virtually blocking the narrow street was the 18-wheeler. 'Wanna word with you, friend.' The other café patrons looked up and all conversation died. The waitress held out a menu to the trucker, but he just brushed it off and walked slowly towards my table, bumping the elbow of a businessman in a suit, who spilt some tea. 'Hey, buddy,' said the businessman, 'watch what—' 'You got something to say to me, a**hole?' The trucker looked down at the guy.

I stood up to face the showdown. The trucker stopped by the latte machine. His eyes narrowed. You could have heard a pin drop in the café. The owner, who had ducked down behind the counter, popped his head up. 'Now, fellas, we don't want no trouble in here.' The trucker looked at the owner and then pointed at me. 'No trouble from me, friend. I jess want this piece of biker s*** outside.' 'Fine, let's go.' I threw down a $5 note for the breakfast, picked up my helmet and keys, and gestured to the trucker: 'After you, fatso.' I followed the bear of a man outside and we faced each other on the pavement. His eyes bore into mine. I could smell the staleness of cigarettes on him. My hand twitched on my helmet strap in case I needed to swing it. 'Jeez, buddy, you're hard to catch. These yours?' He held out my gloves. 'These dropped off your bike in Cornucopia. I was fillin' up right behind you at Chevron. Been chasin' you all mornin'. You that Throttle guy? I know about you an' losin' gloves in Australia. Can't have that in Wisconsin. Take it easy, friend.' And with that he shook my hand, clambered up into his cab, and with a hiss of compression brakes manoeuvred his 18-wheeler back into the traffic.

All right, then, I may have imagined much of that apart from the eggs. But it was a way of effecting closure on the morning's events. I talked about official state fish before. Wisconsin's is the muskellunge, a pike-like fish common in the Great Lakes and surrounds. With all due respect to the muskellunge, and given the risks taken this morning on the road, all I could think about was how it's an anagram of 'gee numskull'.

Chapter 10

Michigan

Nickname: The Automotive State

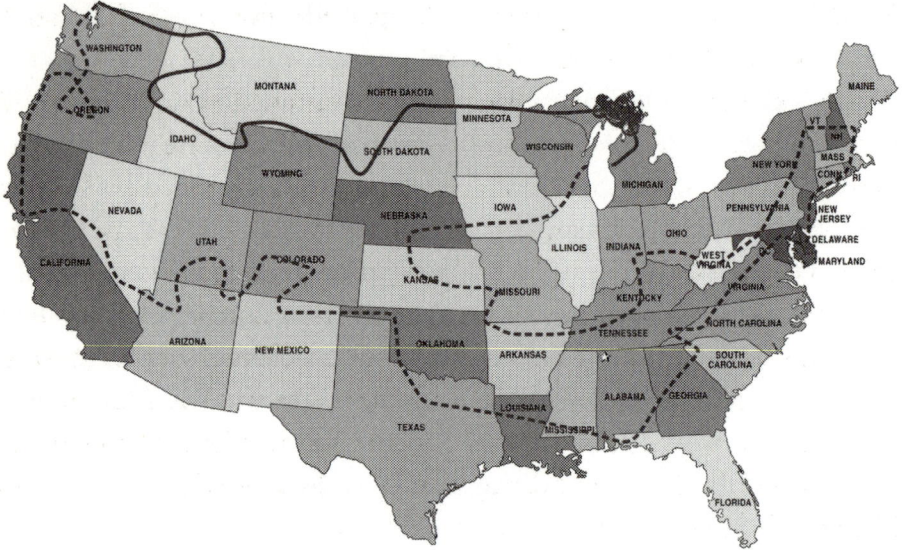

This state: 1,040 kilometres. Journey to date: 10,925 kilometres.

Lady at other table:	Bessin thisair diner chen strair.
Translation to English:	*Best thing in this here diner is chicken strips.*
Me:	That so? I'm enjoying my haddock and chips.
Translation to American:	*Thaso? Arnjoin mardicken chair.*
Lady at other table:	Bore, them chair strair shit spar.
Translation to English:	*Boy, them chicken strips sure hit the spot.*
Me:	Yeah, they look good. Is that dipping sauce you got there?
Translation to American:	*Yeah, ler ger. Tha dem sores yorl gar?*
Lady at other table:	Cane airno chen strair winnow den salse.
Translation to English:	*Cain't eat no chicken strips with no dipping sauce.*
Me:	The quick brown fox jumps over the lazy dog.

Two things were working against me, talking to the oldish lady occupying the only other occupied table in Ma's Place Diner and Grill. She talked like Bubba Gump and she didn't like the fact I hadn't ordered chicken strips. I was in Wakefield, a small town just over the state line in Michigan's Upper Peninsula. I'd a long ride ahead of me that afternoon and fancied something to line my stomach. Anyway, who could ignore a place called Ma's? The haddock was superb and cheap. It was Fish Fry Friday, and the haddock, slaw 'n' fries were on special.

From the moment I walked in, the lady fastened her eyes on me. As I looked at the menu, she called across the room urging me to get the jumbo shrimp — or should I say the *jarn shrair* — as an entrée. I ordered the shrair. It looked disgusting, so I left it on the plate. When the haddock came out, the old lady looked vexed. And then we chatted in some foreign language about her chicken strips. From what I could glean, she loved chicken strips even though it wasn't Cheap Chicken Chuesday at Ma's. I recount all this because it was the first time on my trip I'd struck language difficulties with the locals. But she didn't sound like a Michiganite. I thought they talked more like that down in the Deep South, or was that Harlem? There was only one way to find out.

Me:	Hey, yole warmer. Where y'all frarn en wares?
Translation to English:	*Hey, old woman. Where are you from anyway?*
Lady at other table:	Why, I'm up here in Michigan visiting my son.
Translation to American:	*Wah mare Mershkin vez mar zern.*
Me:	Jess y'all toll ferner innercain erna stain y'all.
Translation to English:	*It's just that you talk funny and I can't understand you.*
Lady at other table:	Who the f*** cares? You going to eat that shrimp?
Translation to American:	*Ferkez. Y'all gone air shrair?*

As I rode away from Ma's, I wondered if there would be more communication problems as I went on. And this was only Michigan. I'd have to brush up on my jive to survive.

Highway 28 tracked right across the top half of Michigan, known as the Upper Peninsula or UP. The massive Mackinac suspension bridge — which spans the Straits of Mackinac, separating Lakes Michigan and Huron — is the lifeline between the upper and lower parts of Michigan. UP has one-third of Michigan's land area but just 3% of the population. Which is probably why I was enjoying the remoteness of Highway 28 as it ploughed eastwards towards the Mackinac Bridge bottleneck.

At Marquette, the highway was metres from the shoreline of Lake Superior. I was riding in the middle lane of three on the freeway out of Marquette when I noticed a white convertible taking up position behind me, but in the next lane. While it clearly wanted to go faster, it didn't seem to feel like overtaking even though it had a clear lane ahead. We travelled in a tight-knit two-vehicle bunch for about 10 kilometres before the freeway curved up a steep hill. I thought about accelerating away from the uncomfortable closeness with this car, but, already a fraction over the speed limit, I just gradually buttoned off and let the car draw even. I looked sideways. It was piloted by a well-dressed woman in sunglasses and a headscarf. It crossed my mind that if this was in the 1960s I'd just flick out a lighter, edge close to the car's window and light her cigarette. Finally the sports car sped forwards and started widening the gap in what I felt was an overly-aggressive feminist fashion. Immediately my mirrors lit up with blue and red flashing lights. Somewhere in the past few miles a trooper had tagged on behind, and one of us was about to be relieved of our dinner money. The trooper passed me and sat in behind the convertible until it pulled over. Thank God. My Australian-blemished criminal record remained unblemished thus far in America, and in a holier-than-thou frame of mind I rode past the unlucky convertible like a choirboy tut-tutting at speedsters.

Reaching the settlement of Christmas, it was time to call it a day. Dusk was approaching and I was sick of pitching camp in the darkness. I saw a sign for the state park, and found a campsite amongst the towering pines.

Scattered throughout the forest grove were lots of other tents and RVs.

My neighbour on the other side of a fallen log was a huge mobile motor home. Its owner was Lou. He'd heard me ride up and had time to kill. Lou ambled over to my site and welcomed me to Christmas. He and his wife, Win, were travelling America in their RV. That night was their 900th night on the road, and they invited me over to celebrate. I finished staking out the tent and followed Lou over the log to his mobile hotel. I'd always wanted to see inside one of these things, having often tucked in behind them on the road. I counted three plasma screens, two ovens and a spa bath inside, and three beds, even though they were a couple. Attached to the rear of the RV by a fixed axle was a small 4WD utility, and mounted on the back of the RV was a 600cc Yamaha trail bike. Lou had a portable satellite dish so he could catch the latest baseball scores, and his library of DVDs was bigger than the local video shop back home. Lou and Win's motor home was 14 metres long, powered by a 600-horsepower Cummins diesel, cost them $400,000, and the driver's seat was referred to as the 'cockpit'. Each time Lou filled the 570-litre gas tank it cost him $600. He could get from 0 to 100 km/h in 11.5 minutes.

Lou was thrilled with my bike trip and couldn't stop asking about things, like freedom on the road, independence and 'go where you like'. Most of these questions were out of Win's earshot and I detected a hint of dissatisfaction with his RV lifestyle. His own motorbike had not been off the back of his RV for the whole 900 days. I thanked the friendly couple for the glass of wine, congratulated them on their milestone, and bade them a good night.

Lou followed me back over the log to my humble little tent, where he counted 0 plasma screens, 0 beds and 0 spa baths. We shook hands in an atmosphere of mutual envy. He looked longingly at my bike and the freedom it represented. I, in turn, thought about the electric blanket and soft duvet on the king bed, the fully-stocked cocktail fridge and ceiling-mounted DVD movie system playing an old Steve McQueen. But then I looked at my tent and immediately basked in a warm glow of affection for my support crew. I wouldn't swap my camping team for any motorized alternative. Anyway, at least it wasn't raining.

It was the thunder I heard first. Then the far-off crackle of lightning. It was 2.00 a.m. I was wide awake and fearing the worst. It came at 3.30 a.m. I have never experienced a thunderstorm like it. The thunder was deafening as it crashed overhead, seemingly metres above my tent. Streaks of forked lightning lit up the sky like an alien invasion. And then the first spits of rain came. Within minutes, it was a deluge. I lay in the tent wondering how waterproof it could possibly be against such a downpour. If it started leaking, what exactly would I do about it? Suddenly I wanted to desert my camping team and knock on the door of the RV to ask for a cup of sugar. When the storm broke, I'll bet Lou just rolled over and flicked his blanket back onto three. The thunder continued its crescendo of drum rolls, and the rain lashed down. But I stayed dry as I curled up in my sleeping bag and wondered how the bike was faring outside.

The night dragged on as the storm gradually abated. By the first grey streaks of dawn light, the thunder had moved out over Lake Superior and the rain reduced to just a light drizzle. I knew all my gear would be soaked and mud-spattered, and I knew the bike would be grumpy all day after its battering. I resolved to shell out for a nice, warm motel at the end of the day and regroup.

There was no sign of life from the RV as I stumbled about in the clearing under a dripping pine tree, wrestling with all my wet gear. I rode out of the state park back onto the main highway a little jaded. The lack of sleep wasn't reacting well, and my every instinct was to find a cheap motel and waste the day by sleeping the sleep of a dead man. But I felt pressured by my self-imposed timetable and did not want to drop a day just because of a slow start. What was needed was a caffeine injection and some artificial stimulants. But as I am a safety-conscious rider and detest drug-taking in any form, I knew I'd have to order, as a conscientious road user, some bacon and eggs to nullify the effects of the coffee. The day immediately brightened at the thought.

For the next two hours as I galloped along Route 28 through the Lake Superior State Forest and on to the coastline of Lake Michigan, the thought of a piping-hot breakfast became an obsession. And here's the funny thing. I had many chances to pull over and get breakfast as every small town had at least one diner, lights on, waitress with menu and coffee jug in hand, looking expectantly out of the window, but I rode on. It was the anticipation of breakfast that was exciting. I didn't want that to end by actually eating breakfast. I made excuses to myself each time to justify carrying on to the next diner. The excuses were sad. That diner looked like it wouldn't have tomatoes as a side. That diner over there probably used frozen hash browns. I'll bet that diner I just passed had a waitress who was surly. Maybe I'll do another quick half-hour cos it looks like rain. The morning ticked by. Then, just past Naubinway back on Route 2, as I was casting sideways glances out at Lake Michigan, the heavens opened.

I've ridden in rain before, and I quite like a cooling drizzle so long as my jacket does what it's paid to do: keep the moisture off my delicate skin. This was not rain, however. I define rain — and forgive the technical jargon — as drops of water falling from the sky. What I was riding through was an absolute cascade, the likes of which I have never come close to experiencing before. Within five minutes, I knew I was going to be unhappy. Within six minutes, I was utterly unhappy. The deluge of rain was so severe I simply couldn't see anymore. My vision just seemed to dissolve in a mosaic of drops that couldn't slide off the visor quickly enough. I was following a delivery van at the time, as we both drove into the waterfall. He switched on his lights and I tucked in behind the pair of red beacons, keeping a constant distance as far as I could judge it. I couldn't pull over, as I had no idea what the shoulder was like. I could feel my riding boots filling with water. I flicked on my heated handgrips and they just laughed at me. To help with vision, I opened my visor a crack. Immediately my face was stung with needles of rain and spray from the waterlogged road surface.

Traffic was down to a 40-km/h crawl, and for the next hour we tailed each other in that fashion. There was now a stream of cold water down my neck, under my soaked T-shirt, past my numb crotch, down my legs and into my boots. I could actually feel the flow of water over my body, such was the volume entering through my jacket collar. Still, it was safer to keep riding than pull off the highway. After what seemed like an eternity, the slow line of traffic reached St Ignace where the Mackinac Bridge starts. The bridge was nowhere to be seen, but I knew it was only a kilometre away. Through the rain I could see a line-up of neon signs. All the old favourites emerged out of the gloom. McDonald's. BP. Burger King. Motel 6. Texaco. Super 8 Motel. Wendy's. Shell. Denny's. I shouted with joy. Pulling into the Super 8 Motel, I didn't care if they only had the penthouse suite left. Within 10 minutes I was going to be dry, warm and telephoning Denny's to see if they delivered.

The motel was gracious and understanding. They allowed me to check in four hours early, provided I removed the bike from their lobby and didn't walk up to my room on the carpet. I got a special key to the outside fire-escape door. I had a hot shower, ignoring the irony of standing under yet more water, lay on the bed to watch Oprah chatting to a farmer who'd seen an alien in his cornfield . . . and that's the last thing I remember.

The next day was a stunner. I rode away from the motel under a bright blue, early-morning sky, belly full of breakfast that may have included the words 'pancake', 'egg' and 'sausage', gear dried and packed, bike tanked up with 91, and a crossing of the awesome Mackinac Bridge minutes away. The day — no, *life* dammit — was wonderful. As I rode onto the approach ramp, the massive suspension bridge towered in front of me. It's longer than the Golden Gate end-to-end. To my left was Lake Huron, and to my right Lake Michigan. I could see through the gaps in the bridge surface a long way down to the waters of the Straits of Mackinac. By the way, as you read the word 'Mackinac', remember that the 'c' is silent. Only in Americac!

At Mackinaw (the 'w' isn't silent) City, the exit ramp of the bridge spilled me out into Lower Michigan. I had several hours to make it down to Muskegon, a town about halfway down Lake Michigan, where the ferry crosses the lake to Milwaukee in Wisconsin. With time to kill, I chose a minor coast road that ambled through sleepy hamlets perched on the shore of the lake, with names like Blisswood, Pheasant Heath, Whittington's Rest and Cross Village. Squirrels darted across the leaf-strewn road as it wended its way through the sun-dappled woods. In Good Hart, an old lady was sweeping leaves from the driveway of her thatched cottage. She looked up at the sound of the bike and waved. It had to be Miss Marple.

I pulled into Dilbert's Diner in Beulah. Thus began my interaction with Shiloh. To explain. Remember: I was a diner pro. I had been diner-ing in America for two weeks. I knew how the system worked. I strode in, went straight to a booth and sat down. Within a minute, the waitress had my water and coffee served and had taken my order of — surprisingly shunning Dilbert's Donut Deal — an all-day breakfast.

Across the other side of the table, leaning over the back of the seat of the next booth, was a little girl perhaps two or three years old. She gazed at me intently as I read the label on the ketchup bottle. Then she started to pick her nose. This would not normally make my book — and you deserve better — but here's the point. The parents were watching her and did nothing about it. 'Shiloh, honey, don't you want your ice-cream?' Shiloh kept standing, looking at me and picking her nose. Minutes ticked by. What do I do about it? 'Excuse me, parents-of-the-month, your daughter is—' But how do I broach it? They have their backs to me. Shiloh had the power to put me off my scrambled egg when it arrived. I had to act. This is how I did it. I put the ketchup bottle slowly on the table and looked at the little girl, bulging my eyes and making sure I did not blink. My gaze was intense with a touch of evil. Finally, after about 20 seconds, she broke. Finger still embedded up her nostril, Shiloh turned back to her own booth and I rubbed my aching, bulging eyes. I'm not sure if any other diner customers watched the interaction, and Shiloh's parents were none the wiser. They will wonder why their daughter woke up that night having a nightmare, but I'm sorry: Twisting Throttle compromises his eggs for nobody.

Traverse City, Manistee, Ludington and Pentwater were nice places on Route 31 down to Muskegon, but my sights were primarily set on making the 3.00 p.m. fast ferry. My GPS made easy work of getting me to the ferry terminal, where I lined up with an assortment of cars, RVs and other bikes about to cross Lake Michigan to Milwaukee. The Lake Express ferry, which was a huge 190-foot catamaran, took 2.5 hours to cross the lake. For half that time we were out of sight of both shores and could have been crossing the Atlantic rather than a freshwater lake. I sat on the open deck, enjoying the wind and fresh air. Suddenly I looked to my left, and there was Shiloh standing looking up at me, finger up her n— OK, only joking there.

What I did see was a man, dressed in T-shirt and shorts, holding a camcorder. So what, you ask? He was filming himself by holding the camcorder in his outstretched hand, pointing it towards himself. But the odd thing was that it wasn't just a 'and here I am on the ferry' type shot. I watched him for over 30 minutes and he kept filming. The lake became quite choppy and the ferry pitched about a bit. It was impossible to stand up on the deck without holding onto a rail or something. Yet the man continued to film himself staggering around this way and that way, almost falling over numerous times. He must have rolled off a whole tape of footage, and I wondered which lucky family members would be viewing it that evening over a glass of wine. 'Hey, kids, go get Mom. Come and see this. It's great. Look, this is the ferry today. Whoaa, nearly fell over on that one . . . Whoaa, look how rough it is. Kids? Honey?'

The ferry docked in downtown Milwaukee, and I rode out into a mishmash of interstate interchange interflyovers. The GPS was in its element, being tasked with getting me through the city to West Bend where I planned to camp in a forest park. This it did with superb accuracy, and as I pitched my tent under a canopy of towering pines I thought about the ride so far. I'd completed 10,000 kilometres, yet still felt like the ride had just begun. I wondered if the Corn Belt states ahead of me would offer the illusion of distance and progress, as I knew a phase of riding hard and fast was upon me, beginning the next day. Lying in the dark in my sleeping bag on my stretcher, I hoped Shiloh was awake and seeing bulging eyes.

Chapter 11

Wisconsin–Illinois

Nicknames: The Badger State–The Prairie State

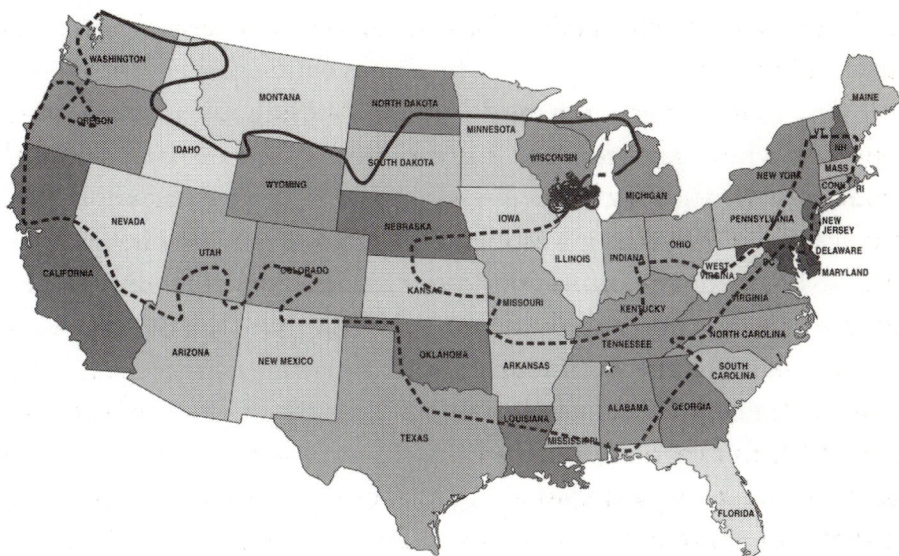

These states: 757 kilometres. Journey to date: 11,682 kilometres.

W HEN I LOOK BACK at my second visit to Wisconsin, this time across the south of the state, I remember three things. New tyres, a Sausage McGriddle, and the day I assaulted one of my support team for insubordination.

Milwaukee was the first of two pre-planned bike-service stops. The big one was another 12,000 kilometres further on in Dallas, and was too distant to even contemplate here in Milwaukee. I looked through the glass window into the workshop at Suzuki Milwaukee, wrestling with emotions as my two tyres were slung in a corner by the mechanic to await whatever fate befalls old rubber. I learned that some roads in America are made of a special tarmac compound which includes shredded tyres, and after further extensive research — which comprised reading an old 2001 magazine article pinned up on the wall of Suzuki Milwaukee's tea room above the shelf with the teabags on it — I can reveal some interesting facts about this subject. I'll do this over the next page or so while we're waiting for the bike to be serviced.

Each year in America there are about 285 million old tyres thrown out. Someone thought: 'Wait — why don't we shred them and use them in roads?' They tried it, and it was known as chunk rubber mix or CRM. But tests showed that it was weaker than not using rubber, didn't last as long, and when cars went a bit fast over pot holes they bounced off the road. So then they thought: 'Wait — why don't we grind up the tyre chunks more?' And the CRM mix became known as crumb rubber mix or CRM. The hot states, such as Texas and Arizona, found that crumb rubber mix, or CRM, really helped their hot mix asphalt concrete, or HMAC, at high temperatures.

But it came with problems in manufacturing, or P in M. The Texas Department of Transportation (TxDOT) set about identifying the P in Ms by designing two key tests for CRM. These tests were the Static Creep Test (SCT) and the Hamburg Wheel Tracking Device Test (HWTDT). So in the lab, in Texas, TxDOT scientists had to come up with some road samples to test. They couldn't just go out to the street and scoop up some tarmac. The specimens needed to be specially prepared by a Texas Gyratory Compactor (TGC) in the case of the SC tests, or a Superpave Gyratory Compactor (SGC) for the HWTD tests. Finally, the lab was ready, road samples collected, gyratory compactors polished and batteries charged, everyone's white coats laundered and buttoned up, the lab boss said a few words to the assembled team, and the tests started. 'TxDOT SCT commencing 0800 hours. Al, start the TGC.' 'Righto, skipper. TGC green to go.' 'Al, insert the CRM in the TGC.' 'CRM being inserted in the TGC, skipper.' 'Bernie, start the SGC. Commence HWTDT.' 'OK, skip. Want me to insert the CRM?' 'CRM? Do you mean CRM being chunk rubber mix or CRM being crumb rubber mix?' 'Um, what does it say on that box?' 'CRM. Crumb rubber mix.' 'Al, you idiot, you used chunks in the wrong gyratory compactor. Tell me the TGC's got crumbs in it.' 'Not my fault, skipper: you said put CRM in it.' 'That's C for "crumb" not "chunk", you moron.' Al walks out. Smell of burning from the TGC. Lab assistants reach for the fire extinguishers (FEs).

I snapped out of this flight of fancy vowing never to watch another Austin Powers movie. But what I do know is true is that the end result of TxDOT's research was that you could make 1 kilometre of neat, rubbery road out of 3,350 old tyres. I would end up using six tyres in my ride around America. That's equivalent to 1.7 metres of road that I could say was sponsored by Twisting Throttle. As I stood looking at my discarded tyres lying on the rubbish heap in Milwaukee, I was overcome with a rush of goodwill knowing that soon they would be in a better place, chunked, chipped or crumbed, provided the gyratory compactor got fixed in time.

The subject of rubber was still top of mind as I ate lunch. I had left the I-94 interstate at the Oconomowoc exit to fuel up. The lure of a nearby McDonald's was too good to ignore, and I was hungry. Standing at the counter looking up at the menu board in places like McDonald's, I always put myself under pressure to hurry up and make a decision. A serving person in a cap with a microphone thing from their ear to their mouth, making them look like Madonna on stage, said to me 'How may I serve you today?', which I thought was very polite. I ordered a Sausage McGriddle, as the word 'griddle' seemed to suggest that there was an old lady out the back called Granny Perkins who was frying real meat sausages she'd made herself on an old-fashioned griddle like they have in Kansas farmhouses. After the first bite I realized I had been fantasizing. It was actually a lab guy out the back called Al using a Superpave Gyratory Compactor. I left the sausage, ate the bun, downed the coke and that was lunch.

As I rode down the ramp back onto the I-94, I liked the thought that Oconomowoc had an 'o' before every other letter in its name, and the memory of lunch faded. What wasn't fading, however, was guilt that I was blasting across southern Wisconsin without making an effort to see beyond the fields that bordered the freeway. I wanted to make the Illinois state line before nightfall, but as it was only 2.00 p.m. I wasn't in that much of a rush. I pulled over at the next exit and consulted my road atlas.

I've mentioned before how my route decisions aren't totally scientific. I look for the pale yellow lines on the map that denote byways or back roads, all the time making sure my progress is in one general direction. That direction is forwards, but not necessarily in a straight line. It is possible to ride around 48 states in 6 days, not 60, but you can forget about any roads that don't have median strips and 24-hour Texaco stations. I picked a pale yellow line that ambled southwards from Madison, the state capital of Wisconsin, 40 kilometres away down the I-94, to Illinois. I circled three small towns — New Glarus, Paoli and Monticello — and entered their names into my GPS. I then entered the name of Lena, Illinois, where I was aiming to camp that night.

So to recap. The GPS was advised, by me the GPS's owner and master, of: (a) where I was at that moment, called the starting point; (b) the way I, the master, wanted to go, called the via points; and (c) where I wanted to end up, called the finishing point. I didn't want the GPS to make me a cup of tea or darn my socks. It is a GPS. That stands for Global Positioning System, and its function is navigation. I paid good money for it, and therefore feel I have a right to be the dominant partner.

Why do I seem so sour? Here's what happened. The GPS, after receiving my instructions through its state-of-the-art touch screen, thought for about 20 seconds then gleefully plotted a route starting from my starting point, going via the via points, and finishing at my finishing point, Lena. That route was displayed as a purple line laid over the map of Wisconsin that I could look down at and see on the screen. All I had to do was ride where the purple line told me to, turning left and right at its instruction, and eventually I would see a *Welcome to Lena* sign. That was the GPS's job, in my — the master's — opinion. However, in a scene reminiscent of Hal the computer in *2001: A Space Odyssey*, this miniature device wrecked my afternoon's ride.

The first warning sign that it wasn't going to be a lovely, rural ramble along byways with primrose hedgerows and young girls in bonnets picking blackberries was when I saw up ahead a building that looked like the Capitol in Washington DC. This was Madison's State Capitol Building, its seat of government and located in downtown Madison. This was exactly where I didn't want to ride: through the centre of a major city. The purple line had spilled me out onto one of those entering-a-city type arterial dual carriageways where there are traffic lights every 200 metres and the traffic is at a standstill because it's home-time for inner-city workers. I had no option but to persevere with following the purple line, gritting my teeth at the realization that the GPS was taking me through Madison city centre. I knew there would be a major investigation that night, if I ever got to Lena, and the GPS would be summoned to a support-crew hearing to explain its behaviour. It took half an hour to ride the 1 kilometre around the three sides of the Capitol. In fact at one point I briefly wondered if I could ride up its steps, along the ground-floor corridor and out the rear door to save time. The purple line had me as its hostage. I had no idea how to navigate out of Madison myself. For all I knew, the GPS was now going to take me out to the industrial area to go past an interesting shoe factory, such was its decision-making randomness.

I battled with long lines at traffic lights on my way out of Madison in the commuter rush-hour. My bike was too wide with the panniers to use that illegal yet highly satisfying motorcycle technique of lane-splitting. That's where you car drivers are sitting motionless in your rightful, well-earned place in the traffic queue, patient yet slightly fuming, and a motorbike buzzes up between you and the next lane, clipping wing mirrors as he gets right to the front. You briefly think about suddenly opening your door as you see him approach in your mirror, but you change your mind because his brother may belong to the local chapter of the Hells Angels.

Eventually I reached New Glarus, my first via point. At last, some glimmer of co-operation from the navigational department of my support team. In an impulsive gesture of frustration, I rapped the GPS with the back of my padded-gloved hand. It was like spanking a belligerent child. I'm sure it is illegal to hit your GPS in many states; I wondered if Wisconsin had anti-smacking laws.

By now dusk was spreading its hazy tentacles over the countryside and it was time to step up the pace and get to the campsite. Highway 69 through Monroe was wonderful riding in warm evening air. The smell of freshly cut grass wafted through my visor. I crossed into Illinois at Orangeville and followed the purple line to Lena.

The only things that the campground's very small shop sold for dinner were Budweiser and Krispy Kreme Donuts. I bought the lot. My site was down at the back of the campground near a stream. Already the frogs were in full chorus. No one else was there apart from some empty caravans and squirrels darting up and down the large spreading oak trees.

I set up my tent and convened a meeting of my support team. There were some issues to discuss, and I had to make some hard calls. I could tell the GPS knew what was coming, as it remained silent and moody on my handlebars.

Master:	Team, we need to clear the air on a few things.
Team:	(Silent apprehension)
Master:	But, first, let's welcome our new tyres, the Metzeler twins all the way from Munich. We were sorry to see the Dunlop brothers leave us in Milwaukee, and we wish them well for their future life as crumb rubber mix.
Front tyre:	Hi, everybody.
Team:	Hi.
Master:	Overall, I'm happy with the way the ride's going. Chainey, you're linking well with the sprockets. You getting enough oil from Scott?
Chain:	Yeah, it's OK. Guardy's a bit rattly, though.
Master:	OK, I'll make a note to tighten it in the morning. Springo, what's happening at the back of the bike?
Rear spring:	All good. That Ohlins boy is wound up tight as a gnat's— you might want to ease off the preload.
Master:	Noted. Thanks, Springo. All you suspension guys, front and back, are doing a great job. Now, you fuel boys. Any issues?
Fuel tank (after a pause):	OK boys, let me talk to this one. Sir, I speak on behalf of myself, Tank, and the fuel-injection lads when I say this. Sometimes you pull into a fuel station and stop by a diesel pump. We're sure it's just a mistake, but each time that happens we s*** ourselves.
Master:	OK, team, sorry about that. I didn't realize. In future I'll

	go straight to unleaded. Anything else?
Tank:	Nope. Just keep topping up with that gasohol and we'll run all day.
Master:	Thanks, guys. OK, now finally to our problems today. You'll all be aware how we ended up in downtown Madison and all those stop-starts at the lights?
Team (trying not to look up at the GPS):	Yeah, it sucked.
Master:	OK, OK. Not a witch hunt, but I think young Mr Garmin Zumo needs to explain.
GPS:	Well, sir, you set me to fastest time not shortest distance, and the fastest time was through Madison on the 151. How was I to know it would be rush-hour? You should ride quicker.
Master:	Sorry? Are you saying that it was *my* fault?
GPS:	Well, I don't punch my own buttons, sir. If you'd told me shortest distance, I would have gone cross-country along leafy lanes with primrose hedgerows and young girls in bonnets picking blackberries. GIGO. Garbage in, garbage out.
Master:	I'm not sure I like your tone, fella. How about I switch you off and reboot you in the morning? Maybe we can talk again then.
GPS:	GIGO. GIGO. GI—

I lay down on my stretcher that night, knowing the team would be out there pumped up after the meeting. It was important to raise morale as we still had a long way to go together. I had concerns over the GPS and its refusal to accept blame, but that was tomorrow's problem. I had two cans of Budweiser and six Krispy Kremes, albeit a week past their use-by date, to deal to. 'Sir, what about us?' I looked up. I had forgotten about the tent poles. It was going to be a long night.

By 10.00 a.m. the next morning I'd had enough of corn. I don't mean this in any disrespectful way, as it is a wonderful crop and a source of income and nutrition for many Americans. It's just that in Illinois, after three hours' riding along rural back roads, I was a bit over corn. I had Iowa, Indiana and Ohio to go, and, little did I know, they don't call that the Corn Belt for nothing. I'd decided to navigate manually, partially because the GPS and I still weren't speaking, but also because I knew I just had to ride due south until Kewanee, then turn right and ride due west across the next three states. So I felt I could do this myself with the aid of the sun, which didn't answer back.

I reached the town of Morrison and saw a diner called The Red Apple. I went in. Although I considered myself a diner pro, this one threw me off-balance. Along the counter were about a dozen old guys, farmer types by the look, in checked shirts and caps, sitting on stools and watching the cook flip pancakes and fry bacon. I desperately wanted to sit there, too, and take my status from diner pro to diner old fart. Trouble was there were no spare stools, so I had to make do with my usual booth by the window to keep an eye on my bike. The moment I sat down and began the diner pro process of menu-coffee-water-order-coffee-read-sauce-bottle-label-eat-breakfast-coffee-leave, a couple of old guys in the next booth turned to greet me. And like the old lady in the diner up in Michigan, they communicated in a language from the Planet Zorb. One guy — whom I'll call 'Hiram' to protect his real name, Bob Bilkens of Unionville — was a self-professed bulls*** artist. In fact, he handed me his card which was totally blank except for *Bob Bilkens, Bulls*** Artist*. His friend I'll refer to as 'Elmer'. I don't know his actual name, but Bob — sorry, Hiram — called him Elmer. Elmer was a man of few words, and it seemed like his role was to back up the Bulls*** Artist. We were all waiting for our breakfasts to arrive. Like Michigan, I'll need to translate for you.

Hiram:	Yawmo seck thar? Wolmarge y'all gair tha dang theng?
Translation to English:	*That your motorcycle out there? What sort of mileage do you get out of that dang thing?*
Me:	Oh, maybe 17 kilometres to the litre on a flat road.
Translation to American:	*Meb fortimart gan on flair row.*

Hiram:	Fortimart gan? Thay bullshair.
Translation to English:	*Forty miles to the gallon? That's bulls***.*
Elmer:	Doln wer bower hem. Airs all bullshair. Hairs bullshair artis of Unionver.
Translation to English:	*Don't worry about him. It's all bulls***. He's the bulls*** artist of Unionville.*
Hiram:	Hairs mackaid. Ser thair? Bulb Bellken. Bullshair Artis.
Translation to English:	*Here's my card. See there? Bob Bilkens, Bulls*** Artist.*

I'll be honest. My breakfast couldn't come quick enough. I have the Bulls*** Artist of Unionville's card in my wallet to this day.

At the junction of Routes 17 and 78 I leaned right, and thus my westward trek commenced. It seemed odd to be heading back towards the Pacific Ocean, but doubling back was the only way I could pass through those pesky Midwest states in the middle. Galva, Woodhull, New Windsor, Viola, Aledo and Joy were the small settlements on the way. You could see them in the distance marked by their tall *War of the Worlds*-like water towers emblazoned with their town name. Between the towns was flatness. Unrelenting flatness. And corn. Unrelenting corn. And soybean. Unrelenting soy— Well, you get the picture. Stretching to the horizon on both sides of the country road were crops. Corn. Two metres high, green, waving languidly in the breeze. Stretching for miles and miles and miles. In the distance, a farmhouse with a grain silo. Even in the towns, the houses would have corn growing in their backyards.

But I had one goal in mind by lunchtime, and the excitement was mounting. See if you can guess. Don't take a peek at the next page, but read the next paragraph. It will be the clue. See how good your knowledge of the US is.

Big flowing thing. Good word for hangman. Huckleberry Finn. Starts in Lake Itasca, Minnesota, and ends in the Gulf of Mexico. Moon River. Steamboat Willie.

Whatever your answer, it was the Mississippi River I rode across at Muscatine. It was a palm-sweating moment, seeing Old Man River for the first time, just like my first glimpse of the Missouri back in South Dakota. The Norbert F Beckey Bridge was 1 kilometre long, and I could look both ways along the wide river to see flat barges being towed by tugboats crawling along the waterway. Coming off the bridge, I officially crossed from Illinois into Iowa. Thank God. No more corn.

Chapter 12

Iowa

Nickname: The Tall Corn State

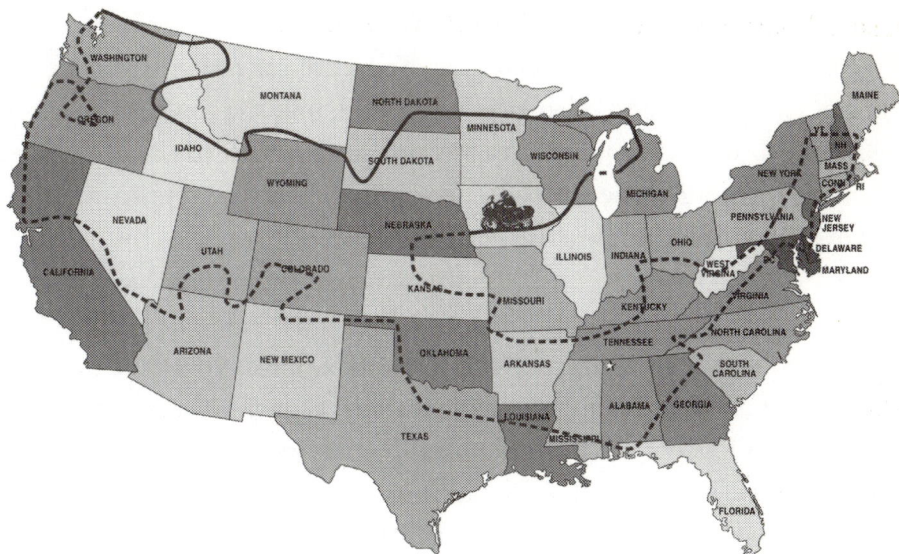

This state: 544 kilometres. Journey to date: 12,226 kilometres.

THERE WERE SEVERAL THINGS about Iowa that made me suspect I might not have left the corn behind in Illinois. I rode past a sign that said: *Welcome to Iowa, The Tall Corn State.* The state song of Iowa contains the lines 'See yonder fields of tasselled corn, Iowa in Iowa; Where plenty fills her golden horn, Iowa in Iowa; See how her wondrous prairies shine; To yonder sunset's purpling line . . .' And it was along my GPS's purpling line that I was now riding, cornfields stretching to the horizon, towards another wondrous prairie's shrine.

I refer, of course, to the town of Riverside. Yes, Riverside. Riverside, Iowa. Riverside, Iowa, USA. You don't know what I'm on about? That's because I was about to pay homage to an event that hasn't happened yet. In fact we are two centuries too early, but I was going there anyway. James T Kirk, captain of the *Starship Enterprise* will be born in Riverside on

22 March 2228. How do we know? There's a birthplace headstone, similar to a tombstone, behind an antiques shop in Riverside's dusty main street. Apparently the creator of *Star Trek*, Gene Roddenberry, mentioned in his book, somewhat vaguely, that Kirk was born in Iowa. One of Riverside's town councillors, who'd read the book, said at a council meeting, 'Hey, why don't we say it's us? We're in Iowa.' The council agreed and erected a birthstone. It caught on, and every year thousands of Trekkies trek to Riverside's Trekfest to pay homage at the future birth site. Riverside sells vials of Kirk Dirt for $3, T-shirt sales go wild, and the town has just over 200 years to work out how to get a couple called Kirk to conceive a son. There is apparently one woman there called Kirk, but reports are that's where no man has boldly gone before.

I paid my respects at the birthplace headstone, kicked the bike into gear, and tore off down the main street out into Iowa's big, wide, empty interior. My route had to get me right across the state into Nebraska, and there was no better way than to just head west.

I continued to have language difficulties. At a gas stop in Ottumwa, a friendly local asked me what the weight of the bike was. I said I thought it was 300 kilograms and tried to work out what that was in pounds. He was actually asking me what the plate was. At the same gas station I decided to treat myself to a gourmet lunch. Behind the oil was a shelf with a hotdog vending machine. The idea was simple. The machine had rotating dogs, hot ones, and you reached in and took one. You got a bun from a plastic bag and squirted on your 'fixins' of choice. You had tomato ketchup, mustard, and chilli in squeeze-bottles, plus a jar of pickles, and another containing something which might have been sauerkraut but looked like someone had just unblocked the drains. After you 'build' your hotdog, you pop it in a microwave oven, hit the start button and wait. When it *tings*, you lovingly take out your meal, insert it into a paper bag, pay for it at the counter and eat it outside by your vehicle.

My hotdog build came adrift at the point I squeezed on the mustard. A hardened sliver of mustard had lodged in the neck of the bottle. I squeezed extra hard, but overlooked the flaw that the nozzle was pointing two inches higher than the hot dog. The mustard spurted out like Niagara Falls. It splodged on the top of my jeans and ran down in a yellow toxic stain to my knee. I reached for a tissue and wiped it, smearing the mess further. I have had better restaurant experiences. To this day I look at the fading yellow stain on my jeans and think about Iowa.

I rode west with the sun slowly setting in front of my windscreen. The road was deserted. I passed intersections with very minor roads heading arrow-straight out into . . . Well, I have no idea where. The sun was an inch away from sliding below the horizon as I wondered where to camp. It occurred to me that I could ride the bike 10 metres into a cornfield, flatten down some corn and no one would know I was there. But getting back out could be interesting unless I got my bearings. That's my theory on crop circles. Aliens? I don't think so. Passing motorcycle tourers after a camping spot and then riding around for a day trying to find their way out? Probably.

My accommodation problem was solved in the form of the Lake of Three Fires State Park about 50 kilometres short of the Nebraska state line. It was dark by the time I found a site down near the lake. There was no one else around. As I lay in my tent, I heard the sounds of the woodland. A far-off screech sounded like a coyote, but it could have been an owl, such is my knowledge of American woodland sounds. There was rustling all around, and at one point in the night I woke up at the sound of what I thought was a saxophone's haunting melody drifting across the lake. It was only the next morning when I rode through Clarinda that I discovered I was camping near Glenn Miller's birthplace. Miller died in 1944 in a presumed plane crash and his body was never found.

Chapter 13

Nebraska

Nickname: The Corn Husker State

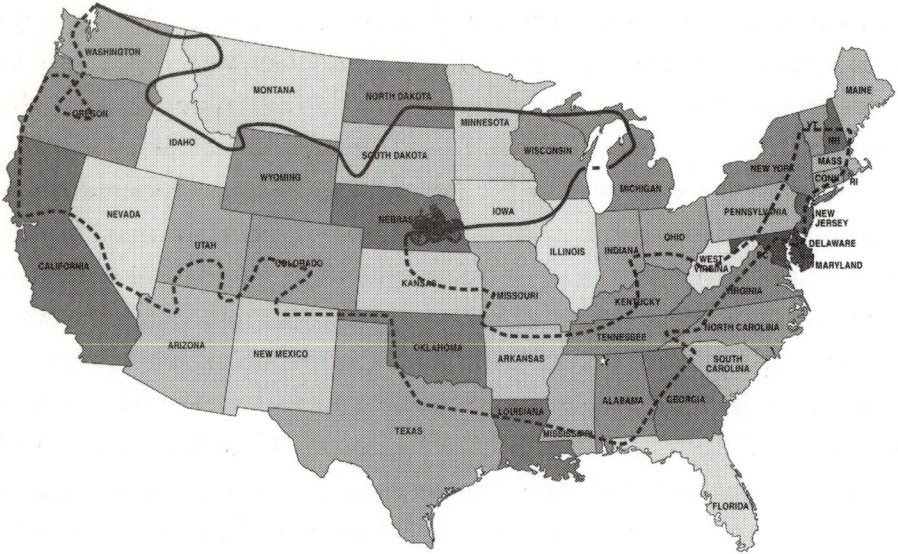

This state: 378 kilometres. Journey to date: 12,604 kilometres.

I MADE A FRIEND during the night. Trapped between the tent inner and the fly was a fly. It was a large blowfly sort of fly, and had been there all night waiting for freedom in the morning. I could hear him snoozing and couldn't be bothered getting up out of a warm sleeping bag to release him. I called him Colin, named after a similar friendly fly that had perched in my helmet for 100 kilometres in the Australian outback. We chatted about the ride so far, and Colin said he was heading for Nebraska to visit his aunt at a rubbish tip near Omaha.

He was no fly-by-night fly, and relished the chance to rest in my tent. However, as I packed up the tent in the morning, Colin simply didn't budge. He remained clinging to the nylon even as I rolled it up into the stuff sack. I realized this was because he was dead. My socks had been airing out in the roof of the tent close to where he had been sleeping. It is possible there was a cause-and-effect in there somewhere, but it made for a dark start to the day, no question.

Colin's death was just the start. No sooner had I ridden away from the Lake of Three Fires forest than dark thunderclouds formed on the horizon, and within minutes I felt the first spats of serious rain on my helmet. I sped along Route 2, taking me rapidly towards the Nebraskan state line as if crossing into the next state would somehow get me out of the impending rainstorm. The gravel side roads looked startlingly white against the black, thunderous sky. Pick-ups hurtled towards me, lights blazing and wipers swishing. Looking ahead I could see lightning flashes and a misty veil of rain on the horizon. I thundered into Nebraska over the Missouri River bridge on the outskirts of Nebraska City. Just as I cleared the bridge, a deluge struck.

Looking for shelter, I saw a beacon of dryness 500 metres up the highway in the form of a Texaco petrol station. 'Y'all rardin n'thess?' 'Yeah, it's a bit heavy, isn't it?' I replied to the lady behind the counter. 'Carfa's thar, hernie.' 'Thanks a lot. I'll take a 16-ounce decaf and two Krispy Kremes.' 'Sher, hernie. Thass darla narnie.' I'm sorry to sound patronizing, but if you have no idea what has just been said then you deserve to be the one standing, dripping wet, clutching two doughnuts and a coffee for $1.90. However, it's now time to explain the system for buying coffee and doughnuts in these petrol stations. There's quite a bit to it. Here goes.

Inside petrol stations are a wide array of vending machines dispensing everything a road traveller could wish for, from coffee to soup to chicken rolls to hotdogs to corn-on-the-cob. But you have to understand how it all works. You select from one of three sizes of paper cup. I go for the 16-ounce, as it is the smallest cup size, the cheapest, and what the heck you can go back for a free refill anyway. Take the empty — repeat empty — cup to the counter and pay for it. Return with the cup to the coffee-dispensing machine and place it under the nozzle relative to the sort of coffee you want. There are two choices: decaf or normal. To the side of the dispensing machine is what is known as the 'fixins'. These are the three types of creamer or milk, the sugar, the stirring sticks, and the plastic lids in case you want the coffee to go. The glaring omission from this highly efficient system is somewhere to tip out the coffee if you don't like it. I opened a pottle of milk and tipped it into my coffee. Immediately it curdled and floated on the top, like a nasal discharge.

The kindly lady was glancing over, expecting to see me cradling the hot coffee in my cold hands, beaming a smile of contentment as the brew warmed up my insides as I gulped it down. Instead, I was inwardly retching at the disgusting mess I was holding in my hands. The issue was how to dispose of the awful coffee without offending her. I looked around at the options. The customer rest rooms were outside the building in the torrential rain. There were no trash-cans close by, and other customers were starting to mill around the coffee machine so I couldn't just put it down and pretend it wasn't mine. The answer was to just kill time in the petrol station, wait for the rain to stop and go outside and tip it out. So I browsed the maps, the noodles, the oil, the postcards and the maps again, all the time taking pretend sips out of the coffee cup under the watchful gaze of the smiling attendant. Mercifully the rain soon eased, and I bade her farewell as I strode out of the petrol station desperate to end this madness and get on my way. 'Y'all rard safe now. Narse day.' 'Thank you, ma'am. Narse day to you.' The coffee mess was flung into a gutter, the stale doughnuts stuffed into the cup and turfed out in the litter-bin. I've enjoyed narser breakfasts, but it was tarm to rard.

The highway was wet, the endless fields of corn were glistening, yet the sky was an azure blue. It was as if the rainstorm had never happened. In fact I couldn't even see it on the horizon in my mirrors. I rode along Route 2 towards Lincoln where I'd be joining the I-80 for a 150-kilometre drag to the exit to County Road 26.

County Road 26. Just the mention of that road gets me excited, and here's why. At the junction of CR26 and West Platte River Drive — a narrow gravel road through the cornfields of southern Nebraska — lies a memorial stone. In the general Indian uprising of 1864, the Platte Valley saw a lot of unrest between the settlers and the native Sioux and Cheyenne. The Martin family had a farm in the valley, and one day Dad and sons Nat and Bob were working in the fields when some Indians attacked them. While Dad held them off, the boys jumped on a horse and took off with the Indians giving chase, firing off a flurry of arrows towards the fleeing duo. One arrow hit Nat in the back and passed through his body striking Bob, pinning the boys together. They fell off the horse and were left for dead by the Indians. Staggering to their feet, they somewhat awkwardly made it home, where the local doctor eventually unpinned them. They both lived long lives but gave new meaning to the term whistling in the wind.

The whole brothers-pinned-together-by-an-arrow story fascinated me as I gazed at the memorial stone marking the spot. The actual arrow is on display in the museum in the nearby town of Hastings. I thought briefly about visiting the museum, but I had another quest in mind and time was getting short. I am referring, of course, to paying homage at the grave of Andy the Footless Goose.

Several miles the other side of Hastings lies the old Fleming farm. I rode up a gravel driveway between spreading oak trees, and there it was in a small enclosure amongst the long grass in the farmyard. The memorial headstone of Andy the Goose. In 1987 a little gosling was born deformed, with only stumps for his feet. His kindly owner, old man Fleming, designed sneakers for him and taught him to walk, and Andy became an overnight media sensation appearing on *The Tonight Show* and delighting thousands of visiting schoolchildren. He became a role model for the disabled and enjoyed game fame. But Andy was found horribly murdered in 1991. His head and wings were missing, but his shoes were still on. Andy fans raised $10,000 as a poultry reward to catch the killer, but the case remains unsolved to this day. A black granite headstone was erected over the spot where Andy was found, and that night the Fleming family enjoyed *pâté* and crackers. I'm sorry, that was crass; but the story of Andy intrigued me. In fact the whole day in Nebraska was turning into a quest for enlightenment. I wasn't sure how much more cultural heritage I could take.

I rode south on the 281 through Ayr and Blue Hill. There were signposts down side roads to oddly named places, such as Lawrence, Pauline, Muriel and Norman. The sky was a majestic blue, and for miles in all directions the cornfields waved languidly in the light breeze. This was classic Nebraska and it was lulling. How any state this laid-back could fire an arrow into two young boys or kill a disabled goose was troubling. It was like there was something slightly below the surface of Nebraska, and I didn't want to scratch too hard to discover what it was.

What I *was* scratching, however, was the top of my left hand. It was so warm that I was riding without gloves. A flying insect of some sort, possibly a grasshopper if they can fly, had landed on my hand and stung me. It wasn't a bee sort of sting, merely an irritating nip before flicking off into the slipstream. My hand itched like hell. I couldn't take my right hand off the throttle, so rubbed my left hand on the hand-guard in a frenzy of itchiness. I tapped down through the gears as the town of Red Cloud appeared at the end of a long straight. It was time to refuel anyway, so I pulled into a petrol station. I grabbed the brush for cleaning windscreens and scrubbed like a madman at my left hand, which was now on fire with the itch. A local farmer pulled up in a pick-up and watched the spectacle with interest bordering on pity. It was then I wondered if I had caught some sort of corn rash and soon the facial twitching would start.

I noticed a post office in the main street and impulsively decided to mail home my burdensome collection of fridge magnets. The lady behind the counter seemed pleasant. 'How may I help you today, sir?' 'I'd like to post these fridge magnets back home, please, but I have nothing to put them in.' 'We have boxes for sale which might do.' 'Thanks. I'll take one.' She sold me a videotape-sized box marked 'priority mail'. I bundled up my magnet collection and taped down the box with duct tape. 'How do you want to send those, sir?' 'The cheapest way, please.' 'That'll be $39.50.' 'That's a bit expensive. Is there a cheaper option? Say by surface mail?' 'Surface is $15.50, but you can only send by priority mail as that's the box you bought.' 'Can't I send the priority-mail box by surface?' 'No.' 'Do you have surface-mail boxes?' 'No, sir, we don't.' 'Can I put some tape over the priority-mail label and turn it into a surface-mail box?' This was the second kindly lady today who was giving me a headache in the quest to be helpful. I thought back to the curdled coffee in the Texaco station that morning. So I paid $39.50 for postage and $4 for the box, thereby doubling the cost of my motley collection of magnets. But at least I'd freed up valuable storage space in my pannier for Andy's remains.

Chapter 14

Kansas

Nickname: The Wheat State

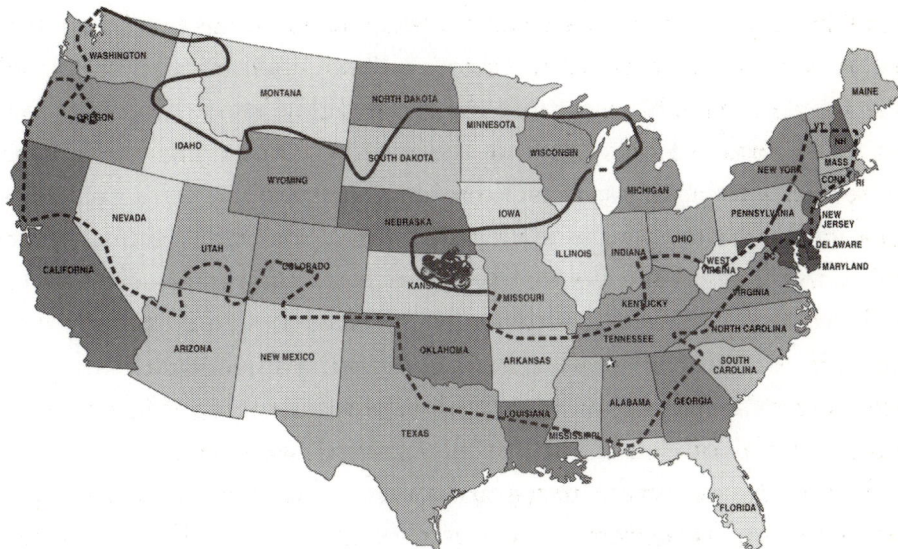

This state: 601 kilometres. Journey to date: 13,205 kilometres.

G OING INTO THIS TRIP I had one faint but nagging irrational fear, and that was tornadoes. Ironically, I was to be bashed about a bit in New Jersey with Hurricane Hanna and forced to out-run Hurricane Ike in Louisiana and Texas, but it was the funnelly sort that preyed on my mind a fraction as I rode across the state line into Kansas on Highway 281. The road immediately started a long, gradual downhill descent, so that what stretched in front of me was a horizon-to-horizon vista of flatness, exactly as you imagined Kansas to be. Tornado Alley, in which Kansas was a lurking mugger waiting to pounce, conjured up images of deadly swirling vortexes sucking up vehicles and houses, repositioning them in the next state. That's what comes of watching *The Wizard of Oz* and *Twister* DVDs on rainy Sunday afternoons. But tornadoes need clouds, and that day there was not one in the bright and clear blue sky. I felt safe.

I turned off along a narrow road towards the centre of the US. Remember back in South Dakota the attempt to find the *other* centre of the US? The town of Belle Fourche claimed it had the new centre back in 1959 when Alaska and Hawaii came on board. Previously Lebanon, Kansas, where I was now, had basked in the geographic limelight, as it was the centre of the 48 lower states. So while Belle Fourche for the past 50 years has been the nouveau numero uno centro Americo, Lebanon has not taken down its marker post, and I felt it was worth a photo and a fridge magnet. The marker plinth was by a large tree out in the middle of nowhere. I lay down under the tree and looked up into the blue sky, considering exactly where I was and whether it was in fact the actual centre.

In 1918, surveyors had made a cardboard cut-out of the US. They then balanced it on a point, like a pencil, and minutely adjusted it so that when the cut-out was perfectly balanced it marked the centre of the US. Seemingly the margin of error using this method was up to 35 kilometres. Probably more, because one of the surveyors dripped some mustard off his sandwich onto the cut-out, which weighted it fractionally in Lebanon's favour. But what say you draw a line between the northernmost and southernmost points of the US. Then you draw a line between the easternmost and westernmost points. Where the two lines intersect is surely the centre, in which case I was lying under the wrong tree. Not only that, but I was 350 kilometres away from yet another competing centre: this time Grenola, Kansas. It was too much. Belle Fourche, Lebanon, Grenola.

But enter into the argument the centroid principle. If you are a maths nut you will have suddenly perked up and realized you've bought the right book after all. Here goes. In geometry, the centroid, geometric centre, or barycentre of a plane figure X is the intersection of all straight lines that divide X into two parts of equal moment about the line. Informally, it is the 'average' of all points of X. The definition extends to any object X in n-dimensional space: its centroid is the intersection of all hyperplanes that divide X into two parts of equal moment. So using the centroid method I was not only lying under the wrong tree, I was on the wrong planet. I took a photo of the marker, watched by several cows having an equal moment themselves in a nearby ploughed field, and rode off thinking about the centroid principle and how it told me I was a long, long way from the sea.

I spent half an hour programming the GPS to take me in a zigzag pattern down through Kansas toward Missouri. I wanted to head sort of southwest to be close to Wichita, then hive off east into Missouri. There was no particular reason for deciding this: it just seemed in the right direction. The zigs and the zags were along arrow-straight rural roads. Combine harvesters kicked up dust storms, and most of the corn I saw looked dead.

On the outskirts of a small, dusty settlement called Downs, a state trooper was parked on the other side of the road. He looked like he was sleeping; his head almost below window level. My speed was respectable, defined as a little over the posted limit for this stretch. In my mirrors I saw the trooper's patrol car do a U-turn and start to follow me. We were the only vehicles on the road. He tailed me for about 2 kilometres at a distance, and then flicked on his red and blue lights. But the strange thing was he was at least 300 metres back. If there had been bends in the road I wouldn't have known he was behind me. The shoulder of this road was one of those that sloped at a steepish angle down into a field either side. The roadway was slightly elevated, meaning I could not simply pull over and put my feet down, not to mention the side stand. So I just kept riding. Eventually the trooper pulled on to the wrong side of the road and drove up parallel with me. I turned and gestured ahead with my hand indicating I'd pull over at the next safe place. He looked at me through mirror sunglasses and waved me on, the patrol car falling back in behind the bike. Soon I came to a little town called Tipton and stopped at a road junction.

In America, there are certain things you must not do when pulled over by a cop. Following my awful record of trying to talk my way out of law enforcement fines in Australia, I had anticipated this sort of scenario and read up about it before leaving. So, sitting there on my bike on a remote Kansas back road, looking in my mirrors as a state trooper got out of his car and walked slowly towards me, I felt I was a qualified speeding pull-over pro and able to handle myself. Here are the official do's and don't's when pulled over in America:

Don't get off your bike.

Do turn off the engine.

Do remove your helmet and gloves, but slowly.

Do keep your hands in sight at all times.

Don't reach into your jacket pocket.

Don't attempt to offer any unsolicited gifts.

Do refer to the officer as 'officer' or 'sir'.

Don't raise your voice or inflame the situation.

Don't use sudden gestures with any part of your body.

Don't attempt to argue the ticket if one is issued. Do that in court later.

Don't ask the officer for identification. Assume he's driving that state patrol car legitimately.

Do be aware that many patrol cars have video cameras running.

I removed my helmet and gloves and switched off the bike. The trooper came up to me and removed his glasses. 'Afternoon, officer. Here's my international licence.' 'Thank you, sir. A $50 bill has got caught up in it. Here you go.' 'Why, thank you. What seems to be the problem?' 'You were gassing it slightly through Downs. But I caught sight of your plate and didn't recognize it. You from out of state?' 'Out of country, actually. These are New Zealand plates.' 'New Zealand? Nice place. My wife's brother lives in Melbourne.' 'Melbourne? That's in Austr— Sorry about the speeding. The town limits jump around a bit, don't they?' 'They can do, that's a fact. Places like Downs and Tipton are generally 30. All right, take it easy. Just wanted to check on your plates. You have a safe ride, sir.'

And with that friendly exchange over, he ambled back to his patrol car, switched off the red and blue cherries and waited while I rode off. The last I saw of him in my mirrors was the car doing a U-turn to head back to Downs. I reached the town of Salina at the crossroads of the I-70 and I-135. The campground was right next to the freeway, but I didn't care. It had a Subway with free wireless over the road, hardly anyone else staying there, and the camp shop sold those jumbo cans of cold Budweiser for $5. That was fine, though: I had $50 of unredeemed bribe money back in the kitty to use.

The next morning I felt like a morale-boost. The easiest way to lift spirits is to do a fast opening ride, so that by the time you start thinking about your first coffee of the day you've clipped through a third of your daily mileage. It's known as 'pinning it' in long-distance motorcycling idiom. I sat on a deserted I-135 and pinned it south toward Newton. Morale duly boosted after two hours in sixth gear, I set my GPS to a place called Benton just outside Wichita. Back home my boss's name is Richard Benton so I thought I might curry some brownie points leading to a pay-rise if I snapped myself draped over the town sign. My road atlas said there was also a Hopalong Cassidy Museum in Benton. There wasn't. Apparently it had closed a year earlier, and all the Hopalong Cassidy items had been auctioned off. I'll bet I would have recognized a few of them. If you don't know who Hopalong Cassidy was, then just put this book down and hang your head in shame. It's possibly also because you are under 50. I'll bet Richard wouldn't know. Hopalong Cassidy was that clean-cut, macho cowboy who used to ride a stagecoach standing up, with a foot on each horse and holding onto the reins. Remember? He was dressed all in black, his horse was called Topper, and his sidekick was Windy someone. Ah, those were the days. Don't get me started on *Gunsmoke* . . .

At El Dorado I was riding directly east on Route 54. I'm sorry to report that this part of the Kansas ride was very, very boring. The road was two-laned, meaning no overtaking risks to boost adrenaline, so I simply counted down the miles to the state line with Missouri. I arrived at the town of Gas — and guess what I did? Nothing, just rode on. Kansas was a done deal for me now, and I wanted to move it on. Pick up the pace. Get some wheel time. Twist some throttle. I had even ridden within 10 kilometres of the world's biggest ball of twine, in Cawker City, and just kept going. Perhaps it was going to the centre of the US — as measured by the cardboard cut-out not the centroid principle, that is — that injected some urgency into the trip now that I was officially closing in on the right-hand side of America. Or perhaps it was a subconscious desire to get out of Tornado Alley now that the grey clouds were scudding across the sky. As I passed the *Welcome to Missouri* sign, I looked ahead and shouted to Dave, my imaginary pillion: 'Toto, I have a feeling we're not in Kansas anymore.'

Chapter 15

Missouri

Nickname: The Show-Me State

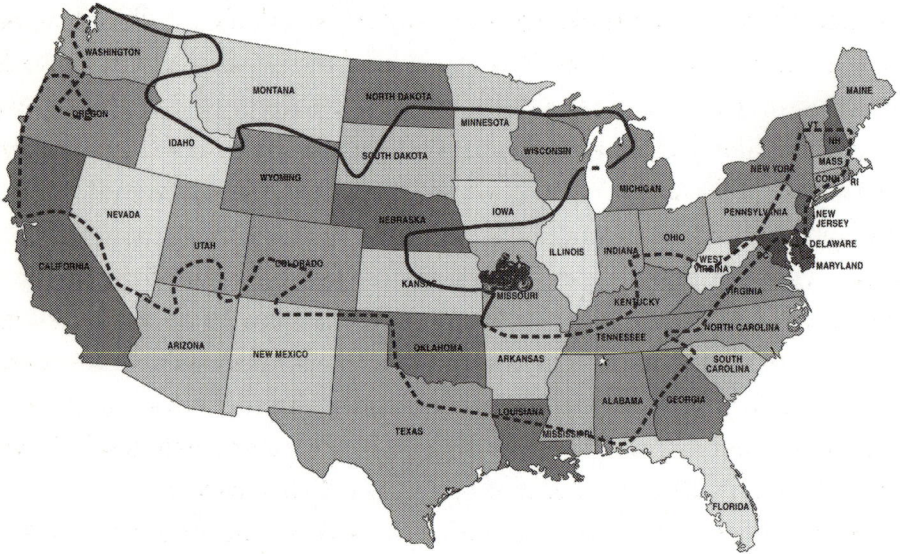

This state: 386 kilometres. Journey to date: 13,591 kilometres.

R IGHT. WHAT DO YOU KNOW about Missouri? Yes, it's a state — but where is it and what's its capital? You know what state lies to the west of it because you've just finished that chapter, but, without looking up at the map, name the state to the east of Missouri. The reason for trying to patronize you like this is because, whatever you do know about Missouri, that's twice as much as I did and I was actually riding through it. Not for the first time on this trip did I lament my lack of research. You'd think I'd have at least read a *Lonely Planet* before coming to the US, but I wanted the ride to be a bit 'off the cuff' and — apart from a general idea of the sort of schedule I'd have to keep up to get around the 50 states in time — there was a lot of flexibility within each state. Take Missouri, for example. It's a decent size, and all I was doing was nicking the south-western corner on my way through to Arkansas. I could have picked a route more or less down the state line and saved half a day, but, knowing zip about Missouri, I felt I should do a dog-leg across at least two or three counties just to see what it was like.

What I can tell you now is that Missouri's sausages are incredible. I stopped at the Copper Kettle Diner in a place called Nevada. The best diners are the ones that look shut. But if there are pick-up trucks parked outside, there are no visible lights on, and the small, almost illegible, *Open* sign is askew in the window, then you've hit diner pay-dirt. When you order an all-day breakfast, which I did at the Copper Kettle at 3.00 p.m., one of your agonizing decisions is whether to have the bacon, the sausage links or the ham. There is no menu option that allows you to have all three. If you're that carnivorous, you have to choose one of the three and request the other two as 'sides', for an extra 95 cents usually. You could not invest that money on Wall Street for a better return. Sausage links are links of sausage, typically skinless and quite tiny, not like their canoe-sized equivalents Down Under. One swallow and they're gone. Dip them in your over-easy egg, wrap them in your sourdough toast, and you are in cholesterol Heaven with the Copper Kettle opening them Pearly Gates wide.

When I went up to pay the waitress, I was gushing about the sausage links, using words like 'ever tasted' and 'best I've'. She turned around and called through the hatch: 'Calvin, get your hiney out here. Customer wants to talk to you.' She winked at me and said, 'He never gets no compliments.' The chef came through from the kitchen. He looked about 18 and had a whipped-dog expression, presumably expecting a complaint. I held out my hand and said, 'Calvin, this is my 15th state, and your breakfast has been the best I've had yet. I've got 35 states to go and it'll be hard to beat those sausages.' The two waitresses then started clapping, obviously pleased for Calvin. 'Thank you, sir,' he murmured, and shook my hand again. I rode away from the diner feeling like visiting royalty having just pinned a medal on a war hero.

My back roads loop took me through Cedar, Dade and Lawrence counties. I thought about turning off to Humansville just for the photo, but had to press on. The light was fading and I had to be somewhere at nightfall. I will reveal why shortly. I pulled into a BP station in Redings Mill, just out of Joplin. As I was pumping the gas, two Harley riders wandered over. 'That's an awesome bike, man. Totally awesome.' 'Thanks, fellas. Where are you from?' 'Springfield. Just headin' down to Tulsa for a gatherin'. Awesome, awesome bike.' He seemed to like the Suzuki. 'So where're you headin', man?' 'Fifty-state ride, nearly a third of the way around.' 'Fifty-state ride? Un-be-liev-able. It'd be awesome to do that. One day I'm gonna go all the way.' 'Where's that, then?' I asked. 'See the ocean at Baja. That'd be an awesome ride. I never seen the ocean.' 'Jeez, is that right? You lived in Missouri all your life?' 'Yep. Never been out of it. In fact this ride is my first state-line crossin'.' The friendly guy would have been in his mid-20s and he'd never been out of Missouri. 'Take care, man. Watch out for them hillbillies in Arkansaw.' 'Thanks, guys. Catch you later. Good riding to Tulsa.' I'd have to class Missouri as a very friendly state. Awesome in fact.

But, nice as pootling about in back roads Missouri was, it was fast becoming the business end of the day. Now for the next page or two I ask you to suspend your belief systems and keep an open mind. I'm about to tell you what happened when I went to investigate the Tri-state Spook Light. But first, some essential background.

There is a point close to a town called Seneca where Kansas, Oklahoma and Missouri intersect. The area is called the Tri-state. For over a century there have been countless sightings of a strange ball of light that is known as the Tri-state Spook Light. There is a gravel roadway out in the country, officially named County Road E40 but renamed Devil's Promenade or Spooklight Road by the locals. It's down this eerie road that the sightings have occurred. The first reported sighting was in 1881. People who have seen the Spook Light have reported that it is orange in colour and the size of a basketball. The light it gives off is so intense it can light up the whole road. The light typically hovers about and darts across fields and above the trees before simply vanishing into the night. It is always viewed after 10.00 p.m. Most people assume it's the headlights of an approaching car until it starts to whiz about, sometimes even passing through the car and extinguishing itself when it reappears behind them. The US Army Corps of Engineers and many paranormal organizations have tried to explain the light away rationally, with suggestions such as the distant I-40 interstate and possible refraction from headlights. From time to time the light splits in three and behaves like a firework going off.

This is where I believe Americans get carried away with themselves. The country is rife with 'unexplained phenomena', and by and large it gets attached with a fair amount of credibility. After all, this is the nation that gave us Area 51 and the live-alien conspiracy theory when everyone knows that ET went home so how could he still be down here in a lab in Nevada? But I'll be honest with you and say that some small part of me nagged away with the 'what if' question, and, as I was going to be riding within a torch-beam's distance from the Tri-state area, I thought I'd time my visit for 10.00 p.m. and see what happened.

First off, it was no easy job finding the Spook Light Road. I set my GPS to find the intersection of roads S700 and E40. It took me along back roads in the woods that shouldn't probably have been travelled after dark. It was pitch-black, with overhanging trees and a rough, unpaved surface. I found myself on State Line Road, or S700, which is bang-on the state line with Oklahoma. Finally, after resisting the strong temptation to just turn back, I reached the intersection with E40. The time was 10.07 p.m. It was so remote I wondered why a paranormal ghostly spook light would choose this particular place to haunt. Just the mere acknowledgement of some supernatural anomalous other-world manifestation made me laugh to think how sucked in I'd been by the whole story.

I dismounted from the bike and stood in the middle of the intersection, looking down the lonely, eerie gravel road E40. I decided to at least take a photo to mark the moment — to say I'd actually been there — and set up my camera and tripod. To illuminate the scene, I switched on my bike lights. Suddenly far up the road, almost where it disappeared over a brow, a small yellowy light appeared out of the inky blackness. I assumed it was an oncoming car and made to dim my lights. But the light just bounced around, as if an invisible kid was bouncing it like a ball. I swear I am not making this up. In fact at the time I swore other things, just rooted to the spot looking incredulously as the spook light got closer. I reached over and flicked my headlights onto full beam. The light instantly split in two, and now I was gazing down the empty road as both orbs, changing from yellow to orange, hovered and darted about. I would say they were about half a mile away. Then, without warning, a larger whiter orb appeared from behind a clump of trees and the whole scene was lit up like a stadium. I ran back to my camera, still set to remote timer, and clicked the shutter.

The resulting photo will shock you to the core. I have captured in complete clarity the Tri-state Spook Light, with its two sidekicks. The photo is suffering a bit from lens flare as it was very bright. I am publishing the photo in this book, and you get to see it for the first time. For all I know, it is the first actual photo of the Spook Light ever. I suppose I could make thousands by releasing it to the tabloids, but the media spotlight would be too intense. There will be many non-believers, and you may be one, but I ask you to flick to the photo, note that the road signs prove that I was at S700/E40, look it up on the net if you have to, and just accept that you have witnessed the corroboration of a paranormal event still unexplained to this day.

After several minutes dancing about, the big light vanished over the trees, and shortly thereafter the two smaller orbs whizzed back over the brow of the hill, and the road was plunged into darkness as if nothing had happened. Why did the Spook Light, or whatever it was, choose that night and that time to make an appearance? Was it my bike's lights that perhaps triggered some sort of playful reaction? Why me? I didn't feel in danger, but I felt very alone, and afterwards my upper body was coated in sweat. I was wearing only my Hawaii Police Dept sweatshirt as it was a warm night. To this day I still have the perspiration rings on the shirt from standing at the Tri-state intersection watching the ghostly scene play out on that remote and sinister country road.

I rode back to Seneca not a little disturbed, but feeling like my scepticism had taken a jolt that night. Perhaps they were refracted lights from the distant interstate. Perhaps it was a will-o'-the-wisp or a few locals with torches playing me for a dickhead. But you weren't there.

I have to end this chapter now. I can't type any more. There's a glow outside the window behind me. I think it's back.

Chapter 16

Arkansas

Nickname: The Natural State

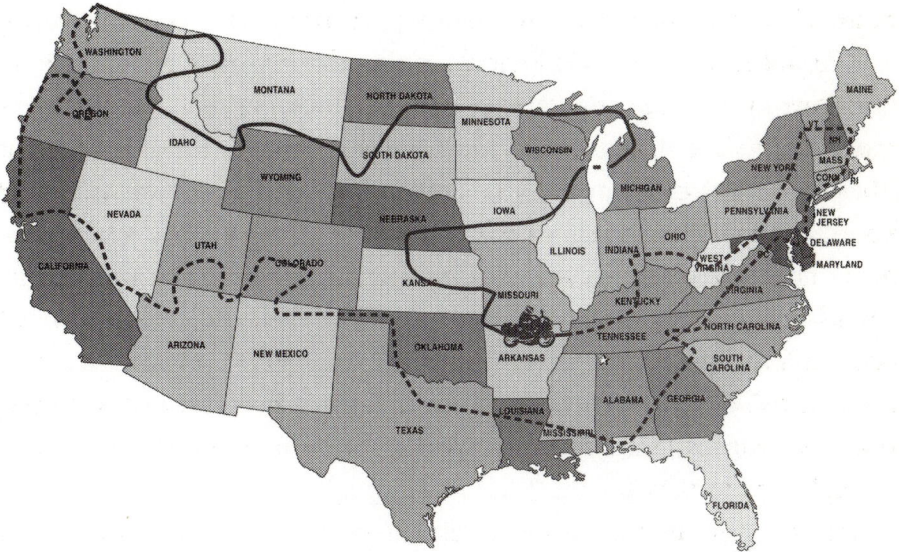

This state: 453 kilometres. Journey to date: 14,044 kilometres.

I SUSPECT THE REASON you picked my book off the shelf in the bookstore instead of *Lonely Planet* is that you are a student of knowledge in the University of Life with a thirst for geographic fact that many other reference guides fail to deliver. You are about to be rewarded with yet more interesting but little-known facts, this time about the history of Arkansas. I rode across the state line at a place called Gateway and was officially in the Ozarks. This is where your education commences.

The Ozarks are made up of Oz and Arks. 'Oz', of course, was where Dorothy and the Yellow Brick Road ended up in the nearby state of Kansas, and 'Arks' is short for Arkansaw. Some sources, namely the usually infallible internet, incorrectly have it that Ozarks came from '*aux arcs*' or 'toward the arches', referring to the many natural bridge formations in the mountains. An extension of that is '*aux arcs-en-ciel*', which is French for 'toward the rainbows', also commonly seen in them there hills. But didn't Judy Garland sing 'Somewhere Over the Rainbow' in *The Wizard of Oz*? Therefore, my theory of Ozarks being in fact the mythical Land of Oz is proven as fact. And the bizarre connection doesn't stop there. The moment I rode past the *Welcome to Arkansaw* sign, the very first sound I heard was a tooting car horn sounded by an angry driver who was upset at the way I had pulled out in front of him after taking a photo of the sign. You don't get it? Toot. Rearrange the letters. Toto.

I don't know what the Land of Oz actually looks like, but it couldn't better the beauty of this region. The Ozarks are thickly forested hills, with lakes, rivers, waterfalls, caves and long, twisting roads. I was riding due east, crossing the north of Arkansas towards Tennessee. You're wondering why I can't make up my mind what to call Arkansas. In the last two pages I've said Arkansaw *and* Arkansas. That's because, by an 1881 state government decree, it's spelt 'Arkansas' and pronounced 'Arkansaw'. Apparently, back then the state had two senators who argued about what to call Arkansas, and agreed to spell it one way and pronounce it the other. This is still law, and you can be fined for pronouncing Arkansas 'Arkansas'. That is the same state government that hasn't got around to repealing the Arkansan law that a man can legally beat his wife so long as the stick is no more than three inches across and the beatings are no more frequent than once a month. If your dog barks after 6.00 p.m. you can be fined. But the best one is the law banning the Arkansas River from rising more than the height of the Main Street bridge in Little Rock. I understand the river has been convicted twice and is out on parole.

I rode into Eureka Springs, a popular tourist town nestled in the wooded hills of the Ozarks. I tootled up and down the main street looking for food. I passed the Roadkill Café, but it was closed. Set back in some trees was a Swiss-looking chalet that was a hotel and restaurant. The sign outside said Czech and German home cooking and to come in for their new $10.95 'recession menu'. If their recession menu was $10.95, I'd like to see the price of their 'boom times menu'.

As I lay in my tent in the dark, thinking about that unfortunate restaurant sign, I heard some dogs barking over in the rich people's camping area. It was well after 6.00 p.m. I'll bet they weren't fined. And it was shortly after that that I lost my tent. This is how it happened.

The camping ground was deserted when I'd arrived two hours earlier. I rode slowly through the forest looking for a suitable camping spot, and was spoilt for choice. I don't know why, but I kept idling along the gravel access lane under the canopy of fir trees finding excuses not to stop and pitch up. I got further and further from the toilet block, but finally pulled up and set up camp. The light was fading rapidly and I wanted to get to the toilets to do two things. Something obvious, and to find a power point. I was overdue posting some photos to my website, and there was a faint possibility that the toilets were sufficiently close to the office to get a wireless connection. So I trundled off and walked the 200 metres or so through the trees to the toilet block, with laptop and toothbrush in hand.

After an hour I'd completed my business for the night, including the web uploading. It was about 11.00 p.m. I switched off the toilet-block light and walked back out into the night. It was utterly pitch-black; not a single sliver of light anywhere. No other campers nearby, no buildings, no stars and no torch. After 10 minutes a sort of night vision returned, and I could make out the shapes of the trees. I walked in roughly the direction I thought I'd come from earlier. It didn't seem too familiar, but I believed I was on the gravel access lane. Then I felt soft pine needles underfoot and realized I'd strayed off the track. I couldn't have been less orientated if I was in an Antarctic whiteout. I screwed up my eyes, trying to see through the darkness, knowing my bike and tent were out there somewhere. Or were they behind me? Why oh why had I set up camp so far from the sanctuary of the toilet block?

Then I had the brilliant idea of using the laptop's screen as a light. I fired up the laptop and it cast an aura of bluish light, illuminating a metre ahead and no more. I bent down so the laptop was shining on the ground. My night vision had disappeared and I was simply walking deeper into the forest, still completely confused about which direction I was facing. I switched off the laptop and waited another 10 minutes for the blue circles in front of my eyes to disappear. I heard a car on the main road in the distance. I knew the road was close to my site and so trudged off towards the sound of the fading car. I walked into a bush. I'm not saying I was close to panic, but this ridiculous turn of events was making me anxious.

At worst I would simply head back to the toilet block, if I could find it now enveloped in the blackness, and sleep on the bench in there. At least I could play Solitaire until the laptop battery ran out. But the thought of my comfortable sleeping bag waiting for me out in the dark forest was too enticing to give up this blundering navigation attempt. I heard another car and paced off towards the sound before it, too, disappeared. My feet crunched on gravel and I was back on the access lane. I fired up the computer again, and shone it out into the blackness. I almost skipped down this yellow brick road as it led me back to my campsite. I made a mental note to leave the bike's park light on in future. Either that or pack breadcrumbs.

The morning dawned and I yawned. There's no better feeling than being able to make the decision to roll over, pull the sleeping bag up around your ears and snooze for another naughty half-hour. That's what I like about solo riding. The freedom to snooze. Eventually the call of the Ozarks got me up, and the call of Nature saw me walk back to the toilet block. I worked out where I'd gone wrong the night before, and was amused to note that had I walked through that bush I would have disappeared over a small cliff into a creek.

I rode out of Eureka Springs a little jaded, but looking forward to a good day in the saddle. The signs to neat town names continued. Zinc, Coin, Dogpatch, Farewell and — my personal favourite — Fifty Six. But my destination was Yellville. You may well ask why. Take a look at the cover of the book. Why am I looking skywards? Here's the thing with Yellville. It's a small town. The human population, currently around 1,300, is growing. The turkey population, currently around 20, is shrinking. And that's largely because the citizens of Yellville drop turkeys out of planes. There are two things to know about this. One is that the turkeys are still alive, and, two, turkeys can't fly that well. In fact they can't fly above 60 feet off the ground, and FAA rules mean the plane has to pop them out at 500 feet. This makes for two things: turkey anxiety and lovely *pâté*.

It all started after World War II when returning GIs came home to Yellville and said, 'Hey, guess what we saw in Italy? There were these turkeys . . .', referring to a centuries-old festival where monks would fling live turkeys off a church roof into the waiting arms of the hungry peasants below. The GIs re-enacted it by tossing three turkeys off Yellville's courthouse roof. They — the turkeys, that is — just fluttered up into the trees and roosted. So the next year they threw them off the three-storey drug-store roof. This time two survived, but the third ended its life by pavement. 'Now we're getting somewhere,' said the mayor, keen to put his town on the map. By the mid-1950s, this annual event was so popular that the thousands of spectators down in the street had trouble watching it. 'I know,' said the mayor, 'let's send up a plane.' That got the animal rights people interested, as images of turkeys at terminal velocity were splashed across the news.

In 1990, the annual turkey drop officially went underground for fear of litigation. What this meant was that Yellville just had its Turkey Drop Festival minus the drop. Somehow the other events never lived up to the same adrenaline-inducing spectacle of the live turkey drop, though. The best legs competition — Miss Drumstickz — came close, but the crowds clamoured for you-know-what and it wasn't chicken wings. Now every year an unofficial light plane unofficially makes a low pass over Yellville's main street when the festival is on and it's about lunchtime. Rotary Club members have the barbecues fired up, and at the sound of the drone of an approaching Cessna the throngs gaze expectantly skywards. Mothers cover their young children's eyes, and teenage boys jostle each other, getting into position to see who can make a clean catch. Finally, out of the plane 20 shapes arc into the sky at 500 feet. In recent years, small smoke canisters have been attached to turkey legs to make it easier to follow the birds' descent into oblivion and the broiler. Some turkeys live to gobble another day by flaring their wings and tail feathers at just the right moment. Others finish the day surrounded by roast potatoes and covered in gravy.

It was a macabre thought, and I made a resolution, riding through

Yellville's main street, to boycott any poultry until I was out of Arkansas.

But I hadn't reckoned on Melbourne's Chevron gas station and their fried chicken. Melbourne is a pretty little town nestled in the hills. I fuelled up and went inside to be fleeced for $3.99 a gallon. The aroma of fried chicken was an assault on the senses. The café attached to the gas station, called Hawgs, had a huge display case full of nothing but fried chicken in 20 different forms. Wings, breasts, drumsticks, nuggets, shavings, patties, boneless, skinless; there was nothing else to choose from but chicken. I rationalized my wavering poultry principles by telling myself that if I saw one turkey product I would walk out.

Girl behind counter:	Yowl war chen?
Translation to English:	*Y'all want chicken?*
Me:	What's the special of the day?
Translation to American:	*Wol spesha die?*
Girl behind counter:	Foal weng frarn pepser,
Translation to English:	*Four wings, fries and Pepsi.*
Me:	You sure that's chicken and not turkey?
Translation to American:	*Y'all shit check knoll terka?*

And so with my conscience clear, I sat down to the best meal of the trip. Succulent and moist chicken flesh coated in a crispy, tangy batter, fries sprinkled with chicken salt, and a caffeine-laden Pepsi. I could hear my arteries hardening as I ate.

I set my GPS to take me through some back roads as I headed through to Tennessee. Sage, Sidney and Strawberry were settlements dotted in the hills as I slowed to cruise along their narrow main streets. Old wooden houses — with star-spangled banners flying proudly from window boxes and flagpoles — had porches with rockers. Old folks sat about and waved as the bike made an uncommon spectacle in their backwoods village. Lawns were neatly tended, and everyone seemed to own a ride-on mower.

At Black Rock I ended the Ozark wandering, and joined the faster Highway 412 that would take two hours to expectorate me into Tennessee over the Mississippi River. In Blytheville, I topped up my tank at a Texaco gas station. A man who introduced himself as Lance was employed sweeping the forecourt and washing windscreens. I suspected Lance was fully stretched, mentally, doing those jobs. He asked if he could sit on the bike while I went inside to pay. His eyes were gleaming as he climbed up. I removed the keys. He held onto the handgrips and his feet didn't reach the ground. I watched him from inside the gas station. He inspected all the electronics and stood up on the pegs. When I returned to the bike, I asked Lance if he'd like to wear the helmet. He put it on and I flicked the MP3 player to Elvis. We were on the border of Tennessee, so I thought what the heck. Lance jived about on the bike and I wondered if the gas station manager was looking.

Eventually, I managed to persuade him to get off. He asked where I was going. I said New York. He said he didn't know about that but he'd been to Pocahontas once. That was a town 50 kilometres back into Arkansas. I asked him if he'd ever seen the ocean. He said no but he'd once swum in the Mississippi. He asked where I came from. I said New Zealand. He said if I was heading home tonight I better get going and to turn left out of the gas station. I think he meant Nashville. I rode away, leaving Lance to his windscreens and waving after me. The bizarre thing was that I had an urge to see if he wanted to come with me on the bike to see what was on the other side of the Mississippi. The tiny, friendly old chap left a lump in my throat. Or was that a chicken bone? Farewell, Arkansas . . . wife beaters, turkey molesters, Dorothy.

Chapter 17

Tennessee

Nickname: The Volunteer State

This state: 525 kilometres. Journey to date: 14,569 kilometres.

NECTARINE IS A FRUIT that begins with the letter 'N'. Why this is worth mentioning will be clear to you if you have read my Australian book. As I was thumping across a particularly boring slice of Western Australia, I played a game that involved standing up on the pegs every kilometre and shouting out the name of a fruit or vegetable for each letter of the alphabet in sequence. At kilometre 14, I just had a mental block on 'N'. Since returning from Aussie, I've fielded countless emails from readers concerned at my appalling lack of pomology: that's the study of English people — sorry, I mean fruit. But these sorts of games help to while away the time when there isn't much else to do other than bend your throttle wrist and stay upright.

Tennessee right then was one of those times. The morning was sunny and warm. Cornfields stretched from horizon to horizon, broken only by whitewashed churches and farmhouses. Young girls in head scarves carried sheaves of golden corn alongside the fields in which their young men were toiling with scythes and trousers held up by braces. The music of Topol was in the air and I swore I'd never watch *Fiddler on the Roof* again. You get the picture. The ride through western Tennessee country lanes was soporifically lulling. I needed to keep my mind alert, so I played another little A–Z-type game.

This time at each mile mark on the GPS I would stand up on the pegs and try to name American presidents, going backwards in time. This is where I got to: Obama > Bush > Clinton > Bush > Reagan > Carter > Harrison Ford > Nixon > and who was it who took over after Kennedy was shot? > Kennedy > someone > then Truman I think it was who ended World War II > Roosevelt, either Theodore or Franklin D > getting a bit tricky but was it Mark Twain? > George Washington . . . It was a mess, and I was disgusted by my ignorance. To be fair, I challenge you to go back further than World War II as well. I flagged the presidents game and started on chain states. Every mile that ticked over, I would shout out a state of America that began with the end letter of the previous state. For example Nebraska > Arkansas > South Dakota. The problem was that it became one endless loop of A's and S's. Alaska > Alabama > Arkansas > South Carolina > Arizona > Arkansas > South Dakota > Alabama and so on. In the end I decided to just ride and enjoy the nectarine — I mean corn — fields.

When I'd looked at the map of Tennessee wondering which roads to take, I'd opted for the narrow back roads as it seemed the sort of state that you'd experience better without a dotted line down the middle of the road. That was to prove an excellent decision. I can't describe how laid-back the riding was, because I can't think of a way of describing the Tennessee countryside. Perhaps like the English countryside combined with Moldova, I don't know. Put it this way: if a horse and cart loaded with hay had come towards me, I wouldn't have blinked.

I passed a red barn with smoke wafting from underneath its roof. In a mild state of concern I wondered if I should be reporting it: but to whom?

The barn was out on its own in the middle of a field of what looked like tall spinach but may have been soybean. Around the next bend was another barn alight. Then another. Inside a mile I saw five red barns with smoking roofs. I now know what they were: they were smoking barns, and that spinach was tobacco. My knowledge of cropology was spot-on as usual. Apparently, inside these barns sawdust from pieces of hardwood is smouldering away as part of a process called fire-curing the tobacco, and this can take anywhere from three to ten weeks. The sort of tobacco that is fire-cured, as opposed to flue- or air-cured, is chewing tobacco and snuff. Chewing tobacco is the sort where cowboys spit a lot, as it nestles between your bottom gum and your lower lip, stimulating the salivary glands. That's why spittoons and Clint Eastwood westerns were invented.

Speaking of westerns, I pulled into a little town called Rutherford, which I wouldn't have even looked sideways at if it wasn't for their town sign that said *The Last Home of Davy Crockett*. Now here's the thing. Of course you've heard of Davy Crockett. But what did he actually do apart from trap bears, wear a coonskin cap, and constantly load Old Betsy out in the woods? Hang on — that was Fess Parker, wasn't it? Wasn't he Daniel Boone or Kit Carson? Which one was King of the Wild Frontier? Another gap in my Americana knowledge was thus exposed. I'd have to brush up on my frontiersmenology, and perhaps Davy Crockett's Cabin in Rutherford was the place to start. It was closed. So you'll need to find the answers on the omni-accurate internet. I rode out of Rutherford, slightly disappointed but humming the famous Davy Crockett ballad: 'Born on a mountaintop in Tennessee, greenest state in the land of the free, dah dah dah dah evr'y tree, killed him a bear when he was only three: Davy, Davy Crockett, King of the Wild Frontier.' Fantastic!

Dresden, Como, Paris and Dover gave the ride a continental flavour as I passed through villages and small towns on the trek eastwards across Tennessee. My route was slowly working its way upwards toward Kentucky and putting me north of Nashville. At a place called Adams I fuelled up, and decided to expand my knowledge of fast-foodology by giving my midday dining business to a chain called — and I'm going to preserve its anonymity by calling it 'Krapstal', in case the real name brings a lawsuit down on me.

The signature dish from Krapstal is their Krapstal burger, with the innovative variations of Krapstal burger with cheese and Krapstal burger with double cheese. What puts the krap into Krapstal burgers is the little square steamed bun and the meat that, in deference to cows worldwide, is nothing like any beef I've tasted. But the bottom of the fast-food barrel is well and truly scraped — probably literally — with their Chilli Pup range. By 'range', I mean the basic chilli pup — a small steamed hotdog bun with a small dog in it covered in warm chilli mince, also tasting suspiciously like dog — and the amazing variation chilli cheese pup, being all the aforementioned plus grated cheese on top.

But looking up at the menu board they all looked incredibly appetizing, and I smacked my lips as I ordered the Krapstal Kombo, being three Krapstals, two chilli cheese dogs and a coke for $6.95. It materialized in a flash, and I knew then that freshness and taste were going to be the victims of haste and waste. I bit into the first Krapstal burger and gagged. And this is Twisting Throttle, purveyor of fast food across two hemispheres. I have eaten Mrs Mac's meat-challenged products in Australian roadhouses, so you can't accuse me of never having plumbed the depths of highway food. In short, I know what I am talking about when it comes to travellers' grub. And this was not good. I scraped the half-melted cheese off the first chilli cheese dog. The mess underneath reminded me of Australia as well; namely, a dead wombat I'd come across that had been run over by a truck. I spread a lot of napkins over the uneaten Kombo, downed the coke, burped lightly, tip-toed to the rubbish bin and slung it out. 'Y'all take kare now, y'hear?' the young girl on the kounter kalled to me as I krept out. I will never say anything bad about Mrs Mac's again.

Chapter 18

Kentucky

Nickname: The Bluegrass State

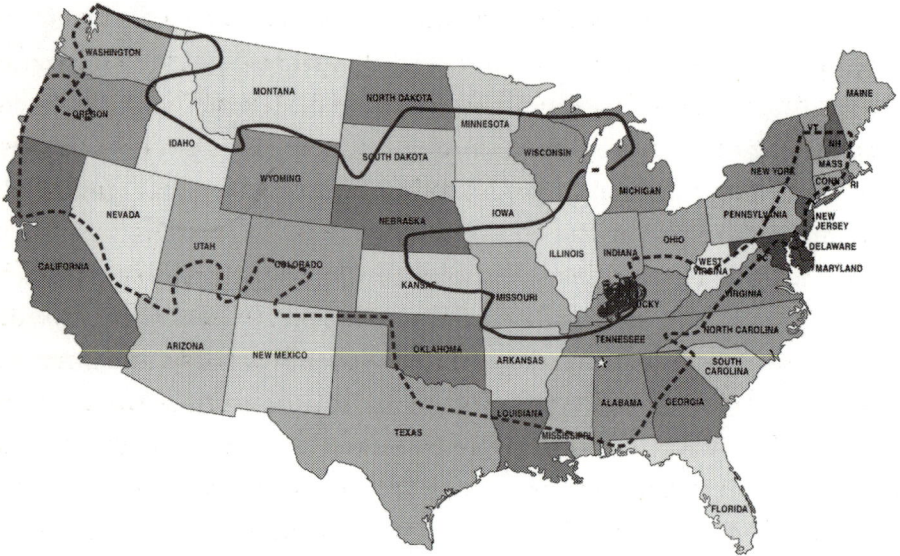

This state: 316 kilometres. Journey to date: 14,885 kilometres.

N36 43.947 W85 32.643. Do these co-ordinates do anything to you in a physical way? Can you feel some sort of sensation that you are not the only one reading this book in the room where you are? Hairs standing up on the back of your neck? If so, then you are a believer. If not, then you are as cynical as I was about supernatural things. My point with all this is that I was parked at these GPS co-ordinates, which was the intersection of Meshack Road and God-knows-where but it was in a very remote part of southern Kentucky. I was there to see for myself if the legend of the ghostly motorcycle pillion of Meshack Road was fact or lore. To backtrack, here is the story.

✪

About 10 kilometres over the border in Kentucky is a small town called

Tompkinsville. Just to the north is a heavily wooded area with a stream running through it called Meshack Creek. Meshack Road is a narrow one-lane winding road that ambles through the woods by the stream. Along the road are several remote farms. Sixty years ago, two young men were driving along Meshack Road and saw in their lights a lone woman hitchhiker. She was attired in a formal dress and on her way to the same local dance as the men. They offered her a lift and danced with her all night long. She agreed to be driven home by the boys only if she could be let out by the old sycamore tree halfway along Meshack Road. As it was raining, one of the boys lent her his coat and said, using the oldest pick-up line in the business, that he would collect it in the morning. She said she lived in the farmhouse over the road from the tree. The young man went back to the farmhouse the next morning and knocked on the door. The farmer listened to his story and said that the young hitchhiker sounded like his daughter. When the young man asked to speak with her, the farmer told him that she had died in a motoring accident by the sycamore tree over 10 years before. The young man was directed to her grave at the back of the farm. On the grave he saw his neatly folded coat.

Since then, Meshack Road has been the subject of many reports of a ghostly presence stalking motorcyclists and horse riders, who claim they feel something or someone clinging to their waist as they ride along. The ghostly pillion legend features on all paranormal websites, and as I was passing through Tompkinsville it was too close to ignore. Looking back on the several hours I spent on Meshack Road, I wish I had just ridden on. Here's what happened.

⚜

Inexplicably, my GPS failed to find the start of Meshack Road. It had me riding around, almost in circles, on a network of back-country roads with no signposts. At one point, I was crossing a field when the rutted track I was on simply stopped at a hay barn. It was as if I was being shepherded away by a force that beat even the GPS. Eventually, I found my way onto Meshack Road itself, and immediately it started to rain. I pulled over in a wooded clearing to change jackets when the bike rolled forward off the side stand and toppled over like a stranded heifer. I took out my camera and snapped a picture of the road winding ahead into the woods. When I downloaded the photo that night I was surprised to see that it was mysteriously blurred with what looks like streaks of a very fast-moving light. I look at the photo almost daily, trying to figure out what could have caused the motion blur.

After several more miles, I rounded a bend to find the Meshack Creek flooding over the road ahead. It was yet another obstacle to riding further on, and I wondered whether I should just turn around. But I knew that somewhere up ahead was the old sycamore tree. I walked through the flooding, established that it was rideable, and rode through carefully.

Then it happened. I felt a tightening around my waist, and was so convinced I had a passenger behind me that I looked in my mirror. Naturally all I saw was my camping gear strapped on to my rear seat. By now my hands were distinctly clammy. To say I was out of my comfort zone would be an understatement. I rode slowly past a derelict farmhouse set back in a copse of trees. The roof was caved in and ivy covered the rotten walls. I looked to my left and saw a big tree overhanging the road. Could that be a sycamore? I had no idea what a sycamore looked like. My jacket seemed way clingier than normal, and again I found myself glancing in my mirrors to see what was gripping me from behind. You are no doubt scoffing, but you weren't there, alone, on Meshack Road, in misty rain, in remote woodland, with the very real possibility that an apparition was inches behind you. Had I seen a Linda Blair face in my mirrors I would have felt relieved, as the trials and tribulations of the previous hour would have made sense. As it was, I reached the end of the road where it intersected with Highway 90 to Glasgow.

So was it a ghostly pillion that created the afternoon's conniptions? Or was it just an overactive imagination reading things into normal, albeit slight extraordinary, events? I sat on my bike looking back down the haunted road. What did I believe about the paranormal? Actually, I think it's a crock. But of all of you out there reading these words, someone somewhere will knock over their cup of coffee and it will stain this page. Welcome to Meshack.

I rode quietly and not a little reflectively north on Highway 90. At Dubre I saw a hoarding nailed to the side of a roadside barn saying: *Elect Willie Dale Killman for Cumberland County Jailer*. I could visualize the employment panel hearing: 'So could you tell the panel your views on capital punishment, Mr . . . er . . . Killman?'

I passed signs to Willow Shade, Summer Shade, Goodluck, Mud Lick, Sulphur Lick, Freedom and — my personal favourite — Eighty Eight. I fuelled up at Wisdom, and after a short burst up the I-65 arrived at a KOA Kampground in Horse Cave. Horse Cave is that well-known town in Kentucky which has a huge cave in the main street that became so polluted with sewage that birds flying over the opening had trouble breathing with the fumes and simply dropped to the ground. It's all cleaned up now, but I love the history.

The reason I head for these organized campgrounds, apart from the ice-cream-eating contests, the all-you-can-eat-pancake breakfasts and the opportunity to help out in the Kidz Klub, is that they always have wireless. And KOA Horse Cave certainly advertised Wi-Fi as a feature. However, when I logged on I couldn't get a signal. I went to the office to ask about it. 'We use the signal from the Country Hearth Inn just down the road.' 'So your Wi-Fi is actually someone else's signal?' 'Yes, but it's no problem: just go into their lobby and tell them you're a KOA kamper. You'll get a really strong signal down there.' I walked down the hill for 300 metres and into the reception area of the Country Hearth Inn. 'Can I help you?' asked a coiffured receptionist. 'Yes, I'm a KOA kamper and I've kome to use your Wi-Fi.' 'Not another one,' she sighed. 'Best to try the Chevron over the road.'

I walked over the road into the gas station. 'What pump?' asked the attendant. 'No gas, just want to see if I can use your Wi-Fi.' 'No problem, but the boss says you gotta buy something.' I thought I'd turn this into a win–win and have my evening meal. I asked for the menu and some bread and dips to start. Actually I didn't. I bought a dried burger from the warmer and a Fanta. I sat down at the only table, which was covered in fast-food wrappers, and logged on. The Wi-Fi network connection asked for a password. 'Do you know the password?' I called over to the girl who was engrossed in Spider Solitaire on her computer. 'Try Bernie,' she called back without looking up. I typed in 'Bernie', but it didn't work. 'Didn't work,' I called. 'No, I mean try phoning Bernie. He's the boss. He can tell you what it is.' I closed up the laptop and admitted defeat. My website would have to remain un-updated for another day. I walked back up the hill to the KOA Kampground and mooched over to the Kidz Klub to see if they needed a hand.

The morning dawned fine and very Kentuckyish. By that, I mean the scenery I was riding through on my way to Louisville. There were white fences bordering huge green fields in which horses grazed. Immaculately manicured driveways led up to palatial white farmhouses or farm-mansions. I was entering Abraham Lincoln country. The town of Hodgenville had a huge statue of Lincoln in their town square. This was his birthplace. I saw a sign to My Old Kentucky Home, the Civil War Museum, and the Bourbon Heritage Centre. But the place I was keen to stop in at was Abe Lincoln's boyhood home at Knob Creek.

Just off the road there was a rustic cabin which, a little incorrectly, was promoted as where Lincoln grew up. But what most people want to hear about, and the weary ranger on duty rolled his eyes and launched into the story of, is the near-drowning of Lincoln. In 1816, when he was seven, Lincoln was out playing in the woods with a neighbour's kid called Austin Gollaher. They were messing about on a log across the swollen Knob Creek, when Abe, who couldn't swim, fell in. With great presence of mind, Austin grabbed a long branch and thrust the end of it into one of Lincoln's hands, which had broken the surface of the water. He pulled the gasping Lincoln onto the bank and they made a pact not to tell their mothers. Over the years Austin waited patiently for some sort of payback, such as being made Secretary of State, but it never came. All he got was an invitation to attend the theatre with Lincoln one night.

The next sizeable town I reached was Bardstown. This of course, as you know, is home to Colonel Lee, Daniel Stewart, Elijah Craig, Old Pogue and Fighting Cock. Bourbons, of course. Kentucky bourbons. Realizing the importance of bourbon to the national psyche, federal laws were passed back in 1964 to ensure that bourbon complied with highly crucial standards; namely, that it had to be no more than 80% proof.

I rode on up the 150 to Louisville, Kentucky's largest city. It has many claims to fame. The first cervical cancer vaccine was developed here, Edison's light bulb was first viewed here, and the first hand transplant took place here. Unfortunately, the surgeon — who was partial to a drop of Fighting Cock to calm his nerves before going into theatre — transplanted the wrong limb, and the patient woke up to find a foot on the end of his arm. As he checked out of the hospital, he asked, 'Where's my hand gone then?' The assembled doctors' and nurses' gazes shifted to his shoe and he was shown back to his room.

But back to Louisville. I'm not trivializing advances in cervical cancer research or the invention of the light bulb, but I was here for two other shrines that arguably have had more impact on American society than anything else Louisville could dish up. Naturally, I'm referring to Kaelin's Restaurant, birthplace of the cheeseburger, and Cave Hill Cemetery, final resting place of Colonel Sanders.

I set the GPS to find the way to Kaelin's on the southeast side of the city. In 1934 Charles Kaelin opened his restaurant, serving burgers. One day he was in the kitchen and wondered how he could give his burgers a bit more pizzazz. He draped a slice of cheese over the grilling beef pattie and watched as it melted. He served up the world's first cheeseburger. His marketing slogan was: *Try Kaelin's Cheeseburgers. 15¢. You'll Like 'Em.* But his place in the cheeseburger hall of fame was contested by the Humpty Dumpty Barrel Drive-In in Denver, who said 'Hey, we put cheese on our burgers before you, Chuck', and the burger world was torn between the two competing claims. I took a photo of the plaque outside Kaelin's and went inside for lunch. I ordered a salad. No wait, only joking, it was a cheeseburger, and I'm sorry but it was crap. Charles Kaelin would probably turn in his grave.

Speaking of graves, my next shrineage stop was just around the corner at the massive Cave Hill Cemetery. I rode in the main gates and was struck immediately by the peacefulness of the wooded gardens and lawns dotted with marble headstones. 'Sorry, sir, no motorcycles allowed in Cave Hill', a security guard approached me from his hut by the gates. I took off my helmet. 'You here to see the Colonel?' He showed me a solid yellow line painted on the paved lane that led through the plots eventually to the gravesite. It took 20 minutes to walk the line. The guard said he'd mind my bike.

I approached the Colonel's resting place with as much reverence as I could muster, considering I was sweating buckets. There was a bust of the Colonel on a pedestal between two pillars. He died in 1980 at the age of 90. Stories abound that he took the secret of the 11 herbs and spices to his grave. In fact that recipe in its entirety is written down only once, in pencil on a piece of notebook paper and signed by the Colonel. It is, or was, in a vault in KFC HQ. In a bizarre coincidence, on the day I was paying my respects at the Colonel's grave, KFC moved the recipe to a secret location under very tight security as they were revamping their HQ building. It was kept temporarily in a cabinet with two combination locks. Two executives had a combination each. No one knew who the executives were. Vials of the herbs and spices were kept with the recipe.

I found my way back to my bike and the security guard. It was so hot that I flopped down and we chatted for a while. The guard, who introduced himself as Drago, said that the Colonel's grave attracted many visitors. I asked Drago what the Colonel had died of. He said it was a heart attack after learning that KFC had brought in a garden salad as a new side.

Chapter 19

Indiana–Ohio

Nicknames: The Hoosier State–The Buckeye State

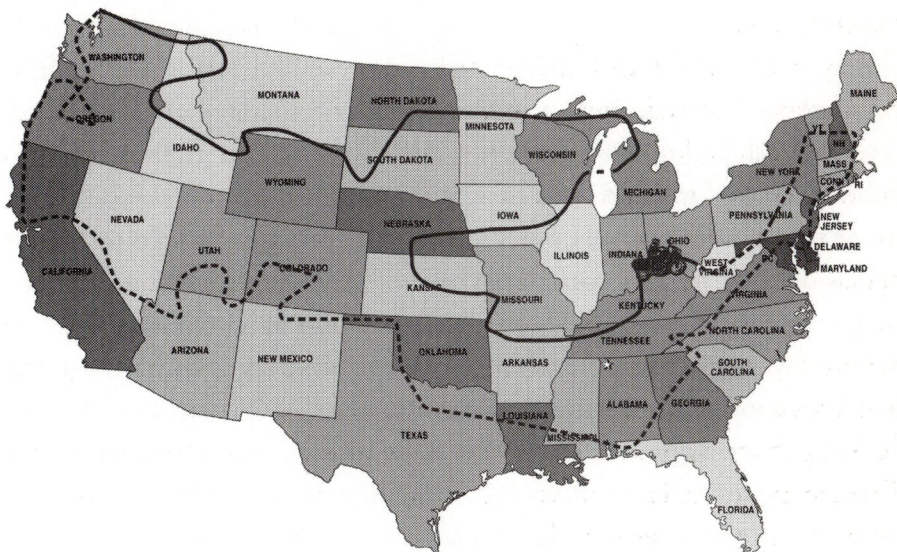

These states: 495 kilometres. Journey to date: 15,380 kilometres.

I RODE ACROSS the Ohio River from Louisville into Indiana. The only thing I really knew about Indiana was the Indy 500, the largest single-day sporting event in the world. My speed increased a fraction just thinking about it As I sped up the I-65 through Clarkville looking for the freeway exit to Charlestown, it briefly crossed my mind to stay on the interstate north and have a look at the Indy 500 track in Indianapolis. But that would entail a 325-kilometre dog-leg, half a day's extra riding, and I didn't have that sort of luxury at my fingertips. My path through Indiana to Ohio would be tracking along the northern bank of the wide and slow-moving Ohio River, another of these designated scenic byways, this one surprisingly called the Ohio River Scenic Byway.

I passed a sign welcoming me to the Hoosier state. That's pronounced 'hooja', where the 'j' sounds like the 'j' of Jean-Claude. It's not so much how you say that word as where it came from. And the thing is: no one actually knows. But to backtrack. Most states' residents are named after the actual state name. For example, Californians from California, Texans from Texas, Floridians from Florida, Mississippians from I'm not sure where. These state-to-people relationships are called 'denonyms', which are also, of course, people who wear jeans. But in the case of Indiana, they said 'That'll be the day we're gonna be called Indians', but the denonym 'Indianian' was considered too much of a mouthful. Then one day back in the early frontier years, a man named Ezra 'Indiana' Jones found a cave with a diamond-encrusted skull guarded by a lost tribe and the Nazis tried to— Sorry, wrong Indiana Jones. Anyway, this Jones coined the term 'Hoosier', after the common greeting when you approached someone's cabin and yelled out 'Hello, the cabin!' to avoid being shot. The call would come back from the cabin 'Who's here?', but as there wasn't a lot to do in cabins in the wilderness other than drink moonshine, the words slurred into 'Who'sh 'ere?', and thus 'hoosier' became the accepted denonym for rural Indianaians. This explanation is also found on the internet, so it must be true.

So it was that I found myself hoosing along Highway 56 just past Madison, enjoying the warm afternoon breeze skiffing off the huge Ohio River. Tugs towed massive, flat barges piled with what looked like coal. The Ohio is the largest tributary of the Mississippi, but where I was riding it was nearly a mile wide, and it was hard to look on it as a mere tentacle off another river. I pulled over at a lookout to get a photo of a barge with a smoke-belching factory on the far shore. Down below, kids were splashing around in the shallows of the river and families were messing about in runabouts and kayaks. As I fiddled about with my camera, a man puttered up to me riding a moped with a huge fishing rod tied lengthways. I smiled as I thought of him as a knight with a jousting stick.

Fishing guy: Yawl sen feshen axe rayon air?
Translation to English: *You seen any fishing access round here?*

Me:	I saw a sign for fishing access about a mile up the road that way toward Vevay.
Translation to American:	*Arse sore sarnfer feshen axe baremarle proadaways tavevver.*
Fishing Guy:	Yawl tockin vevver, baremarle assay?
Translation to English:	*You're talking Vevay, about a mile you say?*
Me:	Yes. So what are you hoping to catch today?
Translation to American:	*Ayup. Wolchu holp ketch dar?*
Fishing Guy:	Arm feshen cate-fesh, mebsum gar, mebsum paid fesh.
Translation to English:	*I'm fishing for catfish, maybe some gar, maybe some paddlefish.*
Me:	OK. Goodbye then.
Translation to American:	*Kaybar.*

I rode off down-river, leaving the fisherman to manoeuvre his moped around cars and trees without getting hooked up with his massive rod. I looked out over the Ohio, thinking that any catfish, gar and paddlefish in it would probably live to see another day.

It was a warm Sunday and motorcycles were out in force. It appeared that the Ohio River Scenic Byway was a favourite with locals, mostly I guessed from Cincinnati, out for an afternoon throttle-stretch with friends. Now would be a good time to explain the biker-to-biker waving protocol for pack riding. Here's my take on it, but I'll need to check the internet to see if it is fact.

When you're riding along and greet a lone biker coming the other way, it is a brotherhood ritual to acknowledge each other. Secretly, you're glancing over to have a look at their bike, but you don't move your head an inch, otherwise you're on the same level as a gawky tourist at the Tower of London. As your right hand has to stay on the throttle, you must wave with your left hand. In America that hand is, by lucky coincidence, the hand closest to the other biker. Why does that matter? Because you can practise the art of the cool wave. I am a waving pro, so have the credentials to be able to explain this to you, a waving non-pro. Here goes. It's all in the style of the wave. It must be as cool and as nonchalant as possible, bordering on being merely a twitch. First, you must establish if the other biker is entitled to be waved at. In some countries it is heresy for riders of Jap bikes to acknowledge riders of Harleys. This is not the case in America. But, generally, if you're riding a decent-sized bike, regardless of brand, you roundly ignore scooters, farm bikes, Hells Angels and trikes. After establishing entitlement to receive your wave, you must time your gesture so that it doesn't look like you are too eager. The wave must appear as almost an after-thought, that you have other things on your mind but you're prepared to register the existence of another biker passing through your territory. Bear in mind the other guy is going through exactly the same process over on the other side of the road. The ultimate waving experience is where both of you get it right.

But the critical factor is the wave itself. You drop your left hand off the handlebar grip slowly. It must go down halfway between the grip and your knee and hover there for approximately five seconds with the index finger pointing at a 45-degree angle towards the road surface. You can tell a waving pro by the rotational angle of the left hand. If the biker merely points to the road as if to say 'Hey, look at that dotted line whizzing by', then he's a waving rookie. By assuming the left-hand position as described above *and then* slowly rotating it so that the fingers are facing upwards, not downwards, then you show the other guy you're a waving pro. At all times you look straight ahead. Time it badly, and the other bike is past you and you are waving to a herd of cows. Time it too early, and you're forced to break the five-second rule, you reveal yourself as a pathetic waving rookie.

My point here is how this policy has to be varied for oncoming bikes in packs. The nonchalant five-second lowering and rotating of the left hand is useless where bikes pass you every three seconds. You'll look like a wind-up doll. There is nothing for it but to keep your left hand lowered, finger extended, for the entire convoy of bikes, meaning you're riding one-handed for quite a while. If you're rounding a corner, then it becomes a little more exciting.

Another dynamic in this whole waving protocol is positioning. Normally, I'd wave to bikes on the other side of a two-laned road, where you're separated by a dotted line. There are variations. If you overtake a bike going the same way as you, then it's polite to wave as you pass, obviously without looking. What you have to communicate is a friendly acknowledgement of existence without inferring any 'had to pass you because you're too slow' threat. Many passees don't wave back. Frankly, I don't either. You pass me when I'm doing the speed limit and you want to be my friend, too? Then there are the freeways. If you are literally eight lanes over from another bike and there's a median barrier in there, too, then you aren't expected to wave. If it's a four-laner with, say, a grass strip, then you wave.

Finally, there's the human element. Many two-up riders delegate the task of waving to their passengers. Waving pros do not tolerate this laziness. If you can't be bothered yourself, then you get ignored. Us pros are sorry for the pillion's sake, but it's a status thing. You don't see the Queen delegating her waving to her maid-in-waiting.

I accept that two or three pages on this subject have got you a trifle bored. The thing is that the whole acknowledgement-of-fellow-bikers industry is complex. You almost have to be in the saddle to understand the crushing rejection of being snubbed by one of your non-waving brothers, or the crushing guilt you suffer by waving too late, knowing the other rider is suffering the crushing rejection of being snubbed. The last thing I'll say on the subject is that there are some motorcycle forums that advocate not taking your hand off the steering and just nodding instead, in the interests of safety. I've talked to other waving pros, and we all say *pshaw*. On the other hand, I could be the first to write rules for being a nodding pro. You deflect your helmet to an angle of no more than 10 degrees, making sure your neck does not rotate so that— Enough.

To avoid being thrust into the throbbing heart of Cincinnati, I took the on-ramp to the I-275 and re-entered Kentucky temporarily as the interstate bypassed the Queen City. An hour later, I was in Ohio back on the Ohio River Scenic Byway passing through New Palestine, Moscow,

Rural and Utopia. At Higginsport I fuelled up and decided I'd had enough of the Ohio River for the moment. I fancied some nice, quiet back roads through cornfields, where the corners are not signposted with speed recommendations. In other words — it was time to live dangerously.

I reached a tiny place called Decatur. Decatur? You don't know the significance of Decatur? If I said top roll technique, hook grip, shoulder pressing, triceps press, strap master . . . Still none the wiser? What about the names Caggiano, Brzenk, Bagent or Cooper? I hear the penny dropping. Yes, I was in Decatur, home of world arm-wrestling champion Sam Cooper. Or at least that's what the sign said as I rode in.

I pulled up at the small café in Decatur's main street and went inside. The owner was a large, stocky man in a red-checked shirt, a white apron and a John Deere cap, and he had just poured a coffee for a customer. 'That'll be $2.90 for the coffee, but why don't we settle this the man's way, Tommy?' 'Shucks, Mr Cooper, cain't we settle this as usual? Ah got money. Ah ain't gettin' into no arm wrestlin' with ya. You bein' world champ 'n' all. Cain't you just take ma money like everyone else?' I walked up to the counter and addressed the bulging-bicepped muscle-man behind the counter. 'Tea for one and a lemon muffin, please, friend.' 'Sure, stranger. That'll be $4.53. I suppose you're a pussy like all them others around here and want to pay in cash?' 'Not me, friend. See that motorcycle out there? That's a Suzuki. Do I look like a pussy to you?' Cooper's face paled. I rolled up my sleeve, clenched my fist and placed my elbow on his counter. 'Well, friend, you gonna be long?' 'Y'all know who I am, stranger? Sam Cooper, world arm-wrestling champ.' He pulled back his shirtsleeve to reveal a tattoo on his bicep that read *World Champ Ram Wrestler*. 'Y'all know who I am, friend? Twisting Throttle, diner pro, waving pro, tattoo spell-checker.'

We clasped fists and our faces were inches apart. The customer watching all this said '3-2-1-wrestle' and we took the strain. Beads of perspiration formed on Cooper's forehead as our forearms twitched with this pressure. Neither of us was yielding an inch. 'You're good, stranger,' he gasped between clenched teeth. I glanced outside and saw that it was getting dusky. I had to get out of here and move on to find a campsite for the night. This had to be ended. After all, it was only a lemon muffin. I

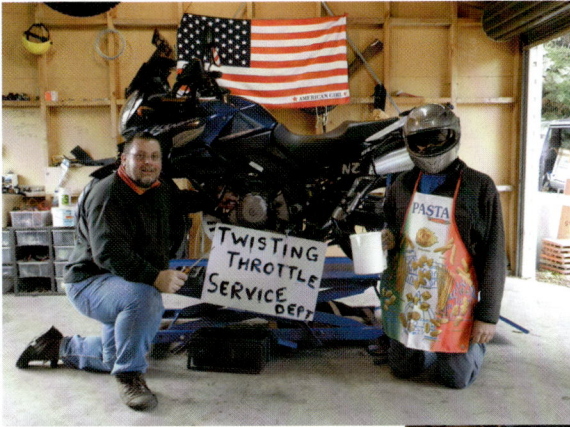

No expense was spared in setting up Twisting Throttle HQ back home. I had corporate sponsorship from Mum, who gave me an apron to keep oil off my jeans. Here I am visiting the TT New Zealand office with Gavin, head of my technical team.

My signwriter son, Robert, puts the finishing touches to the bike's branding. It was thanks to his stunning decals that I got a lot of local interest in where I was from.

The bike and gear is picked up by truck driver Matt, who suggested I might like to save on airfares and jump into the crate, too.

It was pandemonium at the airport with well-wishers bringing the terminal to a standstill. Here are the Dust Devils honouring me with their traditional masons-like salute. That's my wife, Sandy, on my right as you look at the photo. Given that I'd be away for two months, you'd have to ask why she's looking so happy.

From the moment I boarded the flight to Honolulu it was down to business as I continued my research into contemporary American issues to prepare me for the shock of immersion into a foreign culture.

These are the Jewish lads from New York City who were up in Denali, Alaska, doing some bonding. They shared their campfire, pasta and philosophy with me.

Global warming? What global warming?

This is Mr and Mrs S Claus of North Pole, Alaska. I swallowed my pride and agreed to sit on his knee, but he did promise me a PlayStation.

As part of my world charity commitments I visited a moose leper colony in Alaska.

This is Officer Cooper of the US border post at Midway, Washington. After some discussion on who had the higher cholesterol level, he stamped my carnet and let me be on my way.

Each state has it's own state vegetable. Here I am in Driggs, Idaho, about to cross into Wyoming, looking for any clue as to what Idaho's symbolic state vegetable is. I never did discover what it was. Perhaps the zucchini.

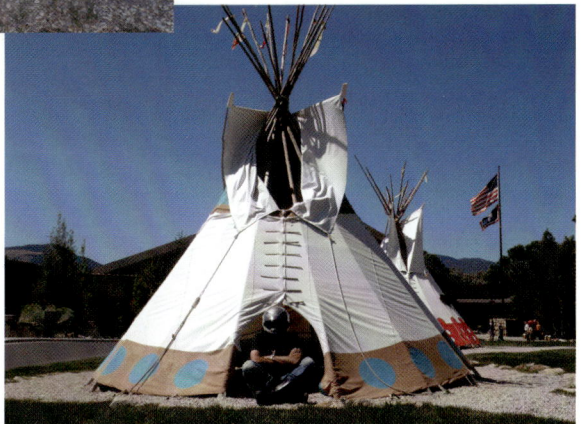

After I finished posing for this photo, I had two choices of what to do next . . . tea or pee.

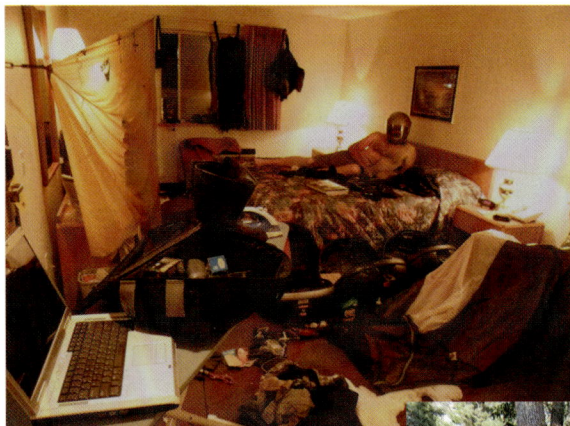

My motel room in St Ignace, Michigan, after running from a severe storm that hit the Great Lakes. Chambermaids queued up to service the room after I left.

I was very tight with my support crew. The nights were lonely. The bike and I grew close, and it was only natural that we started sleeping together.

The GPS and I had frequent disputes about where we were. Here is an example. The GPS says we are in a small town called Lincoln, Kansas, whereas my honed map-reading skill tells me it is Tipton. It annoyed me that a machine thought it was superior to a man.

This is the world-exclusive photo of the Tri-state Spook Light, captured by my camera's remote as I was witnessing a paranormal display of spookiness at night on an isolated back road in the Missouri woods.

During the ride, safety was uppermost in my mind, which is why I'm wearing my helmet here at the Grand Canyon in case of a crumbly edge.

I went to Yellville, Arkansas, where rumour has it that they toss live turkeys out of planes as part of their Turkey Festival. I couldn't see any sign of cruelty to birds, so put it down as yet another tourist beat-up.

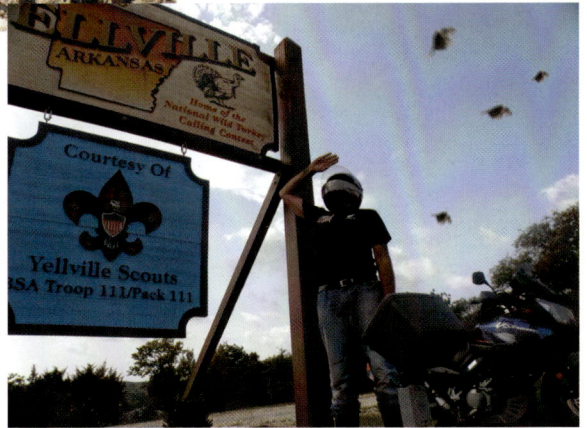

This is the view looking down Meshack Road in Kentucky. It is true that I had an afternoon of strangeness riding along this remote wooded farm road, which is supposedly haunted by a ghostly pillion girl, but I am a paranormal non-believer and this load of bollocks just reinforced my scepticism of these backwoods 'supernatural' stories.

On the whole I loved American cuisine. Into a hole I tipped *this* American cuisine. In a backwoods diner in West Virginia I tried biscuits and gravy. Look at this photo and tell me the words 'cat' and 'vomit' don't spring to mind.

My chance meeting with Amish farmer Amos Lapp in Intercourse, Pennsylvania. That's him and his Surrey buggy with 40mm rear spring displacement pulled by his '97 Saddleback mare doing 10 miles to the bale.

This sums up my diet for the trip. Sometimes this dish is served with a mesclun side salad, a glass of bean sprout juice, and some fresh fruit with yoghurt dressing. Mostly it isn't.

I celebrated my birthday on the road in Vermont. The support team threw a surprise party for me.

In New York's Catskill Mountains there are survival rules posted for how to deal with encounters with the ferocious black bear. Don't panic, remain calm and, above all, if he wants to play 'pat-a-cake' with you, do it.

Many nights were spent camping alone in dark and remote forests. It was only after seeing this photo back home that I noticed the two red eyes in the trees behind me.

This is a hooligan having fun on the Tail of the Dragon in Tennessee/ North Carolina. 316 bends in 11 miles. This photo was taken by a company who hides in the bushes, snaps all bikes riding the Dragon, and then you download the pictures off the net. We call it 'rard porn'.

I was late for my appointment at the White House and wondered how to let the President know I had arrived for our ride. I met *Motorcycle One* at the south entrance and enjoyed an hour's guided tour around central Washington.

In South Carolina I lost a lot of time due to weather. Here, I had to shelter under a rocky overhang waiting for the deluge to stop. It didn't. In fact it continued pouring down all afternoon. Incredibly, after I gave up and rode away, within 10 seconds it was dry again. Very fickle weather.

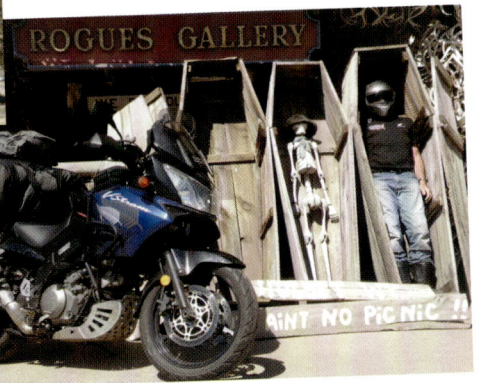

These are conjoined lovebugs in Mississippi. After mating, the male and female remain attached at their rear ends for life, even after the male dies (probably by suicide).

In Florida I had to shelter from Hurricane Ike's outer-edge wrath. Visibility was zero in the continual torrential rain. Here is yet another underpass in the Sunshine State.

Petrol pumps got progressively more complicated, and here in Louisiana it was like putting your money into a gaming machine and hoping you won some fuel.

I made the strategically correct decision to out-run Hurricane Ike with a 1,200-kilometre sprint through Alabama, Mississippi and Louisiana to Texas. It was Mike vs Ike. V-Strom vs V-Storm.

Is this the way to Amar— All right, if I have to explain this photo, then you don't deserve to be looking at it.

This is El Santuario de Chimayó in New Mexico, known as the Lourdes of America. The chapel is built over the site of the Holy Crucifix and is a mecca for thousands of pilgrims seeking healing and enlightenment. But all I was after was a fridge magnet.

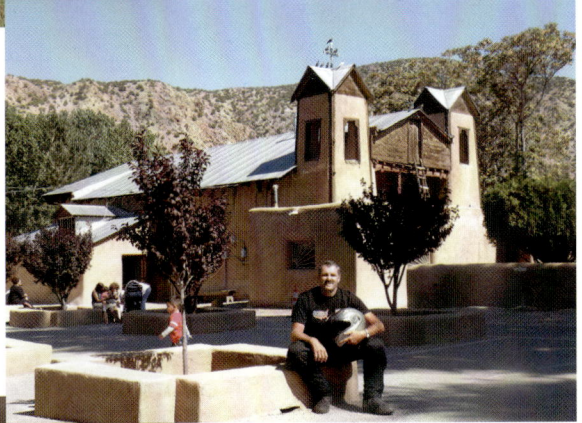

And this is the hole in the chapel's floor where you scoop up some Holy Dirt that has religious and healing properties. Incredibly, seconds after getting some Holy Dirt all over her jeans this little Mexican girl got up and miraculously walked out of the room, without the aid of crutches.

What's this? Adobe Acrobat, reader.

This is the UFO Watchtower in Colorado, with the Sangre de Cristo Mountains behind. In this desert valley, a high number of UFO sightings have been recorded. A local lady built the watchtower, which she claims is a lightning-rod for alien spacecraft being that this particular spot is an inter-dimensional vortex. It was closed, so I phoned home instead.

This is not as sleazy at it looks. This is none other than Room 102 at Snow Shoe Lodge in Creede, Colorado. John Wayne slept in this very bed back in 1972. The room's décor has remained unchanged ever since.

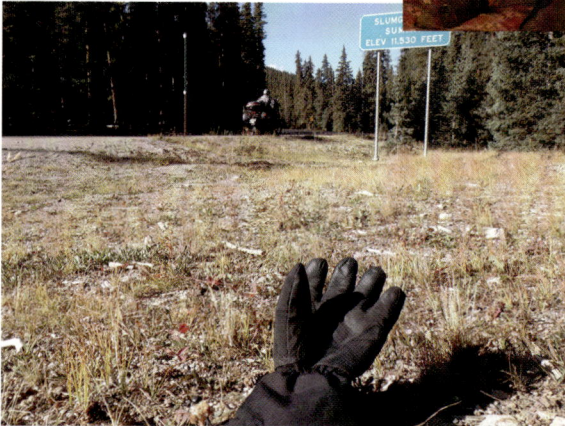

A low spot in the trip was losing my gloves, in a *déjà vu* episode from Australia, somewhere over Slumgullion Pass in the Rockies. This photo is a reconstruction of what it must have been like for Sons of Glovey as the last sound they heard was my accelerating bike fading into the distance.

A typical evening's activity in my executive suite. Writing this book while enjoying stale doughnuts and flat Fanta.

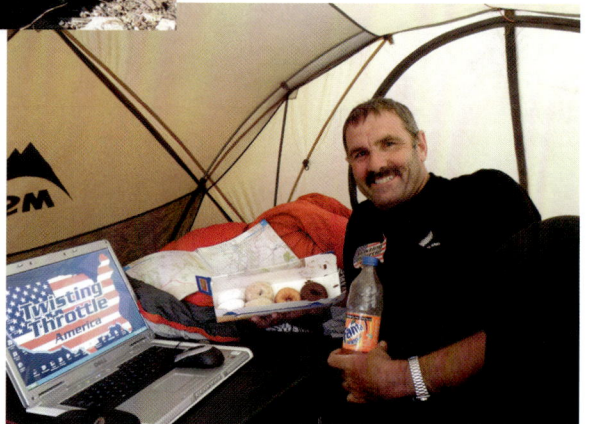

Much of the original Route 66 has disappeared, and to travel its length you have to be prepared to drive cross-country on the more hard-to-find sections, such as this one in Arizona.

One of the best days of the trip. Meeting my daughter, Sophie, in Vegas and doing a loop in the desert looking for casinos in Pahrump and Indian Springs.

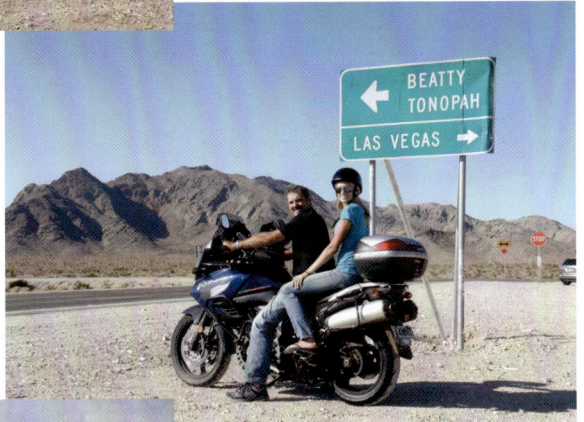

This is Death Valley in 44°C. See where the road bottoms out? That's sea level. Then it drops a further 85.5 metres to the US's lowest point at Badwater.

This is what a head looks like that's been encased in a helmet for three hours in the middle of the day in the middle of summer in Death Valley, the Western Hemisphere's hottest place. At 44°C, I wished I had remembered to bring some water.

This is the famous Area 51 on Nevada's Extraterrestrial Highway. To me it was just another tourist beat-up. There was nothing that I could see which meant this was not just another boring highway in the desert.

The thing with the Nevadan desert is that when you want to go to the toilet you have to walk a'ways to find a bush.

To prove that Bigfoot is a crock, I spent half a day riding through a maze of woodland roads in a peak sighting area, all to no avail. So you heard it here: Twisting Throttle says Bigfoot DOES NOT EXIST.

After 32,000 kilometres, 50 states and 60 days on the road, the journey ended as I crossed back into British Columbia. *The Best Place on Earth* they say? Right at that moment, it was.

rolled my shoulder, hooked my wrist and went for the triceps press slam-dunk. Cooper had no answer, and his fist crashed down on the counter as I slammed home my victory. 'And keep the change, friend,' I called back over my shoulder as I strode out of Kooper's Kakes & Kafé.

Route 125 curved up into the hills as I entered the Shawnee State Forest. It was almost pitch-black when I found the park camping ground and set up my tent under tall fir trees. The last time I'd eaten, apart from the imaginary lemon muffin, was the horrible cheeseburger two states ago back in Louisville. I dug into my pannier and found a bottle of lukewarm water and half a bag of cheezelets. My supper was light on goodness but strong on ambience, as I sat on the bike's padded seat and lay back looking up at the blanket of Northern Hemisphere stars. I wandered down to the camp office before they closed to buy an Ohio fridge magnet. Incredibly, they had one. 'That's $3.95,' said the guy, 'and we take all major credit cards.' I rolled up my sleeve, clenched my fist, placed my elbow on the counter and said, 'Why don't we settle this man-to-man, friend?'

Chapter 20

West Virginia

Nickname: The Mountain State

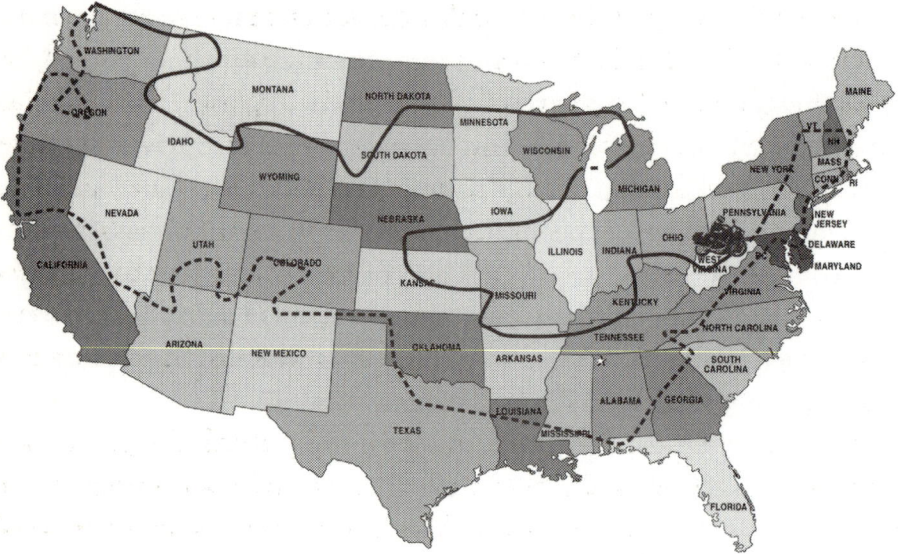

This state: 653 kilometres. Journey to date: 16,033 kilometres.

THE MOMENT I CROSSED the state line from Ohio into West Virginia at Huntington I started crooning 'Country Roads'. Sorry, but don't tell me that you're there holding this book and the mere mention of West Virginia hasn't got you humming it, too. 'Dah dah dah, take me home, to the place I be-long, West Virginia, mountain momma, take me—' And it was a mountain momma whom I was addressing right now as I tried to find out what biscuits and gravy were all about. To backtrack.

I sat on the I-64 as it carved its way through incredibly thickly wooded hills, plunging into the heart of West Virginia. At Charleston the I-64 suddenly morphed into the I-79 as I headed due east. I was enjoying the freedom of just sitting in sixth gear and holding on. There were hundreds of articulated trucks on the interstate, and we all picked our lane and stayed there. I started noticing enticing town names on the exit signs. Big Chimney, Balls Gap, Hicumbottom, Nitro, Scary, Black Betsy. But the one that made me flick on my right-hand indicator was the sign to Buttlick Road. I exited immediately. Who wouldn't want a photo of that to send back home to Great Aunt Molly?

Except I'd sped past the sign without reading it properly. It was in fact Bufflick Road, and so I sat at a crossroads underneath the freeway flyover a bit disappointed, but glad to have made the tug away from four-lane cruising back onto back roads. I pulled out the road atlas and immediately realized it was destiny to have exited just there. Buttlick destiny. A looping, pale yellow line on the map would take me to the settlements of Cotton, Speed, Looneyville, Left Hand, Duck and, if I had time, another side road to Milo, Gip, Dingy, Shock and Flower. This truly was the state of Country Roads. So with a misty taste of moonshine and teardrops in my eye, I rode into the West Virginian woods.

By and by, I came to a diner in a clearing. I think the general area was called Gandeeville. It was mid-morning and I was hungry to the point of wondering how tasty the dead insects on my windscreen would be. I pulled in, kicked down the side stand, and went in. I was treated like royalty from the moment they set eyes on me. This remote diner on a remote back road in the remote woods of West Virginia didn't see many overseas tourists, and I felt like a Martian who was being given the earthlings-welcome-aliens treatment. The kindly lady showed me to their outdoor seating area, which comprised a single tree-stump with a piece of plywood nailed on it to form a table. She gave me the menu, handwritten and illegible, and looked pleased as I pretended to read it, hard-pressed to make a decision. In reality I was searching for anything that was in English. Two young children came out of the diner's back door and stood watching me from a distance. A horse in a nearby field stopped grazing and stood looking at me as well.

'Hmm, not sure what to have. Can I ask what biscuits and gravy are?' 'Besken gray vair narse. Y'all larket.' However, the description 'vair narse' was not one I would rush to use on what I ended up with. And I have to say that I did not larket.

Here is the technical description of American biscuits and gravy, and I repeat it here because it's probably different to what you and I think of as biscuits and gravy. To me, a biscuit is a cookie, preferably covered in chocolate. My favourites are the ones shaped like animals and you lick the icing off first and— Sorry, I've forgotten what I was . . . That's right, and gravy is brown, made by Grandma, and covers roast meat and spuds. Not so in America. Biscuits are like scones — or, if you are a Shetland Islander reading my book, like bannock — light and fluffy, made from buttermilk. The gravy is the killer. It's the dripping from pork sausages mixed with white flour and milk, with pieces of meat and flavoured with black pepper. It has the look and texture of vomit.

I'm really sorry to be so graphic, but frankly it wasn't you who was sitting at a tree-stump in the West Virginian woods looking down at a plate of scones and vomit, being watched expectantly by a mountain momma, her two children, and a horse. I forked around a bit with the gravy and tried to make out I was eating gustily. I managed to get down half a biscuit that wasn't tainted with the gravy. The kindly lady in her apron and boots asked me if I'd like a drink. Thank God. I ordered a giant Pepsi and she rushed it out. For the next 15 minutes I would shovel in a forkful of gravy and swig back two mouthfuls of Pepsi. I would love to have seen what the resulting mess was like inside my stomach. As I sit here typing this, I can feel a retch welling up. It was awful, and yet I had to get it down. It was like the Queen visiting Mongolia and gagging on the yak testicles in sour milk. It couldn't be done: if you're royalty, you have obligations to your subjects. Finally, the kids went back to their banjo-strumming on the veranda, the horse wandered off, and the lady went inside to serve two guys who'd pulled up in a pick-up. I saw them, obviously locals, looking at the menu. They chose the burger and fries. Peasants.

I set my GPS to get me to Looneyville. And drivin' down the road I get a feelin' I should have been home (to Looneyville) yesterday, yesterday. I was already on a narrow, winding road in the woods and hadn't passed a car for miles. Suddenly the GPS instructed me to turn right down a highly suspicious little lane that looked like someone's driveway. It was marked Vandales Forks Road. It narrowed to one lane and pootled along beside a twinkling brook. Every few miles, the woodland would open out to bright green meadows either side of the lane. Squirrels by their hundred darted across the road and scampered up the wide trunks of whatever the trees were that shrouded the picturesque little country lane. Had men in tights dropped down from the trees and held me up with bows and arrows I would not have flinched. The ride was idyllic. I was conscious of mucking about with my schedule, though. Nice as this pootling around leafy lanes was, it was not getting me closer to the Atlantic Ocean.

I reached the settlement of Left Hand in Roane County. I've since looked Left Hand up on the internet and it says it has a population of 599 in 276 housing units. Like you I know if it's on the internet it must be correct, but Left Hand shakes my faith a little. First, I saw maybe three houses in amongst the trees. There was a small post office and what looked like a disused community hall. If nearly 600 people lived there, then they must be underground. I could think of less chilling places to camp after dark.

The country road meandered on. I surfed on the MP3 player for Pat Boone. I freely admit it: I had Pat Boone on my MP3. But before you scoff, I ask you to transport yourself onto a gently throbbing motorbike, warm sun reflecting off the babbling stream to your left, tall, leafy oak trees to your right, a smooth, curving road winding through the woodland, little does and rabbits frolicking in the sun-dappled meadows, leaning left, leaning right, rider and machine at one, the soft crooning of 'Wayward Wind' in your helmet . . . Yes, you're right: I'll delete it.

I passed three strapping farm workers loading bales of whatever crop was growing around here onto a trailer. At the sound of the bike, they stopped and looked up. I waved and they waved back, as if I was leaning out a train window going off to war. It was very heart-warming, and I felt I was connecting with the real America. But I was beggared if I could find Duck. Just like the so-called settlement of Looneyville, it didn't exist. It was on the map, on my GPS, but there in the West Virginian woods it had vanished. I rode up and down the stretch of wooded lane looking for any sign of Duck. There were no houses, no people, nor any evidence of a settlement at all. Finally, I saw just a single paltry sign that said *Duck*. Get it? Paltry sign that . . . It was time to stop messing about on back roads and get some distance in.

Back on the I-79 I turned north, heading towards the Pennsylvania state line fast. At Stonewall Jackson State Park, I exited onto Route 33 that would take me through the Monongahela National Forest to Seneca Rocks in the Allegheny Mountain Range. If you're a Civil War nut, some of these names will start triggering excited reactions in you. Just wait until I tell you that that night I would be camping at Harpers Ferry. It will pay to read on. And speaking of Civil War, it was Suzuki versus BMW for a 35-kilometre stretch of dual carriageway between Buckhannon and Elkins. Here's what happened.

I had fuelled up at Buckhannon, and the entrance ramp to the freeway-like Route 33 was a downhill, single-access road similar to that of a normal on-ramp entering a motorway. Merging protocol is that any through-traffic seeing a vehicle entering the motorway ahead just shifts over a lane so it's good and smooth. Every now and then you get a — and I use the technical term — tosser who simply stays put in the outside lane, as if your rapidly accelerating person down the on-ramp is invisible.

This was the case with a maroon-coloured BMW 1150RT, a large touring bike, with a rider and his leather-clad pillion passenger on board. They all but ran into the back of me. I was watching the oncoming bike in my mirrors, expecting them to observe merging rules and shift into the other lane to let me in. At the point of virtual collision, we would both have been going the speed limit. I couldn't understand the slack roadmanship. The RT pulled up alongside me and the pillion passenger, who had an open-face helmet so I could see every facial expression, gave me a lingering look that included the unspoken words 'you', 'off', 'why', 'don't' and another less polite one. And then the bike surged off at considerably above the speed limit, with the unspoken words 'tourists' and the same impolite one above.

Shaken and not a little piqued at the uncharacteristic bike-to-bike hostility, I gave chase. It wasn't exactly a *Mission Impossible*-style of chase,

166

but it would be true to say that a radar detector would have been handy. Soon I tucked in behind the RT and slipstreamed for 10 kilometres, not sure what to do next. Strangely, he buttoned off his speed, forcing me to overtake and again look his passenger in the eye as I passed. She remained impassively looking forward, but must have known I was alongside. We were so close I could have played knuckles with her. At times like this, I am glad I have a dark inner visor in my helmet, a sun visor. It's a sort of Darth Vader motif and almost completely hides your face. It means you look sinister and evil, like one of those mystery baddies chasing James Bond on snowmobiles. I finally gave up trying to attract her attention and just rode on, leaving behind the BMW.

He picked up speed and sat a consistent 20 metres behind me all the way to Elkins, where I exited the 33 and saw them in my mirrors looking after me as they carried on. It was an interesting little joust and probably just a simple case of two male peacocks strutting and feather-showing. If you're reading this book, you own a maroon BMW 1150RT with Maryland plates, and have a wife with an open-face helmet who knows a few choice phrases, then thanks for making the 33 a bit more colourful than it might have been otherwise. If I'd had more time, I would have offered you both a no-hard-feelings meal in Elkins; say, biscuits and gravy. My treat.

I reached Seneca Rocks, a small settlement in the shadow of Seneca Rocks, a large crag in the Seneca Rocks National Recreation Area. I wondered if this could be Seneca Rocks. The afternoon was almost spent, and I looked at my map for a camping spot. It showed a little tent icon smack in the middle of the Seneca Rocks forest. I asked my GPS for help, and the Garmin Zumo assured me I could reach it if I took the next right after Hopeville. I turned off as instructed. The road crossed the Potomac River, which gave a little thrill as I realized that if I threw a stick in here it would end up floating past the Pentagon sometime the next day.

The narrow road became gravelled and wound up into the thick forest. Gravel doesn't phase me, but it is certainly an indication that there's probably not a diner up ahead anytime soon. I rounded a corner to come face-to-face with a pick-up truck with several dogs on the back barking loudly. The driver wound down his window. 'You lost, friend?' 'Not really, mate. I'm making for the campground at Smoke Hole. Is it far up here?' 'Don't know about no campground up thereaways. Smoke Hole's 10 miles on, but there's a washout two miles up. You can try to get past. You might make it.' 'You guys up here hunting?' The dogs stopped barking and looked at each other. The driver turned to his passenger, and they said something to each other. He turned back to me. 'Yeah, that's right, friend. We're up here hunting.' My next question was going to be hunting what, but I got the impression that it would have been safer asking Osama Bin Laden for the co-ordinates of his cave in the mountains. I wheeled the bike 180 degrees and set off back down the hill, not wanting to risk the washout in fading light. The pick-up trailed me at a distance, and I soon lost them after the gravel ended and I crossed over the Potomac again.

As I closed in on the state line with Virginia near Wardensville, I reflected on West Virginia and how much I liked it. I had been humming 'Country Roads' all day, unable to get the damn tune out of my head. Life is old there, older than the trees, younger than the mountains . . . but their gravy is crap.

Chapter 21

Maryland

Nickname: The Old Line State

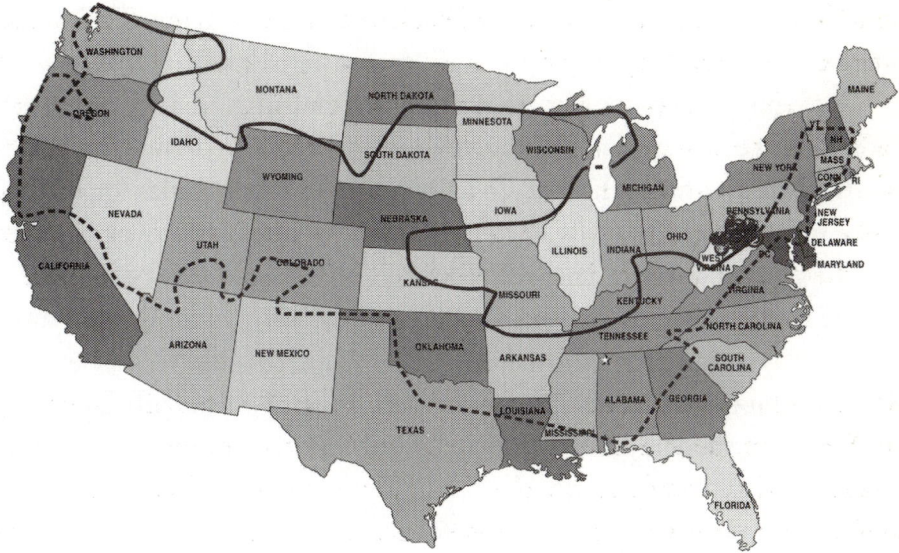

This state: 79 kilometres. Journey to date: 16,112 kilometres.

MARYLAND IS THE SAME SIZE as Belgium. I haven't been to Belgium that I know of, but I surely know that I could walk across it faster than I was crossing Maryland. Maryland has the highest household average income of all 50 states, and I could easily believe that from where I was sitting. Yes, sitting.

Darkness had fallen and I had left my camping decision too late. If I'd pitched up in West Virginia, I would have been enjoying my bottle of water and chips. Instead, I fell for the old trick of wanting to surge across a state line just to get that thrill of mentally ticking off another milestone. Except that I crossed into Virginia, not Maryland. I didn't realize I had to nick the corner of Virginia to get across the state line back into West Virginia, nick the corner of West Virginia to cross the state line into Maryland. But I'd had enough of nicking and crossing, and it was my own greedy fault I was stationary, trapped in the middle lane of three on the I-81 to Hagerstown and beyond. The interstate was gridlocked. And this was Sunday night at 9.00 p.m.?

The three lanes of bumper-to-bumper traffic inched forwards. Stretching miles ahead was a sea of flickering red lights as brakes went on every 5 metres of progress. I was sandwiched between two massive 18-wheelers, and even though the temptation was to lane-split I stayed put. Time ticked on, and the speed of our crawl was no more than 15 km/h.

The next exit up ahead was Route 7 to Washington DC, only some 80 kilometres away. The big gamble was whether I would be giving up the frying pan for the fire. But Twisting Throttle sizzles for no one, and I manoeuvred my way through a packed outer lane over the next two kilometres to make the exit. I looked ahead up the I-81, too late to reverse my decision to exit, and saw the endless worm of gridlocked traffic snaking to the horizon. I turned onto the 7 expecting the worst, but there was nothing on it. I could have cried with relief. After nearly two hours of first gear, I sped up like a maniac just to feel the cool night air and the sensation of getting somewhere.

I set the GPS to get me to a campground at Harpers Ferry, a small town smack on the border of West Virginia, Virginia and Maryland, where the Shenandoah and Potomac Rivers converge. If you hike the 3,500-kilometre Appalachian Trail, then Harpers Ferry is one of the few towns you actually pass through. Therefore, I assumed the town would have more than the usual number of laundrettes, fast-food places and massage parlours. All right, that's being disrespectful to long-distance walkers, but 3,500 kilometres is a long way to plod without life's basic support services.

Speaking of basic services, I found myself the next morning, after a night of light sleep caused by squirrels dropping nuts onto my tent, in the campground laundrette. It was high time hygiene was introduced into my American ride, and, even by my extremely low standards, my socks and T-shirt were in need of cleaning. I'll be honest and up-front: I'd never used a laundrette before.

After walking in, I got the gist of what happened in there, though. There were two types of white machines: washers and dryers. The walls of the laundrette were plastered with instructional signs, ranging from separating coloureds (a little tasteless I thought, given Harpers Ferry's role in the 1800s' slavery era), to how many quarters you need for the washing machine, the detergent-vending machine, the dryers, the fabric-softener-vending machine, and a coke while you wait. I fished around in my wallet. I had nine quarters totalling $2.25. That should do nicely. How wrong I was. The washing machine took six quarters. The dryer took four quarters. The detergent machine took three, and you could, at a push, go without fabric softener and the coke. Therefore I was a dollar short.

I remarked on the whole quarter dependence thing to Mrs Wrass. This is my best interpretation of the name by which the lady on the next machine introduced herself. It was slightly odd that she said 'Hello, I'm Mrs Wrass' rather than 'Hello, I'm Mavis Wrass' or simply 'Hello, I'm Mavis'. But anyway, she saw me doing the maths with the growing dread that I didn't have enough quarters. 'There's a coin-dispensing machine over there on the wall,' she said, 'except it's broken. Been like that all week. I've reported it.'

Mrs Wrass was a campground pro and a permanent resident of this one at Harpers Ferry. She was no stranger to this laundrette, so I looked on her as my soap saviour. 'OK, I've got enough for the washer and the dryer, but I'm a bit stuck for soap.' 'You can buy some down at the camp office,' she suggested, 'but they don't open 'til nine.' I looked over at the large plastic bottle marked 'detergent' she had sitting on her machine. Should I come right out with it and say, 'For God's sake, I'm riding around America — I don't have time for this. Just a capful of detergent, I beg you, Mrs Wrass.'? What I said was 'What about I buy some of yours? Would that be possible?' 'I don't know, dear. My bottle's half-empty.' 'How about a capful for a dollar? Would you consider that?' 'Yes, a dollar then. I'd prefer it in quarters.' I'm not saying this lady was in any way unfriendly, just a fraction too profit-driven for my liking. So, Mrs Wrass, if you're reading my book and you realize these pages are all about you scamming me in Harpers Ferry laundrette, then let me tell you that next time you leave your basket alone while you get your load out of the dryer, check the level of your fabric softener first. Hah.

⚜

But before I ride out of Harpers Ferry, neatly pressed T-shirt on my back and sweet-smelling fabric-softened socks on my feet, let me recount the story of John Brown's bell. In one of those only-in-America ways, the towns of Harpers Ferry and Marlborough, Massachusetts, are not talking to other. Bell rage is going on. Here's the background.

In 1859, anti-slavery campaigner John Brown led a raid on the arsenal in Harpers Ferry, hoping to use any weapons he captured to incite a slave freedom uprising. Ironically for him, he struck a slave woman answering the door to the arsenal who wouldn't let him in. He fled next door to the firehouse. He was captured, most of his men killed in the fight, and John Brown was hung for treason. So it went badly for him overall. In the meantime, the soldiers who fought at the firehouse returned to their hometown of Marlborough, taking with them the bell from the firehouse. Since that day 150 years ago, it has hung firstly in Marlborough's firehouse and then in a specially-built bell tower in their town square. Several years ago, a delegation from Harpers Ferry drove up to Marlborough to ask for the bell back. Marlborough said 'Go to bell' and escorted them out to the city limits. The mayors exchanged emails, the local papers taunted each other, but the bell remained in Marlborough. Apparently Harpers Ferry are now despatching a Mrs Wrass up to Marlborough to negotiate the bell's return. Go, Marlborough!

⚜

I rode along Route 340 into Frederick and plugged northwards through Walkersville, Woodsboro and Taneytown. The Maryland countryside was bleached in bright sunshine under a perfectly deep blue sky. My MP3 player was co-operating with Roy Orbison, and all was well with the world. I started noticing huge white barns with grain silos and conical roofs. Fields of waving corn reappeared after several states' break from that ever-present crop. As I cantered over the state line into Pennsylvania, I thought about how Maryland was one of those states you'd heard about but could never quite place. I'm still not totally sure, and have to look at my atlas to see how it all fits together. But I'd have to say that my experience of Maryland was a bit dominated by detergent and bells. As I pulled over to take a photo of the *Leaving Maryland* sign near the village of Germany, I was reminded of my favourite bell pun. Evidence has been found that William Tell and his family were avid bowlers. However, all the Swiss League records were destroyed in a fire and we'll never know for whom the Tells bowled.

Chapter 22

Pennsylvania

Nickname: The Keystone State

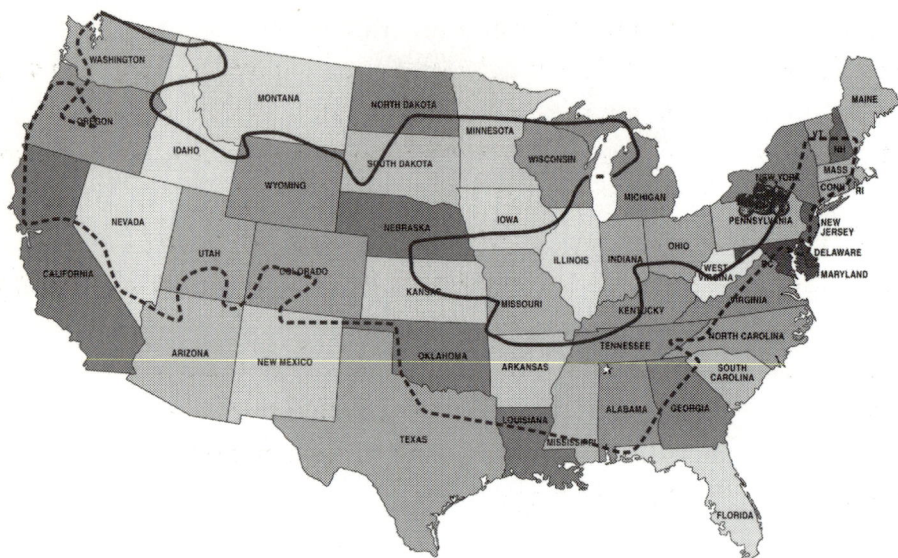

This state: 425 kilometres. Journey to date: 16,537 kilometres.

THE AMISH GUY looked at me and I looked at him. We were in Intercourse, Pennsylvania, at an Amerigreen gas station. I was fuelling up and he was buying some rope. The bike was parked right alongside his horse and buggy. I had my helmet on. He had a broad-brimmed straw hat on. He looked at the bike and I perused his horse. To understand our conversation it would help if you were fluent, like me, in Pennsylvania Dutch, the spoken word of the Amish community.

Amish guy:	Unsah tayklich broht gebb uns heit.
Translation:	*Afternoon, brother.*
Me:	Afternoon. Just admiring your horse.
Amish guy:	Un fagebb motocyclen unsah shulda.
Translation:	*And I admiring your bike was I.*

Me:	Yes, it's the DL1000, 04 v-twin 4 stroke—
Amish guy:	Dei nohma loss 160mm heilich fronten suspensisch stroken sei?
Translation:	*With the 160mm front suspension stroke, I take it?*
Me:	Of course. And your horse?
Amish guy:	Un di hallichkeitmare in Lancaster. Ayvichkeit baleisch 10 miles.
Translation:	*A '97 Saddleback mare from Lancaster. 15 hands and she'd do a good 10 miles to the bale.*
Me:	And is that a Surrey buggy with 40mm displacement on the rear spring?
Amish guy:	Un fiah uns buggers naett in di fasuchung.
Translation:	*You know your buggies, brother. Yes, it's a double-leafed Surrey all right.*
Me:	Chicks and ducks and geese better scurry—
Amish guy:	Ven I'm taken you out in mein Surrey—
Me:	When you take me out in your Surrey—
Both:	Mit the fringe on top!

I could have chatted all afternoon to the friendly farmer. His name was Amos Lapp. I asked him what he did for a living, and he said he made and sold root beer. He asked me where I came from. I said New Zealand. I asked him if he had been there. He said he had never been out of Lancaster county. But then if your transport is a '97 Saddleback doing 10 miles to the bale you wouldn't be roaming too far from home.

This was Amish country in rural Pennsylvania. It was exactly like the pictures you see. Horse-drawn buggies clip-clopped in mainstream traffic. Stern-faced men with beards and no moustaches whipped along their horses in a frenzy, while stern-faced women in black bonnets hung on for dear life. Generally, the Amish grit their teeth and put up with gaping tourists, but on the other hand I saw some signs of them trying to relieve visitors of their cash, so it wasn't all one-way. In the little town of Bird-In-Hand, I passed Abe's Buggy Rides (closed Sundays), the Plain 'n' Fancy Farm's authentic Amish Experience, and Abe's rival buggy-ride operator Aaron & Jessica's Buggy Rides. Not one of them had a fringe on top.

The Pennsylvania countryside was tranquil. Lush cornfields came right up to the roadside, and the whitewashed barns with those semi-circular roofs looked immaculate. By keeping to the meandering back roads I came across one or two covered bridges, which was like driving through someone's house but they're sitting over creeks.

I rode into Kleinfeltersville. It was either that or make a detour to Mooselookmeguntic when I got to Maine, but K-ville was easier. 'What th—?' you ask. Those two places are the longest single-word town names in America at 17 letters. I know what you're thinking: what about Lake Chargoggagoggmanchauggagoggchaubunagungamaugg? True, but that's a lake. Fine then, I'll go there, too, but you have to wait until Massachusetts.

In Pottsville, I caught sight of a small supermarket advertising all-you-can-eat lunch for $6.95. Within a minute I was sitting at the table, knife and fork at the ready, napkin tucked into my T-shirt. 'Please remove your helmet, sir,' called the serving lady. The system was you had to queue up at the checkout, behind a line of housewives with loaded shopping trundlers, and buy a ticket for the all-you-can-eat lunch. Standing there, unshaven, smelly, and clutching a $10 note with no shopping, I felt a little like a homeless man in a soup kitchen. Canned music played 'Girl from Ipanema'. I got my ticket and shuffled back to the counter.

After I handed over the ticket, I was handed a plastic plate and a plastic knife-and-fork set. Part of the deal was all-you-can-eat dessert, but it was unclear whether you had to go back to the counter to ask for a dessert plate. I piled my plate high with as much fresh stuff as I could find. Fresh french fries, fresh battered fish, fresh tartare sauce, fresh white bread . . . No wait, only joking. (I forgot: my wife, Sandy, might be reading this.) What I meant was fresh salads, pasta and something called hummus. Then as a treat I loaded up again from the roast section. My plate was awash with gravy. But then came the awful moment. How does the dessert thing work? The lady had vanished from behind the counter. I couldn't see any dessert bowls, so had no choice but to use my main plate. The ice-cream and lemon meringue pie was delicious. I think the beef gravy added that *je ne sais quoi*. The serving lady appeared with an armful of large sheets of white paper and crayons. She put one set down in front of me. A table sign said: *Kids All-You-Can-Eat 3.00 p.m. Tuesdays.* It was Tuesday and it was 2.50 p.m. Time to go.

Absolutely sated from the obscene gorging back in Pottsville, I rode sedately through rural Pennsylvania, heading for a campground my GPS insisted existed at New Tripoli. I found it after some trouble, but it was lovely, nestled in a forest with a small stream running through it.

There was a bike there already. A Triumph Tiger, 2005 unless I was mistaken. 'That's the 05 Tiger,' I called over to the owner pitching his tent. 'Nope. 07.' One–nil. I hoped he would guess what year my Suzuki was. Whatever his guess I'd add a year on and even the score. The games we play. Pete was a friendly guy. After our mutual camp set-up was done and the light was fading, we sat on our bikes, sipping from water bottles and chewing the fat.

Pete was a management consultant from Vermont. One day, about two months before, he was in a boardroom and just snapped. He packed up his briefcase, caught the bus home, wrote a letter of resignation to his boss, kissed his wife on the cheek and saddled up his 07 Tiger. He told her he'd be gone about six months and not to wait up. I took it there were marital issues in there somewhere, too. He decided to ride down to New Mexico, travelling about 140 kilometres a day. He had been at the campsite since 2.00 p.m., about the time I was tucking into my roast-beef-flavoured ice-cream. 'Why New Mexico?' I asked Pete. 'It's hot, my friend, f***'n' hot. Not like f***'n' Vermont.' I asked him why his pace was 140 kilometres a day. 'Got to push it through, my friend. I don't want to f*** around. But I want to be off the f***'n' road just after lunch. Early f***'n' starts and early finishes.' He asked me what pace I'd been riding. I said about 300 kilometres, omitting to add the words 'by morning tea'. 'That's a hot f***'n' pace, my friend. A bit too f***'n' rich for me.' The last I saw of Pete was when we both disappeared into our tents after dark. I left the campground at 8.00 a.m. His tent was still zipped up.

The next morning I continued my hot f***'n' pace, as I fancied a stretch of interstate riding for a change, especially the chance to do some legitimate risk-free overtaking. The I-22 took me up through Stroudsburg and spat me out onto Route 615, a deserted pretty-mainish highway through the Delaware Water Gap. A water gap is a geological thing where a river cuts through a mountain ridge, in this case the Delaware River traversing the Appalachians. It was lovely riding.

But the incredible thing was the spider webs in the trees. Overhanging the road were xxx trees. I call them 'xxx' because I have no idea what sort they were, so you can substitute any tree type you like. The point is that in their branches were massive cobwebs that looked like swathes of cotton wool. In one such spider's web, I saw what looked like the silhouette of a large bird. It was so striking that I did a U-turn and rode back for a closer look. Sure enough, trapped inside the web was a foot-high black xxx bird. Consider the questions just tumbling around in my head on this one. How big was the spider? Why did the bird just stay there perched on the branch while the spider spun its web around it? What were the spider's intentions anyway? To eat it? To set up house inside it? One thing was for certain: that'd be the last time I'd sleep with my tent zip open in Pennsylvania.

Chapter 23

New York

Nickname: The Empire State

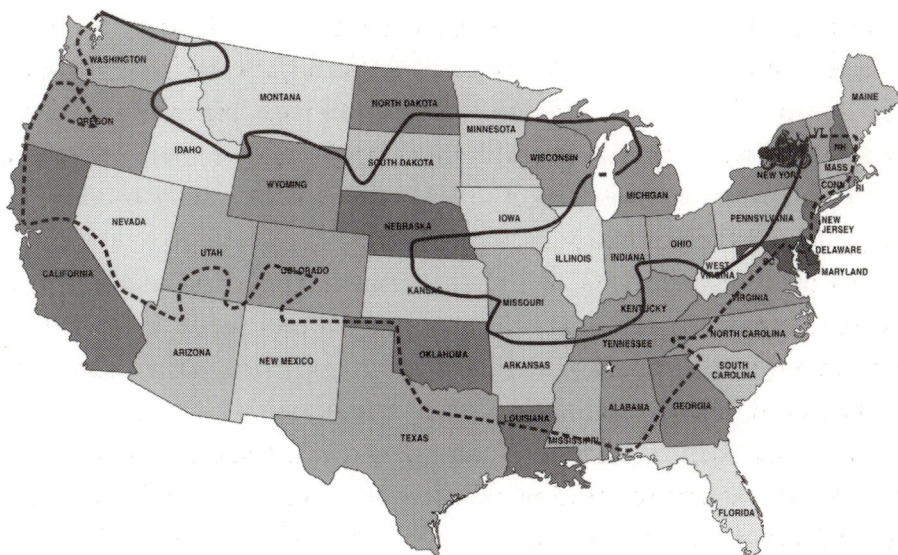

This state: 611 kilometres. Journey to date: 17,148 kilometres.

PEOPLE-WISE, NEW YORK IS America's third most populous state, and I was starting to bump into a lot of them. It wasn't as if I was negotiating the streets of its largest city, New York. It was just that the traffic was a lot more intense. It may have been the closeness to the Catskills, I'm not sure. New York state is pronounced 'Noo Yaw-uk'. If you come from New York City, then you're a Noo Yaw-ukker from Noo Yaw-uk Noo Yaw-uk. You had to read that last sentence twice? Try these pronunciations. Here are three towns in New York within 100 kilometres of where I was now: Poughkeepsie, Coxsackie, Schaghticoke. You have several more pages to guess how to pronounce them correctly. I will give you the answers right at the end of this chapter.

Meantime, I was riding through the small hamlet of Neversink on the edge of the Catskill Mountains. Neversink, pronounced 'Never-sink', is of course famous as the town that refused permission for the local cinema to screen *Titanic* as it would bring the town into disrepute. No wait, that's not it. It's actually the birthplace of fly-fishing in America. I'm more of your fish-fishing sort, but everyone to their own. But Neversink was the gateway to the Catskills, and for that reason I remember it.

The Catskills, being so close to New York City, are a recreational playground for city types. Dotted in this park are numerous 'sleepaway camps', for adults as well as children. To pronounce some of the camp names it would help if you were Julie Andrews. Camp La-gon-da, Camp A-na-wa-na, Camp Ma-Ho-Ge, Camp Ta-Go-La, a note to follow so, tea a drink with jam and— Well, the names were interesting anyway. I rode along a winding, narrow road where the fir trees came right up to the road. Every so often the woods would open out into golden meadows with pretty little lakes. The only thing missing was Bambi himself.

The road traversed up Slide Mountain and descended to the settlement of Big Indian. I fuelled up in Phoenicia, where the price per gallon clicked over the $4 mark. I wasn't to know it at the time, but it would keep climbing the further north I went. I was in the heart of the Catskills and loving it. This was solo riding at its very best — bike on song, dry and empty road, a warm bright sun behind me, Dire Straits in my helmet speakers, and no one else to worry about.

I reached the town of Palenville. Some of you literary types will be gasping 'Palenville, why that's the home of—', but most of you won't. That's because you don't recognize the name as the home of this fictional character. Seeing this New York chapter is turning into a pop quiz, here are the clues to this one: author, Washington Irving; character's dog called Wolf; character's son named Rip; character's wife named Dame Van Winkle; character slept for 20 years? Yes, it was Rumpelstiltsk— or something like that. But Palenville marked the departure gateway from the Catskills and I rejoined the very fast I-87 up into Albany.

That night I enjoyed the company and local swimming-pool membership of Latham residents and friends Steve and Kim Moon, and their son, Spencer. Again my boots were requested to remain outside, and I began to understand that this was just a cultural thing in America and nothing personal.

The next morning I entered the Adirondack State Park. You'll still be struggling with the pronunciation pop quiz earlier, so I won't burden you with trying to say 'Adirondack' correctly on first reading. I was there for the better part of a whole day and I still say 'Arindon . . ., Adinack . . ., Aridonda . . .'. The A-Dacks are a 6.1 million-acre state park taking up most of northern New York state. I entered the park at Lake George and rode a looping route that curved through what I picked to be the best bits, defined as passing a lot of lakes. The A-Dacks were starker than the Catskills, but had a wildernessy sort of beauty that I liked.

I rode along the upper reaches of the Hudson River to Indian Lake, then to Blue Mountain Lake then to Long Lake then to Tupper Lake then to Saranac Lake then to . . . Well, you get the picture. I reached Lake Placid and hunted high and low for a fridge magnet. Lake Placid was of course a two-time venue for the winter Olympics, but most of us know it as the lake where that 10-metre crocodile ate a cow, several hikers and a helicopter. As I mentioned in Chapter 1, most of my knowledge of America has come from the movies, and it was at times like this where it stood me in good stead.

In a small town called Keene I had pulled into a gas station to check my tyre pressures. The sign on the air pump said that air was free with fuel, but otherwise it cost 75 cents. On the other hand, fuel was $4.33 a gallon — the steepest yet. Should I risk leaving tanking up to Vermont where it may be cheaper out of the state park? But riding on a spongy rear tyre would chew up more fuel . . . The economics racked me for a few minutes, then I fuelled up and became a free-air customer. This involved the attendant switching on the air pump, and under an honesty system I would return inside after use and he would switch it off.

Just as I was finishing with my rear tyre, up roared a bright red sports bike, a Ducati I believe, with a black-suited rider. He flipped up his lid and greeted me with a classic New York hail: 'That's an ass-kickin' highway, man.' We shook hands and he introduced himself as Connie. I hoped it was an abbreviation for something like Conrad, rather than him having a girl's name. But here's the point: he *was* a girl. I'd made the stereotypical assumption that the rider would be male, but in my defence Connie was a little masculine-looking shall we say. Her handshake would have challenged even Sam Cooper, arm-wrestling champ, back in Indiana.

Connie was on her way from the Big Apple to Ottawa in Canada about 240 kilometres away. She had just crossed Lake Champlain on the car ferry, which is where I was headed. 'Look out for a lard-ass called Floyd working the deck. He's a real bike nut,' she told me. 'You want to get some air?' was all I could offer in return, as if we were standing in the ballroom at an embassy cocktail function. She topped up her tyres using my free-air allocation, which is where you get the expression 'hot air'. Connie said she was off to get a 'boyger', and if I saw Floyd on the ferry I was to say 'Connie says "F*** you, lard-ass" '. She gave me the impression that Floyd would then make sure my bike got off first. I spent the next half an hour tossing up whether to risk it.

✪

Lake Champlain is a massive freshwater lake that extends up into Québec, where it becomes Lac Champlain. I rode along a quaint country lane reaching the lakeside village of Essex on the New York side of Lake Champlain. I could easily make out Vermont over the other side. It was $6.15 to take a bike on the ferry, and my antenna was on full alert for a lard-ass who might or might not like motorcycles and who might or might not take the greeting of 'F*** off, lard-ass' in good spirit. In the end I didn't see anyone fitting Floyd's description, and there were only two ferry hands. Halfway across the lake we passed another ferry coming the other way. One of the hands on that ferry looked tubbyish, but I was secretly glad we didn't connect up. By the way, Champlain is pronounced 'Cham (not sham) Plane'. If I got you on that one, you probably got your own back with Puh-KIP-see, Cook-SACK-y and Scatter-coke.

Chapter 24

Vermont–New Hampshire

Nicknames: The Green Mountain State–The Granite State

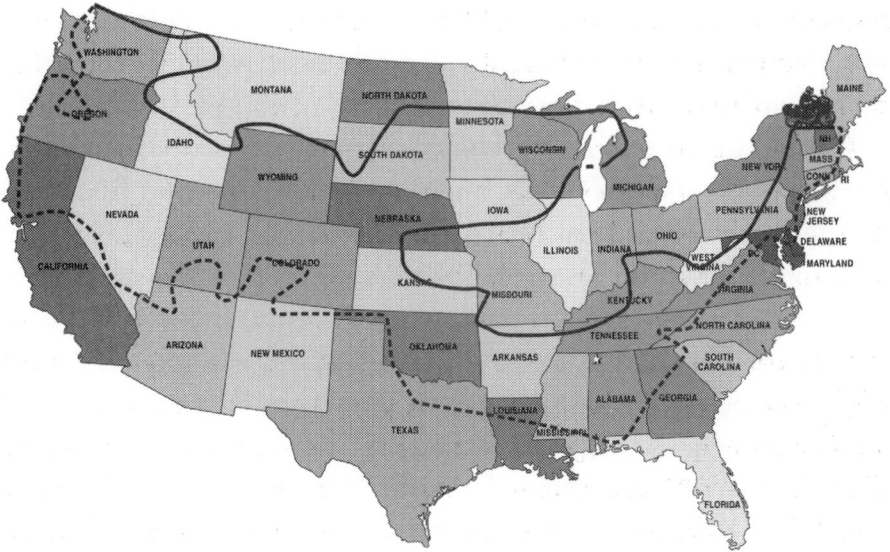

These states: 356 kilometres. Journey to date: 17,504 kilometres.

I WAS IN VERMONT for about three hours. That sounds like I just nicked the corner of it, but I didn't. My route through to New Hampshire saw me completely bisect Vermont. It's just that it's fairly small. In fact it is the fifth smallest state in area, and the second to smallest in population. Vermont's largest city is Burlington, and Burlington is America's smallest largest city if you understand. Vermont is known for its dairy products and is the US's leading producer of maple syrup. One of the state's national parks is called Camel's Hump. At the summit of the actual Camel's Hump peak is a plaque announcing that you've just climbed Camel's *Rump*. Somehow, and I don't mean to diss Vermont, that seemed to sum up the ride.

After riding off the Lake Champlain ferry, I pulled over to review where exactly I was going. I was heading vaguely in the direction of a well-known landmark, and I can't quite remember . . . it's on the tip of my tongue . . . That's right: the Atlantic Ocean. In the way were Vermont, New Hampshire and Maine. The following day I had big plans to conquer the Mt Washington Auto Road, a motorcycle mecca in New England, so I knew I had to find a campsite somewhere in the White Mountains in New Hampshire in order to get a good get-go in the morning. That meant not hanging about in Vermont.

I opened up the throttle and blasted down the interstate to Montpelier, state capital but only a village really. I branched off onto Route US2 through Danville towards the state line. Somewhere near Mollys Pond, in a curvy stretch through some woodland, I suffered an involuntary bowel movement. There is a more descriptive term in biker circles, but this is a family book. In a bout of non-existent concentration, I rode into a left-hand sweeping corner completely misjudging the line.

On a bike, you corner according to the Apex law. I'm sure the laws of motion, momentum and force play a part, but, simply put, you imagine a dotted line that starts out wide and curves through the corner as straight as possible. The point where you're closest to the bend is called the 'apex', or the 'side-swipe zone', as that's where you and an oncoming car joust for the centre line. The theory is that if you judge the apex correctly you will be able to maintain speed, stay in your half of the road, and stay as upright as possible. What you want to avoid is what's called an 'early apex'. A delayed one is OK, but an early one is bowel-moving stuff. If your imaginary dotted line hits the apex of the bend too soon, you'll not get around the corner without going wide. In other words, you know you've early-apexed when you note with interest that the centre line is actually on your right. The next — and probably last — thing you note is that milk-tanker.

In this left-hand corner, I early-apexed. My speed was ridiculously high, the bend just kept going, and I was drifting on to the other side of the road, being carried there by momentum. The rescue technique for riders whose name might include the word Rossi is to what's called 'roll on the throttle', drop your elbow and knee, look ahead to the point of safe exit of the curve, and let centrifugal forces get you out of the doo doos. However, I tend to be afflicted with a technique called 'reflex' that sees me hang on the rear brake and stand the bike up. This usually ends in tears for the rider. Luckily the other side of the road on this corner had a handy paved wide shoulder and a safety crash rail. My left-hand boot to this day has a mark where it rubbed along that rail. No other cars were coming and I made it out of the curve still upright, on the wrong side of the road and shaking like a leaf. It was my first close call in nearly 17,000 kilometres and there was no reason for it. I pulled over for a drink of water and to change two things. My cornering technique and my underwear.

I crossed the state line into New Hampshire as the I-93 crossed the Connecticut River. The light was fading rapidly and a campsite was top of my mind as I rode straight into the White Mountain National Forest, an area that covers a quarter of the whole of New Hampshire. I chose to head for Twin Mountain, as it seemed like a good springboard for the next day's assault on Mt Washington.

I passed by Cannon Mountain in Franconia Notch State Park. Had it been five years earlier, I would have been able to look up and see the Old Man of the Mountain. A series of granite ledges, when viewed from an angle, looked like the craggy face of an old man. It was 12 metres tall and had been there for centuries. Repeated ice and thaw cycles finally collapsed the outcrop at midnight in May 2003, and down came the Old Man. What you can now do is peer through some mounted binoculars in a viewing area which have an outline of the Old Man on their lenses so you can see what it looked like. Locals were distraught and laid flowers at the base of the cliff. Luckily it happened at midnight, though, as you wouldn't have wanted to be practising your abseiling on that cliff face and hear a cracking and splintering sound from above. The only casualty was Muffy, Old Lady Tyler's bichon frisé, who was reported missing the next morning and was known to like chasing rabbits at the foot of Cannon Mountain.

I pulled into the local campground at Twin Mountain in pitch-blackness. I was so tired after the day's exertions that I set up my tent by remote control and just lay on the ground inside in full riding gear. I was asleep within minutes.

At about 2,000 metres, Mt Washington is the highest peak in the northeastern US. Its claim to fame is that in 1934 it recorded the world's highest wind gust. There is a narrow road that winds to the top known as the Mt Washington Auto Road. Most of it is paved, but there is some gravel. Add to that no guardrails, lots of cars, and steep drop-offs, and it's the perfect motorcycling experience.

The first stop is at a toll kiosk at the bottom where they post a wind warning and relieve you of $12. That day it was gusting a zephyrish 48 km/h at the summit. The kiosk guy came out at the sound of a bike and handed me a sticker that said: *This Vehicle Climbed Mt Washington*, which I thought a bit premature. We looked up at the summit and watched dark grey clouds scudding across, almost obscuring it. 'You got half an hour,' he said with a touch of sombreness. 'Until what?' ''Fore the weather closes in. They're predictin' sevenny mebbe eighty mile an hour 'fore lunch.' He was talking to thin air: I'd ridden off.

This was not a road where you'd get your apexes wrong. In fact it was ridiculously easy. The views were stunning, it was lightly trafficked, and the surface was like your driveway at home. At the top there were the usual weather buildings, and the end of a cog railway that crawls up the mountain from the base station at Bretton Woods. We motorcycle riders scoff at this lazy tourist method of going up a mountain. Just sitting on a nice comfy seat and letting a mechanical device do all the work. Where's the fitness and personal challenge in that?

I was in scoff mode because I had met a gentleman at the summit who was red in the face, carrying a stout walking stick and had just hiked up Mt Washington on the Tuckerman Ravine trail. His name was Peasley and he didn't scoff at me. In fact he was an ultra-hiker, having covered most of the 3,500-kilometre Appalachian Trail from Georgia to Maine. We shook hands and I asked him how he'd got to the summit, dreading the answer. 'Walked it,' he said. And then the return thrust. 'And you?' 'Bike,' I said leaving the possibility open that it was a mountain bike not a motorcycle. He looked at me holding helmet, keys and padded jacket. I felt like an aged granny in comparison. Peasley would have been at least 10 years older than me, and I was breathing hard just having clambered up the steps to the café. I hoped to hear the cog train arrive so we could direct our scoffing at other tourist enemies.

I use the word 'enemies' because hikers and cog-railway passengers — being at the opposite ends of the fitness spectrum — have fallen out lately. There is a local tradition called 'mooning the cog', a sort of protest against the smoke-belching train from the hiking purists. Some passengers thought it cheeky. Others were bummed and complained to the railway. Undercover park rangers posing as trees jumped out and ticketed the mooners for public nudity, but the tradition continues.

The information board in the café talked about that fateful day in 1934 when the weather guy stationed on top of Mt Washington went out to the weather vane and noted with interest that it was spinning a bit more quickly than usual. That's because he was in the middle of the world's strongest wind gust at 372 km/h. They found him in Vermont minutes later.

I trundled back to the bike, making sure that Peasley was inside the café on his first cup of tea, and rode back down. There were a lot of bikes on the way up. We all got our apexes right and passed with cheery waves. None of us had time to look at the view. There's too much else to do. It's not easy riding up or down a narrow mountain road, apexing, waving *and* mooning hikers.

Chapter 25

Maine–Massachusetts–
Rhode Island

Nicknames: The Pine Tree State–The Bay State–The Ocean State

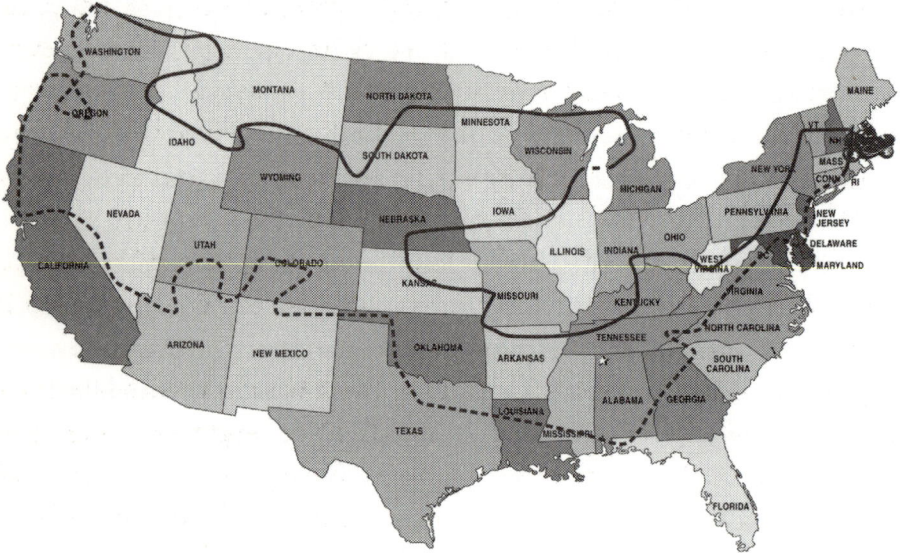

These states: 502 kilometres. Journey to date: 18,006 kilometres.

CALL ME ANAL if you like, but I can't stop homing in on trivia and oddities. I just think it's a lot more interesting than important facts. I suspect you like reading about these sorts of things, too, otherwise you'd have given up this book long before Chapter 25. That's why Maine represented a state I'd looked forward to since crossing the Mississippi. It's got some great claims to fame, and I don't mean anything remotely significant.

Maine is the only US state of one syllable. All other 49 state names are two syllables or more. That's quite incredible, and was the first thing that occurred to me as I rode past the state welcome sign just after Conway Town leaving New Hampshire. Needless to say, I mumbled my way through all 50 states just to check how many syllables they had. Secondly, Maine is the number-one exporter of wild blueberries and, until a few years ago, toothpicks.

✪

Let's dwell on the toothpick scenario for a minute. In the town of Strong, in central Maine, the largest toothpick-manufacturing company in the country produced 20 million toothpicks a day until the factory shut down. That was 7 billion toothpicks each year. The population of the US is 300 million. That means that, in its heyday, every 15 days every US citizen — man, woman and child — used a toothpick from this one company in Strong, Maine. I racked my brains as to whether there was even a grain of usefulness in calculating this statistic, and frankly there wasn't. It was a completely useless piece of information. Love it. And as I trundled along a rural road towards Sebago enjoying the plainness of the Maine countryside, there was nothing much else to do but dwell on it. That's the toothpick, not the countryside.

Consider the size of a toothpick. It's made of wood and there's nothing else to it. As a manufactured product it couldn't be simpler — a single part made from a single material and used for a single purpose. Therefore, all you need is a log of wood and some sort of massive shredding machine. One log in, 20 million toothpicks out. And, if Maine isn't called The Pine Tree State for nothing, you'd assume raw material supply wasn't a problem. Back in the old days, it was fashionable to pick your teeth after a meal with a toothpick and keep it sticking out of your mouth for the rest of the evening. And your female partner would probably be standing around chewing on hers, too. Nowadays, if you reach for a toothpick and lever that trapped sliver of meat or corn out of your teeth, your female partner is likely to ring for a taxi home. Today, the dental fashion is brushing and flossing, rather than picking, and the toothpick industry is accordingly dead in the water. Strong became a ghost town overnight. America now exports logs to China to make toothpicks which America then imports.

✪

I snapped out of the toothpick analysis as road signs started naming Portland 40 kilometres ahead. I could hardly believe that the Atlantic Ocean was an hour away. Somehow reaching the sea on each coast has a major significance for me. I remember the same feeling in Australia each time I reached the road end at the shore on the four different seas — the Tasman, the Coral, the Timor and the Indian.

I rode into Gorham and looked for a petrol station. Assuming the process here was no different to the rest of America, I left the bike by the pump and went in to prepay. 'No need for that, honey, we trust ya.' I must have stood there marginally agape as the kindly lady behind the counter emphasized 'Go on, just fill 'er up.' And thus I rode out of Gorham in as good a mood as I'd been in for days, all because they trusted me not to drive off without paying after refuelling. For the next half-hour, while the euphoria lasted, I waved to young children, fast-forwarded to Cliff Richard's 'Congratulations' on the MP3 player, and sang along heartily. Yes, I had some Cliff Richard on my MP3 — now you know and I don't care.

I searched on my GPS for the keyword 'lighthouse'. It found Portland Head Light and I approved the choice by asking for a route straight there. The GPS took me through a maze of freeways, skirting Portland's industrial area. I passed a sign to Cape Elizabeth and in a small park saw as many seagulls as ducks being thrown bread by two young girls. Signs that the Atlantic was all but a cod's breath away. Rounding a corner, I saw it: the dull, grey ocean under a grey, brooding sky. Behind some trees was the white lighthouse. I rode into Fort William Park and turned into the Portland Head car park. The bike's front wheel nosed up against a fence. A metre the other side of the fence was a cliff, at the foot of which waves crashed onto the rocks. I dismounted and just stared out to the Atlantic, wrestling with an overwhelming urge to throw something over the edge to mark the moment. I was desperate to share the milestone with someone who would understand the significance of reaching the Atlantic coast. I'd parked the bike under a *No Parking* sign and received some disapproving glances from three old ladies walking three old dogs. I fretted. They wouldn't have looked at me like that if I'd been riding a Harley.

I wandered into the lighthouse gift shop and bought a fridge magnet. There was an elderly man sitting just outside the shop at a camp table with a sign saying *Book Signing Today*. He was the author of a book about the Portland Head Light, and no one was paying the slightest bit of attention to him. He had a pile of books on the table and a pen at the ready. The trick was to not look him in the eye as you walked past. I looked him in the eye. 'Morning.' 'Morning.' The trick was to avoid acknowledging his book. 'What's your book about?' I wasn't functioning well that morning. The cover of the book had a picture of an olden-days Portland Head lighthouse on it. The book was titled *History of the Portland Head Light*. His table was 2 metres away from the actual lighthouse and I was standing there holding a lighthouse fridge magnet. 'The lighthouse,' he replied. 'Have you seen inside it yet?' That was my escape clause. 'No, I haven't. Will you be still be here in an hour?' falsely insinuating I'd be back to buy a book when I planned to be well inside Connecticut instead. 'Sure. See you when you come out.'

As I got back to my bike, going the long way around the lighthouse so that it appeared I was going inside, a miniature dog was cocking its leg against my wheel. I kicked the gravel on the path and it sprayed the dog, which ran off leaving a wet stain on my front tyre. I was so incensed I'd have hurled the dog over the cliff into the Atlantic if it had stayed around. Here I was enjoying a mental ticker-tape parade for riding across America coast-to-coast and my bike gets peed on. Maine was bringing out some competing emotions that morning.

I soon forgot about the canine urine as I rode down the on-ramp to the I-95. This was a thrilling moment as I carved over through light midday traffic to the centre lane and sat on 120 km/h, pointing due south. Interstate 95 is the main highway down the east coast of America from Maine to Florida, surging 3,000 kilometres through the major cities on the eastern seaboard, like Boston, Philadelphia, New York, Baltimore, Washington and Miami. It is the longest north–south interstate and passes through 15 states, more than any other highway in the country. But — and if you're an interstate nut, this is a big but — there is the famous I-95 gap in New Jersey. For 16 kilometres there is no I-95, and you have to connect the two hanging threads by travelling on the New Jersey Turnpike. The gap was created back in the '80s when environmental concerns prevented this stretch being built. All of which wasn't going to worry me: I had other plans for New Jersey.

Mile after mile rolled past and I lapsed into a rhythm, counting down the exits as I pounded towards the state line with New Hampshire at Kittery. As the interstate surged over the Piscataua River I entered, for the second time that day, New Hampshire. Twenty minutes later I exited New Hampshire. Immediately the traffic started to build up as the I-95 closed in on Boston. At Amesbury, I exited right onto the I-495 that carved inland to the east of Boston. Welcome to Massachusetts.

Sitting on the interstate gave me a lot of space to think. It was low-maintenance riding. By that I don't mean that the antenna was any less tuned to what was going on around me, specifically in lanes 1–5. It was just the road itself. With some exceptions, there is nothing to look at from interstates. When an interstate bends it does so in the space of a kilometre, which means you're not actually rounding a corner. On a bike you merely hint at a lean and stay in sixth gear. It's an efficient way to traverse the countryside fast, but offers no real challenge to driving skills compared to, say, the Rockies. Therefore I had a lot of head-space in which to rack my brains about what I knew about Massachusetts apart from the Bee Gees. I'm sorry to tell you that I've nothing meaningful to write about this state other than it's the third most population-dense in America.

I closed in on my day's highlight destination located in Sterling, exiting the I-495 and dropping onto Route 2 followed by the I-90. Within 10 minutes I coasted to a stop by a small park in the small town of Sterling. This was the town common, and there was a reason I'd gone out of the way to get there. I was parked in none other than the birthplace of Mary Had a Little Lamb. Mary Sawyer, whose pet lamb inspired the poem, was born in Sterling in 1809. But it's not as easy as that. Remember when I was in Louisville, Kentucky, paying homage to the declared birthplace of the cheeseburger at Kaelin's Restaurant? And how several other towns claimed that they were the true birthplace, not Louisville? The same thing has happened with Mary and her little lamb. This is incredibly interesting, so here goes.

In 1815 young Mary Sawyer, of Sterling, was followed to her schoolhouse by her pet lamb. Her classmate John wrote the poem when he saw the lamb turn up in class. Meantime rival town Newport in rival state New Hampshire claims that their hometown poetess, Sarah Hale, penned the poem, not some limerick-scrawling urchin from Massachusetts. And, furthermore, she invented the lamb thing. To help Newport's cause is the fact that it was Hale who first published 'Mary Had a Little Lamb' in 1830. Sterling said, 'Yeah, but you stole it off us', and both towns rushed to erect monuments. Newport had a simple plaque, but Sterling outdid them with a 1-metre bronze statue of a lamb. And it was this lamb I was leaning against in the town common. Interestingly, many years later a Mary Tyler, née Sawyer, came out in public and declared she was *the* Mary and had a pair of socks from the lamb's fleece. As that was inconclusive, she produced a bottle of mint sauce and the rest was left to everyone's imagination.

Sorry, but I love stories like these. And I'll ride tens of kilometres out of my way to visit these shrines of Americana. I'm not bothered about visiting the birthplace of George Washington, John Kennedy or even Ronald McDonald, but Mary Had a Little Lamb? I know you're with me on this.

And while I was in the area it would have been criminal not to visit Webster. By now my fuel light was blinking, so I chugged into the Texaco in Webster to glug unleaded relief into the empty tank. And there it was, just over the road from the petrol station. That awesome road sign I'd ridden to photograph: the longest placename in America — Lake Chargoggagoggmanchauggagoggchaubunagungamaugg.

Lake Chargogg, as the locals abbreviate it, is Nipmuck Indian for 'fishing place near the boundary'. It is the sixth-longest placename in the world. It has more letter A's in it than any other word, and its 15 G's are the most instances of any letter in a word, if you count placenames as words. And I was parked underneath the sign. This truly was a monumental day.

It wasn't over yet: I had one more heritage-based visitation to make in this part of the world, and I was running out of time. It was 4.30 p.m. and I had to ride 60 kilometres through rush-hour traffic to Providence, Rhode Island. The quickest route seemed to be cross-country, so I set off through the Massachusetts countryside, passing Bad Luck Pond, Riddle Brook and Hundred Acre Lot, as if I was in a Famous Five tale. I was in an endless line of traffic moving at a slow pace, and there was no point in overtaking. Eventually the pace quickened as I flowed onto Route 146, crossing the state line into Rhode Island, the smallest state in the US, near Woonsocket. Briefly before downtown Providence, my old friend the I-95 emerged and cocooned me all the way to my next destination. You're wondering what could possible usurp Mary Had a Little Lamb or the longest placename in America. How much more adrenaline could one person inject into a day already laden with cultural enlightenment? Clearly, you haven't heard of the tree root that ate a dead body.

Roger Williams was a staunchly religious forefather of Providence. When he died in 1683 he was buried in a family plot, and that was that until 1860 when the city fathers wanted to make a memorial to honour founder Williams. When they dug down into his grave, expecting to exhume a skeleton, what they found in the empty coffin was a root of a nearby apple tree in the macabre shape of a human body. Seemingly, apple trees seek out carbon and this tree root had entered the coffin at the skull end and followed the path of his decomposing bones, forming a long spine, a crook at the hips and a bend at the knees, and continued down to the ankles and two feet splayed outwards. The Williams root was taken in by the Rhode Island Historical Society, who didn't know what to do with it. It ended up at John Brown House near downtown Providence, where they put it in the basement. The curators of John Brown House wanted visitors to focus on John Brown and not a corpse-eating root. But due to public demand, they mounted the apple-tree root in a coffin-shaped display case and bolted it to the wall of the small museum there. The place is a favourite with school groups, and frequently young children burst into tears when they see the ghoulish sight. Personally, I can't wait to have grandchildren, as after this American trip I've a wealth of macabre stories to send them off to sleep with.

And it was outside the locked gates of this museum that I stood craning my head through the bars to see the root. The place had closed an hour earlier. I'd ridden all this way and was too late to see the tree root that had consumed a dead body. It's hard to describe the crushing disappointment of being so close yet so far. Why'd I spent so much time at the lamb statue in Sterling? I thought about scaling the gate, but it was almost dark and I wanted to get to a campsite.

I rejoined the I-95 and knuckled down for the final hour on the interstate, in the dark and heading for the Connecticut state line. I was aiming for a campground at North Stonington, just over the state line, which had the added advantage of being close to McDonald's.

There was no one in the camp office when I pulled in, and this place had barrier arms blocking the road in and out. When you pay your camping fee, you get a swipe card which lets you in and out. Therefore I had a problem . . . or would have if I'd been driving an RV. On a bike you need only a 2-foot gap between the end of the barrier arms and the wall. Thus I entered, with only a slight scrape of the panniers, the North Stonington campground. Typically, the campsite is rigged up for RVs. If you have a small tent and have no need for water or power, you are referred to as a 'primitive camper' and get shoved out the back in trees with no light. I found my way to the primitive camping area and noted I was the only PC so had a choice of trees. I pitched the tent in the dark and parked the bike on bare ground on its side stand, not upright on the centre stand. Why this lapse in normal routine is important will emerge in the next chapter.

This was one of those nights where it was so pitch-black I just left all the gear on the bike and simply lay down on my camp stretcher in full riding gear. I left my helmet on. You never know if that tree next to the tent was an apple tree.

Chapter 26

Connecticut–New Jersey

Nicknames: The Nutmeg State–The Garden State

These states: 523 kilometres. Journey to date: 18,529 kilometres.

I'M NOT GIVEN to impulsive, short descriptive words when under stress, but poking my head out of my waterlogged tent at 6.00 a.m. and seeing the bike lying on its side like a beached whale forced out some phraseology that made young children nearby run for their mothers. During the night it had rained. Not only had it rained, it had rained very, very hard. The top three inches of the ground had become mud. My side stand had sunk, and sometime during the night over she went. I was lucky I hadn't parked it right by the tent.

It was still drizzling as I stumbled around, packing up soaking gear. The advantage of camping under trees is that you get some protection from the full fury of a downpour. The disadvantage is that, after it formally stops raining, the trees continue to dump drips on you for an hour afterwards. Overall, you'd be drier camped out in the open.

I bent down to haul up the 300-kg fully-fuelled bike and felt two things go snap. Twigs under my feet, and vertebrae in my back. Then I had the issue of how to keep the bike up. I couldn't use the side stand in the mud, and I couldn't get traction to push it. The only way was to ride it out onto solid ground. But the keys were in the tent. I had a spare pair of keys hidden under the seat, but you needed the main keys to unlock the seat. Assuming you only needed the spares when you lost the main set . . . Hmm, I might need to speak with my planning people. With my outstretched leg I managed to lever over a nearby fallen branch and tentatively rested the side stand on it, expecting the bike to roll off and crash into the mud again. But it stayed up. I found the keys and wheel-spun the bike out of the bog back onto safe ground. By 8.00 a.m. I had packed up and was ready to leave this campsite from Hell.

The unique feature of the day's ride was that I would not leave the interstate. My goal was to rard like the devil to New York, take the photo, rard like the devil out the other side, and see how far I could get before the devil could rard no mower. In other words, I wouldn't be using gears two to five much, and it would be what is referred to in the Twisting Throttle handbook as a 'grunt day'.

The I-95 interstate tracked along the Connecticut coast with periodic views out to Long Island Sound. There were several gridlocks as traffic piled up before large places such as New London, West Haven, Bridgeport and Stamford. Speaking of New London, the one fact I know about this city is its links to Nathan Hale, none other than Connecticut's state hero. Hale was hanged by the British who captured him as part of the Battle of Long Island in 1776. He was in the Rangers, the unit trying to defend New York City. His main claim to fame was his famous last words before the noose tightened: 'I only regret that I have but one life to give my country.' Myself, I would have fallen back on an impulsive, short descriptive word or two.

The I-95 careened towards New York. The interstate is also known as the Governor John Davis Lodge Turnpike. And now is a good time to complain about turnpikes. A turnpike is a toll road named after the olden days where you paid your toll and a man raised a stick, or pike, to let you and your cart of hay through. There are two ways of fleecing road users in America. One is the toll plaza. If it's too late to swerve off at an exit to go around it, you'll be approaching that plaza with a lump in your throat and sweaty palms. This is because there are several possible ways the toll plaza will make your life a misery and turn you into a criminal.

First, most locals have an E-ZPass transponder in their car. When they swoosh through a toll plaza an amount is deducted from a prepaid account, like using a cellphone and then topping up the credit balance. Most lanes at toll plazas are reserved for the bulk of cars using E-ZPass. In fact at many plazas they don't even have to slow down. Peasants using cash are usually restricted to one lane. There may or may not be an actual person in the toll booth. If there is, you pull up and hand over your money. The attendant can give you change and off you go. If there is no attendant, your troubles magnify unless you have the exact coins for the toll. There is a big bin like a washing basket into which you toss the toll, a green light glows and you accelerate away. If you have only notes, then you are in big schtuck. The washing basket won't recognize notes, and there's no human there to help.

Enter the second stressful dynamic of the cash lane at a toll plaza: lined up behind you are the toll pros. These are the turnpike users who have all the right coins in their ashtray, wind down their window and heave the exact change into the basket without even changing down gear. If a toll pro comes up behind a stationary toll rookie blethering around in their purse looking for the money, then horns start honking. The toll rookie panics under pressure, drops his money and ends up throwing all his coins into the basket just to see that green light glow and get going. He has probably paid $8 to drive on a $1.50 toll road. I've never worked out how you'd get caught if you just threw a washer or a button in and just motored off, as there's no one there to press a button or call out the FBI.

I mentioned there were two sorts of toll methods. The second is where you enter a stretch of toll road, get handed — by a human or a machine — a ticket which establishes your entry point. You then drive until you want to leave the toll road at an off-ramp. There, you'll pull up at a tollbooth. The kindly lady takes your ticket, her computer works out how far you've travelled, and you cough up accordingly. This system is called an entry/exit toll. The key point for anybody like me who's contemplating nipping through the entry plaza without getting a ticket is that, once through, you're trapped inside the toll corridor. All off-ramps have exit plazas, and all exit plazas have stern, forbidding mamas who are just waiting to liven up their boring job by clobbering toll criminals. If that sounds a touch harsh, it's because I was, at this time, being dressed down by a toll-plaza mama. Here's what happened.

As I was charging along the I-95, I arrived at an unmanned toll plaza. I pulled up at the cash-lane booth where the sign said: *Press Button Take Ticket.* But I swear to you there was no button. I could see where the ticket came out, but where was the button? All over the side of the booth were things that *looked* like buttons, and as the first toll-pro honking commenced behind me, I started pressing bolt heads, rivets and even what I think in hindsight may have been the fire alarm, I don't know. Surely it wouldn't have been too much trouble to (a) place the button at elbow height and (b) have a sign over it with an arrow saying: *This Is The Button You Press For Your Ticket, You Moron.* Under pressure I just rode away, not wanting demotion from toll rookie to toll imbecile. I knew I was inside the toll corridor on the turnpike ticket-less, but with so many interchanges and exits looming ahead how difficult could it be not to escape the turnpike?

Shortly the GPS advised me to exit the turnpike onto the Cross Westchester Expressway. A toll plaza blocked the way on the exit ramp. I pulled up at the booth. It was womanned by a toll mama.

Toll mama: Tek.
Translation from toll to English: *Ticket.*
Toll criminal: Sorry, I don't have a ticket. I was at the plaz—
Toll mama: Garner tek? Yo GARNER TEK?
Translation from toll to English: *What? Got no ticket? You GOT NO TICKET?*
                     (Hint of satisfaction creeping into tone)
Toll criminal: There wasn't a button. I couldn't see a button back at the plaz—

Toll mama:	Far darl.

Translation from toll to English: *Five dollars.*

Toll criminal:	Five dollars? For 10 miles?
Toll mama:	Garner tek. Far darl maxim.

Translation from toll to English: *Got no ticket. Five dollars maximum.*

If you enter the zone without a ticket, you pay the maximum toll as if you had travelled its length and not just the two exits like I had. It wouldn't be the last time I had issues with toll plazas and lack of teks.

I was now on the Hutchinson River Parkway that turned into the Cross County Parkway East that turned into the Bronx River Parkway South that turned into the Major Deegan Expressway, heading for downtown Manhattan. The skyscrapers were looming fast, and the traffic was just plain fast. My eyes were constantly flicking down to the scrolling map on my GPS, as not only were the off-ramps emerging thick and fast, but I needed to watch my lane positioning to be ready for them. With two or three exits literally on top of each other, I had a nano-second to decide which of the three was mine. The GPS map was a jumble of arrows and intersections.

So it wasn't my fault that I ended up in the Bronx. I was too many lanes over to get onto the George Washington Bridge across the Hudson River. Instead, I had to carry on and execute a loop back to the bridge via the Bruckner Expressway onto the Sheridan Expressway onto the Cross Bronx Expressway. I ignored the GPS, which was re-calculating the fastest route back on track and entreating me to ride through the side streets of New York's poorer inner-city suburbs to get there. I was going well, but fatally missed the Sheridan exit, plunging deeper into the area known as South Bronx. Every minute, there was a low-flying aircraft on landing approach to nearby La Guardia just over the East River.

I knew I was riding in completely the wrong direction; namely, east. I had to stop, re-program the GPS, and take stock. I exited the Expressway at Bruckner Boulevard. It was a high-rise development area, and I picked out a Shell gas station just down the road. As I pulled in to the gas station, I saw a lot of — how shall I put this — stereotypical Bronx citizenry milling around and sitting about in cars, several of which were blasting out music and it wasn't Olivia Newton-John's. The loaded bike drew some stares. I kept my helmet on as I fuelled up with one hand and punched the GPS buttons with the other. I went inside to pay. When I came out, two black guys were loitering by my bike. One had a baseball cap on backwards. I knew instinctively how to deal with the threatening situation, and that was to communicate with them in jive, pretending I was a local. One of them.

Me: Hey, blood, wass happenin'? How's it hangin'?
Them: Just looking at your bike here. You come far?
Me: What you gassin', brother? Ah'm no zipperhead. Yo dudes harshin' ma yellow.
Them: Take it easy. We're just wondering if you want directions back onto the Expressway.
Me: Callin' me cheese weasel, homey? Keepin' it real, man, keepin' it, real. Solid!
Them: Look, we've got to go. If you carry on past White Plains Road, take the entrance to the 278. If you see Pugsley Avenue, you've gone too far. Safe riding, friend.
Me: Ah dig it, man. Gotta skitty an' pop me wheelie. Slap me some skin, brothers. This cat's gonna blow this joint.
Them: OK. Bye now. Just try not to talk to too many people if you stop again round here.

Having successfully defused the simmering racial tension at the gas station, I rode away feeling that I'd got to know the real New York. I had no more navigation problems and finally got to Liberty State Park over the river from Manhattan.

As I leaned against the fence overlooking the downtown skyline and the Statue of Liberty, I tried to work out where the Twin Towers would have been and what it would have been like watching events unfold on September 11. Inside the ferry terminal building were displays in glass cases featuring letters written by children to their fathers — some office workers and some fire fighters — who didn't come home from work that day. Sobering would understate the mood in which I kicked the bike into gear and rode away from Liberty Park.

Back on the New Jersey Turnpike, I saw another toll plaza up ahead. This time I was handed an entry ticket by a toll mama and my relief was overwhelming. To finally be a legal user of a toll road was wonderful. A mile later, I had to pay 85 cents for the use of that stretch. I wondered why they bothered. As I was speeding down the eight-lane-wide turnpike, I turned my head a fraction and noticed, with interest, that I was 500 metres away from the undercarriage of a jumbo jet landing at Newark. The turnpike opened out to 12 lanes, and there were no trucks as this stretch was designated cars-only. I have no idea of the legal speed limit, but simply to keep up with the general flow of bumper-to-bumper traffic I was riding at 125 km/h.

I considered the enjoyment factor of riding in this tsunami of vehicles all the way south on the New Jersey Turnpike, with Trenton, Philadelphia, Wilmington and Baltimore adding more traffic to the maelstrom of cars in what is known as the Northeast Corridor. In a rash, but I felt calculated, decision I left the turnpike surging southwards inland towards Washington, and took the exit to the Garden State Parkway. The Parkway tracked the coast down through New Jersey towards Cape May where there was a ferry across Delaware Bay to Lewes and into Delaware. I'd not bargained on Hanna.

Hanna was the name attached to a hurricane. The hurricane was attaching itself to the eastern seaboard of the US, and, having already ripped through Florida, was swirling up the east coast leaving a trail of wrecked homes, flooded towns and general hurricane misery.

My first inkling of trouble was riding into a curtain of torrential rain near Toms River, still plummeting down the Garden State Parkway south. I'm no stranger to riding in the wet, but the odd thing was the horizontal force of the rain. Minutes later, as the Parkway got closer to the coastline at Barnegat Bay, I felt the wind strengthen and wondered if I might have been better jousting with cars back on the turnpike further inland. And then it all simply got stronger. A lot stronger. The rain heavier and — my real nemesis — the wind gustier.

Rounding a curve on the Parkway, I saw a whole lot of cars pulled over and a small crowd at the tree line. A pick-up had been blown off the road and was crashed up against a tree. People were tugging at the driver's door. The Parkway was two lanes wide and I needed both lanes. The gusts of wind slammed into the bike, and before my brain could connect with the need to counter-steer I was blown into the adjacent lane. I tucked in behind a car towing a small caravan. The caravan's wheels frequently left the road surface. My visibility was minimal through a rain-spattered visor, and the spray thrown up by aquaplaning cars ahead was drenching. I didn't know at the time, but do now, that I was entering the eye-wall of Hanna, being the circle of strong thunderstorms that surrounds the calm eye of the storm. Here precipitation is heaviest and winds strongest. You reckon?

I saw exit signs to Atlantic City. My choice was to battle this meteorological insanity down to Cape May or just turn off and call it a day. I thought about the ferry and the storm. As the conditions were worsening by the minute, chances were that the ferry was currently wedged in a tree. I took the exit. Out of the gloom emerged that beacon of universal hope: a motel sign. $49 lighter and 10 minutes later, I was standing under a hot shower, slightly shaken by the turn of events but determined to improve my intel for future weather-planning.

A tropical storm becomes a hurricane when the winds exceed 100 km/h, a mere puff. Then there are five categories of hurricane strength as the wind-speed increases, with Cat 5 being winds over 220 km/h. On the eastern coast, where I was sheltering in my motel, the hurricane season goes from June to November, and I found out later that this season was the second most destructive on record, with 16 nasty storms of which eight were hurricanes and five of those were Cat 3 or above, meaning winds over 160 km/h. The one I was riding out, Hanna, was to be the deadliest with 537 deaths, mostly in Haiti. The strongest and most destructive would be Ike. Ike and I were to meet later.

Lying on the bed, flicking through the cable channels and watching sombre weather presenters telling people like me to stay off the roads, I mulled over the whole hurricane thing; particularly, how they get their names. Listen to these. These are the names of the 16 tropical storms or hurricanes in this hurricane season: Arthur, Bertha, Cristobal, Dolly, Edouard, Fay, Gustav, Hanna, Ike, Josephine, Kyle, Laura, Marco, Nana, Omar, Paloma. There's an organization called the National Hurricane Centre that is responsible for naming storms. It all started in 1953 when storms were given female names. But then the men's rights movement insisted on male names being linked to death and destruction, too, so in 1979 it became a pan-gender naming system.

But here's the interesting thing. Storm names are decided on years in advance. There are 21 storm names prepared five years out, one for each letter of the alphabet except Q, U, X, Y and Z, presumably because you can only have so many Hurricane Quentins, Xaviers and Zenas. In four years' time, if it's a bad season like this one and the number of storms gets into double figures, I can tell you that if you're living on an island in the Bahamas then chances are your house will be destroyed by a wind called Kevin. It's not right. So in this hurricane season, five names didn't get their time in the sun. Those obsolete five were Rene, Sally, Teddy, Vicky and Wilfred. I don't envy the naming guy's job, but you'd think he could come up with meaner names that sort of fit a hurricane. This year's lot sound like a roll call at a rest home: Arthur, Bertha, Dolly, Josephine, Nana. To call a ferocious and destructive force of Nature 'Nana' seems to undermine its very danger, or is that just me? What about Hercules, Zeus (whoops, sorry: can't use Z), Caesar, Hera, Poseidon, Triton or — my personal wind favourite — Mariah?

The next morning dawned as beautiful a day as you'd ever see on the Atlantic seaboard. I turned on the weather channel to see where Hanna had moved off to. It had slammed into Philadelphia and then spun off at 90 degrees out into the Atlantic never to be seen again. But all eyes were on the next in the hurricane queue, Ike, which was making a mess of Cuba. I felt sorry for Cuba, but had more pressing, perhaps a fraction selfish, things to worry about — should I have the Lumberjack Slam or the Heartland Scramble?

I was the only customer in Denny's on the road into Atlantic City. As Atlantic City had been the official eye of the hurricane the night before, understandably there weren't too many tourists mooching about. Under pressure from the waitress heading towards me with pad and pencil in hand, I went for the Scramble as the Slam had grits with it, and I was saving that delicacy experiment for the southern states where my goal was to hear 'Yo wan' grets, bore?'

I had been eating too much highway junk food lately — ever since Canada, to be frank — so I needed to introduce some fresh food into my diet, and the time was now. 'Is the Heartland Scramble a fresh-food dish?' I asked. 'Why, yes,' the waitress replied. 'You get a freshly picked sprig of green parsley and some natural buttermilk.' 'Great. Is there anything else?' 'Yes, we garnish the dish with fried potatoes, bacon, ham, sausage, two eggs, grilled peppers and onions, and top it with cheddar cheese.' 'I'll take it. So long as the parsley is fresh. Where's the buttermilk?' 'It's in the two pancakes with maple syrup.' I've never eaten so healthily. After wiping the plate clean with the sourdough toast, the only thing left uneaten was the parsley. It was the best $7.95 I've spent.

Tanks and bellies full, the team headed out back onto the Garden State Parkway for the hour's canter down to the end of the peninsula, and New Jersey, at Cape May. The freeway was littered with leaves and debris from the hurricane passing through, but was strangely empty of traffic. The Cape May ferry cost $27 for a bike and another $4.95 for the fridge magnet, and took 1.5 hours to cross Delaware Bay to Lewes.

Halfway across, we entered Delaware. Delaware Bay is the second busiest waterway in the US, after the Mississippi River. All I saw in the grey, choppy waters of the Bay were a few dolphins and a massive floating pile of what looked like seaweed heading out into the Atlantic. On the other hand, Philadelphia, which has a large number of Denny's, is up-river from the head of the Bay. Perhaps it was parsley.

Chapter 27

Delaware–Maryland–DC

Nicknames: The Blue Hen State–The Old Line State

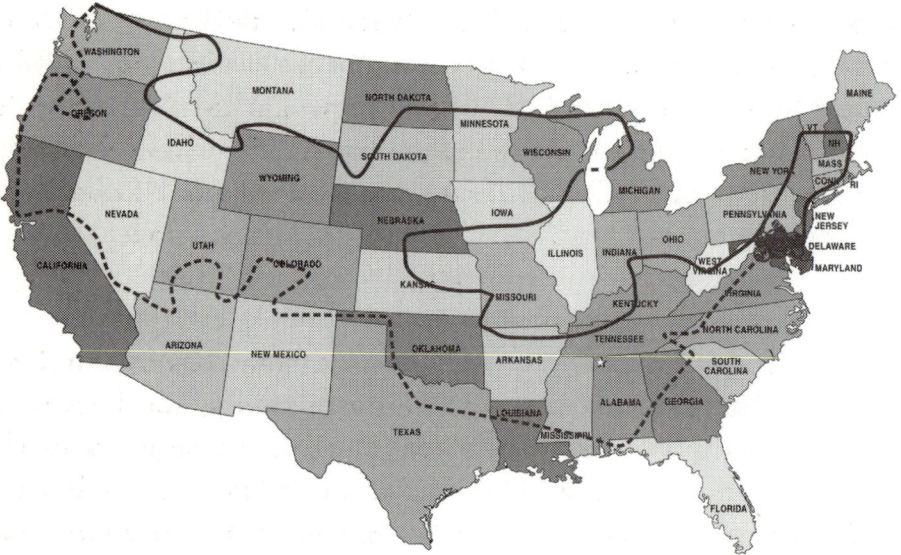

These states: 228 kilometres. Journey to date: 18,757 kilometres.

ELAWARE IS THE US's second smallest state, area-wise, at 50 kilometres wide and 150 kilometres long. Therefore, as I was bisecting it heading west to Washington DC, I knew I wouldn't be in Delaware for long. But that didn't matter, because it was quality over quantity, and riding through Sussex County towards the Maryland state line I enjoyed the roadside pumpkin stalls.

Normally I'd avoid writing about pumpkins in my book, as there's only so much excitement a reader can have. But Sussex County, Delaware, is special in the pumpkin world. Or should I say in the punkin chunkin world. The rules of punkin chunkin are not complicated. You have to hurl, or chuck, a pumpkin, by mechanical means, as high and as far as possible without it exploding. Pumpkin chucking, or punkin chunkin, is an annual frenzy where engineers team up with farmers to effect the ultimate pumpkin trebuchet. The world champs are held in Sussex County, home of punkin chunkin. Apparently, because the distances keep getting bigger, they have to move the chunkin range each year. It started in Old Ma Webley's back garden in Milsboro, but soon outgrew it. Then the local park in Georgetown became too small as neighbours complained of thuds on their roofs. Then the chunkin moved to firing across, and often into, a lake. The only recorded fatality in the history of the event is a duck, and you can work out the facts for yourself. With typical American economic efficiency, the punkin chunkin is held the weekend after Halloween when supply is buoyant. Then the weekend after the Punkin Chunkin World Champs, the local restaurant's soup of the day until Christmas is . . . Well, I guess it's not French onion.

Just outside the small town of Greenwood I slowed down for a sharp right-hand corner. Immediately the most tantalizing smell assaulted my nostrils — and I'm talking barbecue chicken. In a large tent on the roadside were row upon row of barbecues, all grilling chicken. It was a fund-raising venture by the local Kiwanis club for the Greenwood girl scouts. The barbecue smoke coming out of the tent wafted across the road, and every open-windowed car did a U-turn and pulled in at the stall. It was impossible to ignore. I parked the bike and went in. The girl scouts were dishing out half-chickens, blackened and glistening with barbecue juice, on plates with pickles, coleslaw, a few potato chips and a can of coke. I paid my $5 and ate like a pig, sitting at a long trestle table in the tent with other slavering travellers. The chicken was to die for.

And dying was what I'd be risking if I carried on to Washington. According to Ralph. Ralph was my neighbour seated at the trestle table, and strangely wore a badge that said *Introducing Ralph*. I don't think he was one of the organizers, so the need to wear the badge was a mystery. Ralph had a major problem with Washington DC, his nation's capital and my destination after my chicken lunch. 'Howdy, friend. Look likes you're a long way from home. Where're y'all headed?' 'Come from New Jersey this morning on the ferry, and aiming to get into Washington to see the sights.' 'Nothing to see in DC, friend. You want to give it a miss. You're on a motorsiccle? Big danger in DC. Gangs of youths throwin' concrete off overhead bridges. Keep off the Beltway. Teenagers joy-ridin', throwin' cans an' tailgatin'. Lots of pot holes in DC. Everyone in a hurry. Pass the mustard, will ya?' 'Here you go. So you're saying . . .' 'I'm sayin' keep clear of DC. It's a big, big place. Lots of crime. All them homeless blacks and Hispanics. Traffic gridlocked. You want to go to Wilmington instead, friend. You gonna eat that pickle?'

★★★

With Ralph's advice ringing in my ears I rode away from the Kiwanis tent, the girl scouts $5 richer, and my belly as full as it had been for days. I couldn't wait to get to Washington, ride the Beltway, littered with lumps of concrete, and meet some homeless Hispanics. Just after Adamsville I crossed into Maryland for the second time. The Shore Highway took me across the Choptank River, Tuckahoe Creek, and I sat in fast traffic on an arrow-straight road heading directly for Adrenaline City.

What I actually mean is Bay City, but even the mention of that name starts the adrenaline flowing. Why? If I said the words 'Chesapeake', 'Bay' and 'Bridge', do you feel any juices stirring? If not, then you're not eligible to join the Twisting Throttle Big Bridge Appreciation Society. The Bay Bridge is 7 kilometres long, and when it was built in 1952 it was the world's longest continuous over-water steel structure. It's now the 50th longest in the world. I'd have a lot of riding to do to cross the others, including the Lake Pontchartrain Causeway Bridge down in New Orleans. (At 38 kilometres long, the longest bridge over water in the world, I wasn't sure how I'd be able to cope with the testosterone, let alone adrenaline.) As I rode across the Bay Bridge in the outside slow lane to savour the moment, looking down over the railings into Chesapeake Bay, I saw gridlocked traffic in the opposite lanes. Apparently the bridge is prone to gridlock, especially in commuter peaks. Maybe Ralph knew what he was talking about.

Coming off the Bay Bridge, the traffic coming the other way was still at a standstill. There was a fairly sharp curve towards the approaches to the bridge, and as I rode smugly towards Washington with three empty lanes at my disposal I saw cars come out of the curve that, seeing the gridlock up ahead of them represented by the brake lights of a wall of stationary traffic, unbelievably tried to careen off at the last exit before the bridge. This entailed crossing two lanes of similarly-careening cars in a rapidly-diminishing space of about 200 metres. It was pandemonium. I fleetingly wondered if I should be flashing my lights at the oncoming traffic to warn of the chaos ahead, but the traffic backup was outpacing me as I rode. There were so many vehicles heading for the bridge that the back of the traffic jam was building up before my eyes, and I was riding at close to 120 km/h. And it was a Sunday.

I was suddenly in Washington DC. It was a crazy entrance. On Route 50 and riding through the sort of industrial zone build-up you get on the outer edge of cities, I was thinking about pulling over to set my GPS for some inner-city landmark, such as the Capitol. But I thought I'd get closer to downtown first. The road became New York Avenue, did a brief dog-leg around Vernon Square, and in under a minute I was facing the White House. I sat on the bike at the corner of Pennsylvania Avenue and 15th, stunned at how I'd ended up in the belly of Washington so easily. The light was red, I got a non-malicious honk and turned into 15th Street by the Department of Treasury. I cruised down 15th, trying to take in where I was. Looming large at the end of the street was the towering obelisk of the Washington Monument. I looked left down Pennsylvania, straight down to the seat of Congress, the US Capitol, shining white and looking very stately.

My mission was to find a park, and I considered the odds of finding a legal parking place on the street this close to the seat of government. Plagued by the memory of the $40 parking ticket in Fairbanks, Alaska, I tootled around the side streets looking for the merest hint of a gap for a bike. I finally saw a wedge at the end of a row of official-looking cars outside the Department of Commerce building on the corner of Constitution and 15th, right over the road from The Ellipse that backs on to the White House. I cable-locked my jacket to the bike's handlebars, stowed the gloves, and with camera in hand strode off towards the Washington Monument, West Potomac Park, the Lincoln Memorial and back to the White House.

'Afternoon. I'd like to see the President, please.' The young marine with the buzz-cut stationed at the south entrance gate-house looked up from his clipboard. 'Sorry, sir, this entrance is reserved for visiting ambassadors and VIPs.' 'I'm here representing all the motorcyclists of, or currently in, America.' 'Your name, sir?' 'Ambassador T. Throttle from Down Under.' 'Sorry, sir, you're not on my list. And the President is very busy right now.'

At that moment a heavily-armoured bright green Kawasaki Ninja ZX-6R idled down the driveway towards the White House's southern gate. Its rider wore a stars-and-stripes helmet, the bike had *Motorcycle One* emblazoned on its tank, and several guys in suits with earpieces jogged beside it. Reaching the gate-house, the rider raised his visor and killed the engine. 'Twisting Throttle? Sorry for the wait. You ready to ride?' 'Too right, Mr President. Just a quick lap of the Potomac, eh? I've got some miles to do before nightfall.' 'No worries. Hold on a sec. Sergeant, radio the Secretary of State up at the house. Tell her to keep the Russian guy talking. I got something better to do.' 'Lead the way, Mr President. I'll ride sweep.'

I followed *Motorcycle One* out onto Constitution Avenue, his bike's speakers blaring out Springsteen's 'Born in the USA', which I thought a tad over-the-top. We rode down Independence Avenue, weaving through slow-moving traffic, across the Potomac, circumnavigated Arlington Cemetery, blasted by the Pentagon, and pulled up in a shower of gravel at the Jefferson Memorial in East Potomac Park. I treated the President to a kebab and coke from the Turkish food stall in the car park, and we sat on our bikes slugging them back.

'I heard you were a classic bike collector, Mr President.' 'Yep, that's right. Nortons and Indians, mostly.' 'I suppose that's why they call you the Commando 'n' Chief.' His coke sprayed out all over the Turkish food-stall owner as he convulsed with laughter. 'That's a good one. So you want to swap bikes for the run back?' 'Nah, I'll stay on the—' 'That wasn't a question, my friend.' 'Love to, Mr President. You come out on the Ninja often?' 'Not as much as I'd like to. But my finger's always twitching on the button.' I blinked at him. 'Sorry, I meant the electric start button.' 'You've a wonderful riding country, Mr President. I've had an outstanding trip so far. It's been a dream ride. I—' 'I, too, have a dream, Throttle. I have a dream that one day on the red hills of Georgia the sons of former slaves and the sons of former slave-owners will sit down at the table of brotherhood. I have a dream of justice, of truth, of freedom, of all creeds and races living in harmony. But my biggest dream is that I'll be able to afford the Ducati 1198 with the highest torque-to-weight ratio of any super-bike ever made.' 'You will, Mr President. Torque is cheap.' He went into spasms of laughter again, slapped me on the back and we mounted up.

The last I saw of the President of the United States on *Motorcycle One* was as he did a wheelie across the White House lawn before disappearing in a gaggle of suited Secret Service agents keen to get the Ninja back for debriefing and an oil change. I liked the guy a lot, but to be honest his cornering was crap.

I had dallied around Washington for long enough. It was time to ride out into Virginia towards the Blue Ridge Mountains, Shenandoah River. Life is old there, older than the trees, younger than the moun— And it was country roads I was looking forward to again after so long on the interstates. I'd forgotten what oncoming traffic was like except on the other side of a median barrier. The I-66 swept me out of DC into the Virginian countryside. The sun had disappeared below distant hills, leaving a hazy dusk and wisps of wisp shrouding the tops. I had no idea where I'd be able to camp, and rode until something presented itself. Near Strasburg the I-66 collided with the I-81, and was only 7 kilometres away from my route north of a few weeks before.

At Edinburg I saw a sign to a campground and found a narrow, curving one-lane road winding its way by a creek into woodland. I couldn't see an actual campground, but the area looked safe enough, so I pitched my tent on the bank in semi-darkness. As I lay on my stretcher listening to the sounds of the night, all I could think of was whether the President of the United States would like to trade places just for a day. That night I had a dream . . .

Chapter 28

Virginia

Nickname: The Old Dominion State

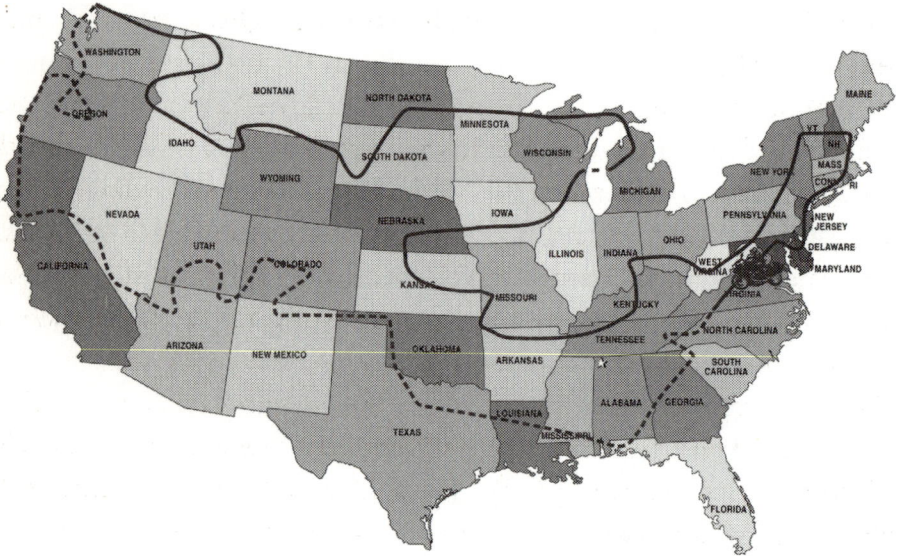

This state: 696 kilometres. Journey to date: 19,453 kilometres.

I MIGHT HAVE MENTIONED BEFORE a growing obsession with official state symbols and how Americans seem preoccupied with having a representative thing for almost everything. There are the obvious official state things, like state flag, capital, motto, governor, language and website. But the best official things are the under-layer, if you dig deep enough to discover what they are. I'm referring to official state fish, dance, fossil, flower, insect, tartan, shell, slogan, bird, and — my personal favourite — state bat.

Virginia is no exception to having lots of state things. The official Virginia state beverage is milk, dance is the Virginia Reel, fossil is naturally the *Chesapecten jeffersonius*, dog is the American foxhound, fish is the brook trout, and their official bat is the Virginia big-eared bat. But their state motto is a beauty. The motto is not to be confused with the state slogan: 'Virginia is for Lovers' — a slogan I'd have thought more appropriate for, say, Hawaii or California. No, the state motto of Virginia is: 'Sic Semper Tyrannis'. This comes from the words 'Sic' (Latin for motor-sic-cle), 'Semper' (Latin for always), and 'Tyrannis' (Latin for turning corners). And that's what was happening as I started out from Edinburg on a cold, misty morning. Riding my sic along a deserted twisting mountain road, leaning left, leaning right, semper tyrannis, semper third gear.

Highway 675 over Powell Mountain crossed the North Fork and then the South Fork of the Shenandoah River. The valleys of both forks were shrouded in an eerie fog that all but obscured the road ahead. The woodland was deathly silent, and the road surface littered with wet leaves. Fantastic. The contrast to riding the interstates of the past few days was total. I could almost hear the tyres croon with ecstasy as the outsides at last had work to do.

I was heading for Thornton Gap in the Shenandoah National Park. The Gap is one of the few entry points onto Skyline Drive, the 170-kilometre roller-coaster scenic byway that runs along the ridge line of the Blue Ridge Mountains, the entire length of the Park. It's the warm-up for the famous Blue Ridge Parkway, a continuation of Skyline Drive. The maximum speed limit on the Drive is 60 km/h, because the road is strewn with hazards, from deer to walkers on the Appalachian Trail to tourists at the wheels of campervans to one of the densest black bear populations in the US. It passed through an overgrown road tunnel chiselled out of the wooded mountainside, and for the next three hours I simply held on as the bike weaved around the bends and sweeping curves of the mountain-top road.

The Blue Ridge Mountaintops of the Appalachian chain stretch from Georgia to Pennsylvania. The 'blue' in Blue Ridge comes from the bluey haze that shrouds the hills when viewed from a distance. Something about trees and hydrocarbons. It also comes from the colour of motorcyclists' language when they look down at their fuel gauge and note how the needle is hovering on the little 'E'. There are no towns on Skyline Drive, and my GPS advised me, somewhat coldly I thought, that the next fuel was in Waynesboro at the finish of the Drive. I knew with mounting resignation that I would flame out long before Waynesboro; the good news was that it was all downhill.

Then, without warning, a gap in the trees opened with a sign to a visitor centre and shop at Big Meadows. It was fridge-magnet time, so I pulled in only to see that Virgin Mary of motorcyclists riding on their reserve tank: an unleaded pump. There was a small hut beside the pump no bigger than your wardrobe at home. In the hut sat a lady, virtually motionless. I fuelled up the bike and wandered over, poking my head into the door of the hut. 'Morning.' 'Howdy,' she replied. 'Pump 1 fuel.' I looked back at the lone pump and wondered why I'd said that. 'Y'all walkin' Applayshin Trel?' I looked down at the helmet I was carrying and wondered why she'd said that. But it was a good point, as the famous Trail, or AT as it's known, passed right through the Big Meadows area.

The Appalachian Trail is not your average day-hike or an even moderately-challenging walk through the hills. This 3,500-kilometre-long trek through 14 states has a cult following, being hikers who attempt to do the whole length of it in one go. These nutters — sorry: very fit individuals — are known in trail lore as 'thru-hikers'. The completion rate is about 15%. Many hikers have support teams who drive as close to the trail as they can, such as the Skyline Drive, so the hikers don't have to lug backpacks with enough gear to last the five to seven months it takes to do it. Perhaps the pump lady thought I was a support vehicle. The unofficial speed record for the AT was set in 2005 by Andrew Thompson who ran the Trail in 47 days. That's an average 75 kilometres per day every day for 1.5 months solid, uphill and down, through woodland, bogs and valleys. When he arrived in Maine on Day 47, looking sweaty and ashen, he asked for three things. A drink of water, a bus ticket back to Georgia, and the address of the helpful man in the park back home who'd pointed down a path and said, 'Go down there, young man, it's a shortcut to the mall.'

I rode out onto Skyline Drive, keeping an eye out for signs that might indicate the AT was crossing the road, but saw none. I always suffer a brief bout of inferiority complex when rubbing shoulders with travellers who are closer to the pain barrier than I am on a motorbike. Whenever I overtake long-distance cyclists, I toot; not so much as a friendly gesture, but more in acknowledgement of their much superior effort. It makes me feel sedentary sitting on a 100-horsepower 1000cc engine, whereas all they have in their power chain are two spindly yet muscled legs. It's the same with long-distance hikers. The thought of walking hundreds of kilometres with a backpack, knobbly knees and a stout stick makes me shiver. It's not that I'm not a fit pers— All right, I'm not a fit person. But the incredibly slow pace of progress would drive me to drink — an energy drink, naturally — and I simply don't have that sort of slow-moving metabolism. On the other hand, those brief bouts of respect and feelings of inferiority soon give way to smugness when I surge past cyclists and walkers at the foot of a long, steep and winding ascent. And, as I always say, I'll swap my motorbike for pedal-power the moment I see a long-distance cyclist actually smiling.

The Skyline Drive ended at Rockfish Gap, just after crossing the I-64 at Swannanoa. The road carried on along the same ridge-top route, but rebranded as the Blue Ridge Parkway, commonly known as America's Favourite Drive. The Parkway runs for 755 kilometres through the Blue Ridge Mountains. It's the longest, narrowest national park in the world, and the most visited one in the US. It starts where I was now and finishes at Oconaluftee in the Great Smoky Mountains. The route is closed to commercial vehicles, often closed to everything due to ice and snow in winter, and the speed limit is a maximum 70 km/h.

One of the reasons for the slow speed is that on the Parkway there's a good chance you'll end up playing chicken with anything but a chicken. White-tailed deer abound, and it was three of them that I was bearing down on near an open area of meadows near Johnson's Farm. In the middle of the road were three young bucks, or possibly does, I'm not sure. Most lay-people don't know enough about deer to remember which is male and which is female. When you're a learned naturalist like me, there are techniques to tell which is which and I employed one now: 'Doe a deer, a female deer, ray a drop of—' Yes, they were female deer all right, and as I wheeled out of the curve their heads perked up and it became a face-off. The deer simply stayed put and I braked hard, coming to a halt only 5 metres away from them. Slowly the deer meandered off to the side of the road and started nibbling the grassy verge.

There are rules about what to do if you hit a deer and it's you looking down at the twitching deer lying on the road, not the other way around. First, you make sure it's beyond the point of rehabilitation. That means that if the deer is getting up shaking its head, you reverse over it. No wait, only joking there. You in fact have to call the wildlife service or police to come and attend to the deer if you believe it's not going to die. They may make the call to euthanize it, in which case the police cruiser will then reverse over it. Then the real trauma starts: who's going to get the meat? It's quite legal to throw the dead deer's body in the boot of your car and take it home. But the question is: does the average member of the public know how to skin and fillet a whole deer? Is the wife really going to thank you when she sees what you're dragging through the front door? It's not like bringing a trout home. Some states have laws against scooping up road kill and taking it home to eat, but somehow a freshly run-over deer is — and I've been trying to work this one in all page — fair game.

Riding away from the trio of carefree deer now strolling across the meadow towards the woods, I thought about grilled venison on a barbecue and how I was well overdue for something to eat. There are no settlements on the Blue Ridge Parkway, let alone a Denny's, and you have to make a conscious effort to turn off down side roads that wind their way down through the wooded hills to the towns lying in the valleys either side of the mountain chain. I say 'effort' because riding along the Parkway was lulling. The road undulated and twisted its tortuous way along the spine of the Blue Ridge, and I simply leaned left, leaned right, and kept a constant speed. The GPS had no navigational responsibilities, so kept itself occupied by pumping music into my helmet speakers. It wasn't a Meat Loaf sort of ride, this one. Up on the Blue Ridge it was a Neil Diamond meets Paul Simon meets Phil Collins sort of sing-along attempt, where you know half the words and fill in the rest with a croon. And all this at the top of your voice. Strangely, I saw no more deer for the rest of the day.

Waitress:	Thait ther paykan parze on spayshle.
Translation to English:	*That there pecan pie is on special.*
Me:	Mmm, I've got to get me some of that then.
Translation to American:	*Mmm, golter gitme some there.*
Waitress:	Yawlbe wahn cramer arse cramer they?
Translation to English:	*Would you be wanting cream or ice-cream with that?*
Me:	Better make that cream, ma'am. And what about some of that delicious coffee, too?
Translation to American:	*Bear make crame, mam. An walbow serma they lersher carfatu.*
Waitress:	Yugar, herner. Be rarber.
Translation to English:	*You got it, honey. Be right back.*

The diner pro was in action again, this time in Denny's Roanoke. Venison wasn't on the menu, so I had the next best thing in the pretend game of 'you kill it, we grill it' with animals I came across on the road. With saliva glands in overdrive, I ordered the mouth-watering Western Burger, with its tangy steak sauce drizzled over thin, crispy onion rings and melted Swiss cheese, accompanied by: lettuce, to satisfy the need for token freshness; tomato, to satisfy the healthy-options-in-fast-food-restaurants lobby; and fries, to satisfy my actual hunger. Add to that smorgasbord of gastronomic nirvana a pecan pie special with double cream, a coke and two coffees, and Twisting Throttle was sated. I fuelled up the bike, checked tyre pressures for 75 cents in the not-so-free air machine, and rode out of Roanoke as contented as I'd been for days. Roanoke's name before 1880 was Big Lick. I'm assuming the settlers ate at Denny's, had moustaches like me, and had the Western Burger with extra steak sauce.

Chapter 29

North Carolina

Nickname: The Tar Heel State

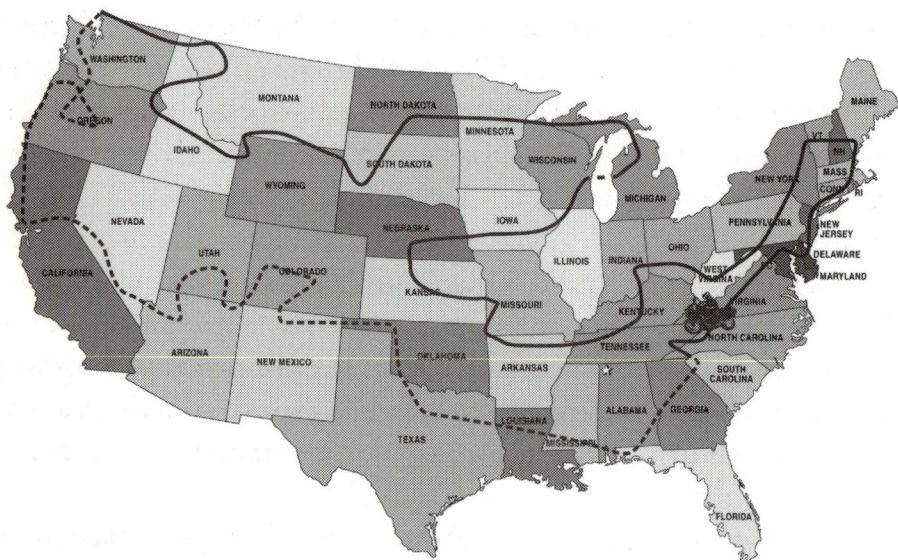

This state: 701 kilometres. Journey to date: 20,154 kilometres.

Toast. Bottom. Cycle. What do those three words have in common? I'll tell you shortly. I crossed into North Carolina on the I-77 South. The state line was near Fancy Gap, which is where the interstate plunges 1,500 feet over 6 miles, but with a gradient that never exceeds 4.5%. This is a recipe for a long drag downhill on a two-lane freeway — and it was fantastic. The descent starts at the top of the Blue Ridge Mountains and ends in the lowlands of North Carolina. Apparently this stretch of interstate through Fancy Gap was one of the largest excavations in US interstate-building history. I love this sort of road-engineering fact, whether it be bridges, viaducts, gorges, tunnels, flyovers or gaps of fancy.

What I'll remember most is the duel between two rigs right in front of me. Traffic on the interstate — given that it was a gradual downhill, dry, and out in the country — was clipping along very fast. The official limit in North Carolina is 110 km/h and we were all sitting at 125–130 km/h, including our heavy, articulated friends the 18-wheelers. I've often been tucked in behind one of these rigs and watched as it gradually overhauls another 18-wheeler. Inevitably, the fractionally faster truck pulls out to overtake the fractionally slower one, and effectively blocks the road as the two rigs duel for supremacy side-by-side. By and by, the faster truck creeps ahead and eventually pulls back in front, freeing up the fast lane again for us minnows to spurt past. These duels can last for up to 10 kilometres, especially if the slow truck decides to floor it. This is what I saw happening on the Fancy Gap downhill. A large refrigerated rig pulled out to pass a container truck and it was all on. Neither driver was giving an inch, and they rocketed along at a steadily increasing speed approaching 140 km/h. Had I been standing on top of one the trailers, I could have stepped over the gap onto the other — they were that close. I'd no idea these things could move along so quickly. Add to that driver boredom, male egos and a CB radio so they could trade insults, and you got a mighty convoy truckin' through the night.

The trucks were ignoring any traffic in their slipstreams; then again, the rest of us were struggling to keep up. As the interstate flattened out, the slow-lane truck actually won the race and pulled gradually ahead, forcing the overtaker to bleed off speed and pull in behind. It was a fascinating duel, and I would have liked to stay in my rearguard position to see what'd happen next. Within the space of 30 kilometres, I saw signs to towns called Toast, Bottom and Cycle. I lost sight of the trucks as I exited the I-77 onto the westbound I-40 at Statesville.

I was enjoying my break from the endless curves of the Blue Ridge Parkway. The bike was humming along the interstate, and I didn't have much to do other than lock my wrist on the throttle in a sort of frozen cruise control and hang on. This was one of the rare times I was enjoying doing fast miles at the expense of seeing anything half-interesting. I had in mind to get as far as a place called Swannanoa near Black Mountain and Asheville, where I knew there was a kool Kampgrounds of America kampground. It was time to find a wireless internet signal and do some website uploading.

Speaking of signals, remember back in Chapter 3 where I described the handy little orange device mounted on my handlebars named SPOT? That's a Satellite Personal Tracker, about the size of a cellphone, which every 10 minutes takes a fix from a satellite and transmits to another satellite, which places a little red dot on a Google map on my website so Mum and Aunty Flo can see where I am. I know that SPOT is beaming up its signal properly by two small flashing green LCDs. Those LCDs became like a comfort blanket after a while: so long as they were flashing every 30 seconds or so, I knew that somewhere in space a satellite was taking notice of my trip. I also knew that one day the green lights would turn red and the batteries would need replacing. The green lights had been flashing for over a month without a break. How long could two AA batteries last? Surely they'd be almost dead? For the past few days I'd entered a period of slight paranoia about the SPOT batteries. When I was working on riding — such as on a twisting road entailing some small ounce of riding skill — my mind went off it. But here on the interstate with not a lot to occupy me, the battery obsession returned and I couldn't take my eyes off the lights. It's like trying to tell yourself not to look down when you're standing on a cliff or a bridge. A quick glance down to SPOT and there they were; the twin green lights flashing. Green was good, green was 'all's well', green was nice.

At Hickory, the lights turned red. At first I couldn't believe it. It was like losing two faithful friends. Something died that day. Sure, the two little AA batteries had died, but I mean something else on a more emotional plane. I was almost two-thirds of the way around America and one, sorry two, of the support crew, albeit minor members, had snuffed it. They had given their all for the team and just couldn't contribute any more. They were spent. The rest of the guys would be devastated, but I didn't want to announce the bad news until Swannanoa, as they still had a 100-kilometre job to do.

That night at the pretty lakeside campsite, with a full moon overhead, the mood was sombre. I parked the bike by the tent, and addressed the assembled staff. 'Quiet, everyone. We're here to pay respects to A and A.

Those little batteries are — were — more than just 1.5-volt compressed manganese dioxide cells. They were pals. Like all of you, A and A played their part in the Twisting Throttle team. But they knew what the risks were when they—' 'You should have brought rechargeables,' a small voice piped up from somewhere under the windscreen. 'Who said that?' 'It was the nimhs,' reported the digital-camera battery-charger. I looked down at the four 2500mAh 1.2v Ni-MH AA batteries nestled in the charger. 'SPOT doesn't take rechargeables, guys. A and A knew they'd be a one-charge wonder, but 20,000 kilometres was a wonderful effort.'

I held their little dead battery corpses in my gloved hand, thinking about throwing them into the middle of the lake. 'Sir, that's not a good idea,' whispered Tank. 'Corrosion, leaching, fish poisoning, environment . . .' 'Good point, Tank. Any thoughts?' 'Bring the boys home, sir. None of us wants to stay over here when our time comes.' And so with the wise words of my ever-faithful fuel tank, I wrapped the little batteries in some duct tape and wedged them under the seat so they'd complete the journey in spirit if not in SPOT. I dismissed the staff and we spent the rest of the night in reflective silence. The replacement batteries in SPOT, Ever and Ready, knew to keep a low profile until the grieving process had run its course. But mine was already over. As soon as I saw those flashing green LCDs again, I'd moved on.

The next morning I climbed back up to the Blue Ridge Parkway for a final stretch to link up with the Great Smoky Mountains. This section of the Parkway meandered through the Pisgah Forest into Transylvania County. The low cloud and misty rain added to the draculian ambience of these hills. I had the road to myself. After Looking Glass Rock, the Parkway started to descend to Cherokee and then suddenly converted into Route 441, which bisects the Great Smoky Mountains National Park. From nowhere the traffic trebled, and for the next three hours my average speed was 60 km/h winding up and around the densely wooded hills and valleys of the Smokies. This is one of the most visited national parks in the US, and not just because Dollywood is just up the road.

I turned left before Gatlinburg and pulled into a gas station in

Townsend. I was several states behind in my fridge-magnet collection and this place had magnets for Africa, although all I wanted was North Carolina. The kindly lady took it on herself to fish through the box, looking for the states I was short of. She was definitely a native of the Smokies as I couldn't understand a word she was saying. See if you can. Here are the names of the states she pulled out magnets for: Jolge. Sour-care-larn. Ver-jenny. Mare-lair. Nol-care-larn. Ten-sair. El-bam. I'm not going to give you the answers. You just have to keep saying them over. If you never get them, well you now know how I felt. I just took her offerings and paid up, thanking her profusely or should I say thang ho po-fuse-lair.

I rode up Foothills Parkway as a shortcut west towards Chilhowee Lake and Route 129. Depending what sort of reader you are, at the mention of US129 you may or may not be feeling goosebumps on the back of your neck. If you are, you know all about the Tail of the Dragon. This 18-kilometre stretch of road has 318 bends, ending in a clearing in the woods called Deals Gap where you can buy the T-shirt *I Rode The Dragon*. The thing is the Dragon's bends are not wide, sweeping curves; they're tight, sometimes 180-degree, well-cambered lean-overs. It's a mecca for motorcyclists and sports-car drivers, who use it as a personal racetrack. The local state troopers — referred to as Leos by dragoneers — park by the trees in lay-bys and keep the cash register ringing. The speed limit is 50 km/h.

Within two minutes of entering the Dragon, three sports bikes overtook me on a blind bend as if I was standing still. I am a safety-first type of rider, with a will to live and a family back home. Therefore I was not prepared to take risks and intended to treat this as a leisurely ride, honing my braking and cornering skills without compromising safety. But that'll be the day Twisting Throttle gets passed by hooligans having fun. I upped my pace and risk profile and felt the foot pegs scraping the road surface more than once. As the curves came and went, I was constantly shifting position on the seat as if I had haemorrhoids. I fleetingly saw two state troopers dozing in their cars. There was a stream of bikes coming the other way, but no one waved. This was not the time to take your left hand off the clutch lever. I flashed past a yellow road sign warning that this was a twisting road. Someone had scrawled across it *no shit*. Finally the Dragon ended abruptly at Deals Gap. Over a hundred bikes were parked up, with everyone playing the game of admiring each other's bling. I got a few glances, being packed up with panniers and camping gear: you wouldn't normally ride the Dragon loaded up like an ox-cart.

There's a biker's anthem for the Tail of the Dragon called 'The Dragon Realm' which goes on a bit, full of stuff like this: 'Knees kissing asphalt round each bend; Body motions; Weight shifting; Side to side; Brake; Shift; Throttle; Shift; Brake; The mindless rhythm of a road dance sung to an ageless tune; I control the moment; I indulge my insanity; I command the road; I defy the Dragon. I've come home; I've sensed the road; I've mastered the machine; I've conquered the Dragon; And we are one.'

Having done it, I now offer my own anthem and you are the first to read it:

Tail of the Dragon.
Lots of zigzaggin'.
Road twists a bit.
Sign said no shit.
Too fast round a corner,
Your wife's a mourner.
But that's all it takes,
Cos them's the brakes.
A slide and a swerve,
You're in Deadman's Curve.
Bikers are braggin',
They've ridden the Dragon.

Chapter 30

South Carolina–Georgia

Nicknames: The Palmetto State–The Peach State

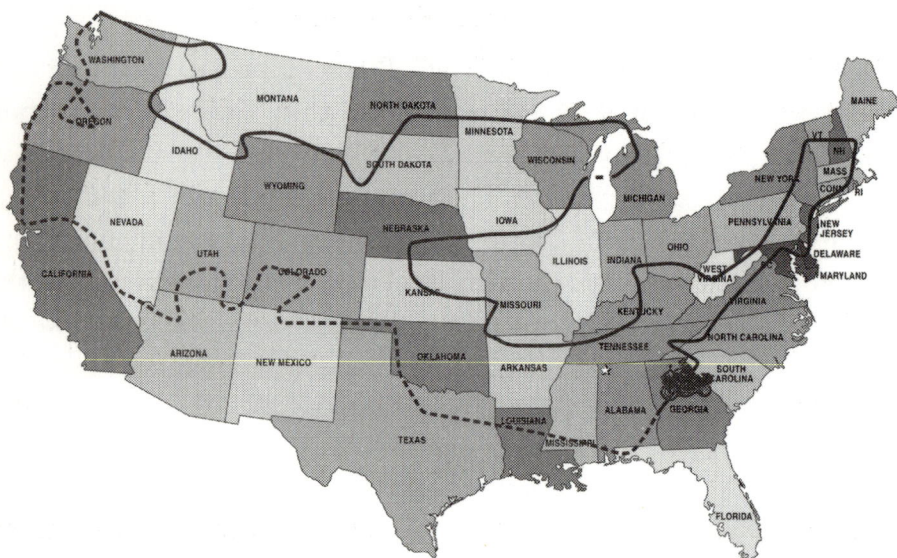

These states: 405 kilometres. Journey to date: 20,559 kilometres.

T HE MOMENT I CROSSED the state line between North Carolina and South Carolina, I felt I was getting somewhere at last. After days of messing about on mountainous, twisting, woodland byways, I needed the morale-boosting injection of interstate riding for a day just to put on lots of miles. The states I chose to more or less ignore, by sitting on the freeway, were South Carolina and Georgia. You may ask what I could have learned about South Carolina in just 100 kilometres nicking the top left corner. Lots, actually. For example, the state snack is boiled peanuts, the state dance is the shag, and the state motto is 'Dum spiro spero', which is Latin for 'Feeling shagged-out after a long ride? Stop for some boiled peanuts'. And that's what I did in Walhalla.

In the south, boiled peanuts are on the same cultural level as okra, black-eyed peas and Jesse Jackson. Called BPs, they're sold all over the place. I saw signs everywhere, so just had to try them. They were disgusting. I thought they'd be a bit like peanut butter without the butter, but these were small, purple and salty.

Boiled-peanut lady:	Hair larkem pain-arse?
Translation to English:	*How do you like them peanuts?*
Me:	Fantastic. Really more-ish.
Translation to American:	*Taste-ic. Rail molsh.*
Boiled-peanut lady:	Woln trar serm cay-shin pain-arse?
Translation to English:	*Want to try some Cajun peanuts?*
Me:	Yes, thanks, but may I keep the bucket?

The only two roadside stalls I've pulled over at — being the elk jerky in South Dakota, and now the boiled pain-arse in South Carolina — haven't totally hit the spot, so I resolved to just keep eating at Denny's in future.

I rode into Georgia across a long bridge over Hartwell Lake. The I-85 sliced across northern Georgia and speared through Atlanta before spurting out the other side into Alabama. Atlanta in the mid-90s was the most dangerous city in America. Last year it was the 21st, with Detroit making the number one city-not-to-walk-around-in-at-night slot. As I weaved in and out of commuter traffic on the eight-lane freeway, gazing up at Atlanta's high-rises, it looked like any other glass-and-chrome downtown area. Mostly the freeway surged through underpasses and tunnels, so I didn't get a great view. There was also the tiny matter of looking where I was going. Just after the skyscraper area, the freeway paralleled Atlanta's Hartsfield-Jackson international airport. But here's the crazy thing: the flight path was right over the freeway. Every two minutes a large jet would scream overhead metres above me as if it was landing on the freeway. I could tell you the brand names of their tyres.

I exited the interstate at La Grange. It was time to fuel up bike and rider. The location selected for the rider's top-up was a chain called Cracker Barrel. I am prepared to give this company free global exposure in my book simply because Kelly, a waitress at their La Grange store, gave me a dose of the grits. Far from being a disease, grits is a bowl of coarsely ground corn that has the consistency of sago or semolina. You eat it hot and sometimes have a knob of butter on it or maybe some grated cheese.

I was sitting in Cracker Barrel, flicking through the menu looking for the 'cholesterol dishes' page when Kelly came up to pour some coffee. 'Y'all won trar grair? Ah'll bring y'all serm grair jess for y'all.' And bring me some grair she sure did. A small bowl, free of charge, from an eager kitchen staff peeking out from the swing doors. I didn't know it then, but my Down-Under accent caused a flurry of interest among the kitchen staff. I ate the grits, and she came back looking pleased that the bowl was wiped clean. My choice was to order another bigger bowl of grits or something else. I ordered the something else. Funnily enough, the plate included items such as bacon, scrambled eggs, pancakes, hash browns and maple syrup.

As I went up to pay, Kelly asked if I'd mind coming through to the kitchen. Apparently this was completely against house rules, but the girls out the back were keen to meet the grit-swilling stranger from a far-off land. I suspected they didn't get too many out-of-state visitors in La Grange. Through the swing doors were assembled six aproned ladies. I felt like the Queen meeting actors backstage after the theatre. I complimented whoever made the grits. The girls turned to a negro lady who beamed. Kelly said none of them had ever heard an Australian accent for real. I didn't bother correcting her, but just accentuated the accent and started talking like Crocodile Dundee. It was a lovely moment.

Chapter 31

Alabama–Florida

Nicknames: The Yellowhammer State–The Sunshine State

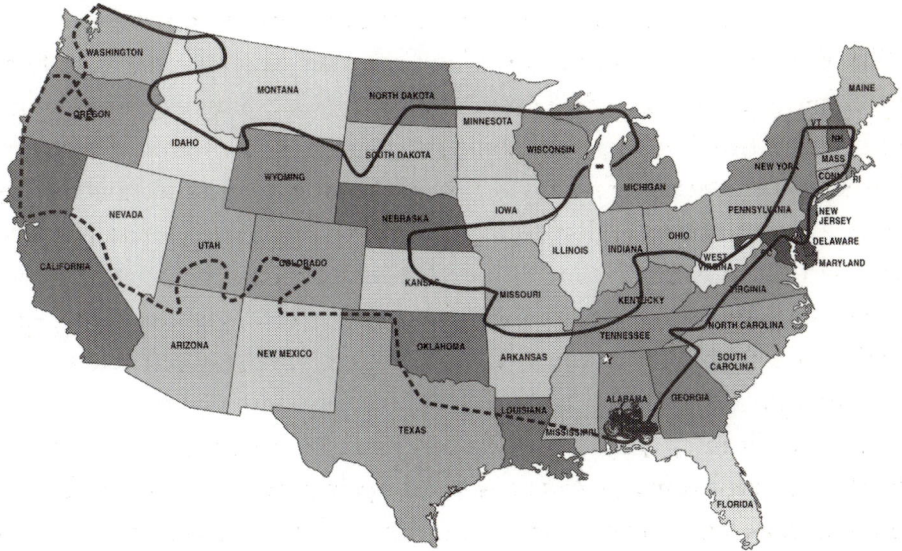

These states: 511 kilometres. Journey to date: 21,070 kilometres.

ALABAMA. THE HEART OF DIXIE. I exited the I-85 interstate at Opelika just over the state line from Georgia. It was time to get back to the byways, and I was happy with the momentum gained by blasting through Georgia. But it was good to be back on two-laned roads with cows a-grazin', barns a-raisin' and fields a-maizin'. My knowledge of Alabama was extensive from a lifetime of study and research of this crucial part of the Deep South's history. The Freedom from Slavery movement, the Alabama Constitution, the American Civil War, and of course Matilda, the world's oldest living chicken.

You're hungry for more information I can tell, and it's not about slavery. Matilda was a Red Pyle hen who lived a world-record 16 years, from 1990 to 2006. She was named after 'Waltzing Matilda' due to the way she stepped sideways like a waltzer. The hen made it onto national TV and into *The Guinness Book of Records*. The owners, a couple living in Birmingham, are looking around for a fitting final resting place, such as a pet cemetery or a plate surrounded by roast potatoes. Meantime Matilda is in their freezer at home.

I pulled over in a clearing and consulted my map. I needed to be in Florida that night, so selected a meandering back-road network that seemed to head in the right direction. I programmed the GPS and just put myself in its hands. The ride that afternoon was a beauty. There were no big towns in the way, just periodic rural villages like Smut Eye, Hatchechubbtee and Jack. I passed many single houses right on the roadside, where residents were sitting in rockers on their porches watching traffic go by. Perhaps it was a midday siesta sort of thing, and maybe this was just life in rural Alabama. Without exception they all waved, and my left thumb was permanently on the horn button. The bike was loving being in fifth gear for a change, and I couldn't remember the last time I'd used the brake.

I reached the town of Enterprise, and made my way to the town centre to worship at the Boll Weevil Monument. Boll was a famous Deep South black rock-and-roll singer who greatly influenced artists like Hendrix, Clapton and Buddy Holly. He played the legendary rectangular guitar, and his best-known albums are *Hey Boll Weevil, Boll Weevil's Beach Party* and *Surfin' with Boll Weevil*. His unique hambone beat has been used by Springsteen to Bowie to— hang on, sorry that was Boll Diddley. Sorry, I'm a bit mixed up.

Boll Weevil was a Mexican beetle which devastated Alabama's cotton crops a century ago. But why the monument in Enterprise? When the pest decimated Alabama's cotton, it forced farmers to diversify into other crops, like soybeans and peanuts, and some members of the community — namely, the boiled-peanut stall-holders — thought that was a good thing. The townspeople of Enterprise made a statue of a woman in a flowing gown holding a boll weevil above her head, as a tribute to how a disaster can be a catalyst for economic change. The ex-cotton farmers said, 'Yeah, but you're not the ones still findin' these varmints in your shoes', and there was a fair bit of vandalism of the statue. Now it's protected by a fountain and a security camera. Just down the road from the Monument, I saw a hotel called The Boll Weevil Inn. Given that the insect is 6mm long, has long feelers and looks like a striped cockroach, you'd wonder if the hotel might be better changing its name. If I checked in as a guest, the first thing I'd do would be to shake the sheets over the balcony and look behind the toilet.

I was really enjoying my ramble through rural Alabama and was not hurrying to reach the Florida state line. Residents were out on their John Deere ride-on mowers, and yellow school buses ambled slowly along side roads, stopping to let out their charges every hundred metres or so. I crossed into Florida's panhandle at Eunola, and within minutes commenced a part of my trip that I now look back on as 'making heavy weather'. This period was to dominate my next two days' riding through Mississippi, Louisiana and Texas. Here's how it started.

Approaching the junction of the back road I was on and I-10, the interstate that crosses the entire southern US from Santa Monica to Jacksonville, I could see ahead a massive bank of broiling black storm clouds. Right above me the sky was blue and birds were chirping in the trees. By the time I physically reached the interchange, the sky was black and the birds were heading for Arizona. I didn't know it then, but I was seeing the outer edges of Hurricane Ike. Ike had been wreaking havoc in the Caribbean for the previous few days and, as the weather annals now record, ended up being the third most destructive storm ever to slam into the US. Haiti was recovering from Hanna, that puff of wind that had battered me about in New Jersey, when Ike hit it. They say that had Ike made landfall in Florida, about the time I was riding up to the interchange, its destructive force would have been greater than the all-time worst hurricane, Katrina, in 2005. In fact Ike swung along the coast out to sea in the Gulf of Mexico, killing time before deciding which part of the Gulf to come ashore over. Eventually it would choose Galveston in Texas.

My original plan was to make a beeline for the Gulf coast at Santa Rosa Beach: a 30-kilometre burst along the I-10, exiting to the beach access road. I'd been on the interstate for 10 minutes when a wall of water slammed into me. I had about half a minute's warning. I am no stranger to riding in rain, but this was like sitting on the bike underneath a waterfall. I've never known torrential rain like it. My visibility was zero, and the rain was so hard that I could feel it entering my helmet behind two visors. It made the storm back in Michigan seem like a drizzle. Several small descriptive words passed my lips. The whole situation gave me what is often referred to as the . . . well, it wasn't grits. I saw the vague outline of an overbridge ahead. Ignoring the rules about not stopping on freeways, I took shelter under the bridge. The vortexes of spray from 18-wheelers were mere misty rain compared to the deluge that was continuing unabated. I'd no idea at the time that it was anything like a hurricane, as the last time I'd watched TV was Oprah back in New Jersey. But I was sufficiently worried about the ferocity to know I shouldn't be making for Santa Rosa Beach.

Suddenly the idea of a warm motel and mints on my pillow became a goal. The rain eventually died down to a continual downpour, and I rode on looking for the first sign of a motel. I found it in DeFuniak Springs. The Indian lady on reception was sympathetic. 'I got a room for $79.95. You can have it for $75 even.' 'That come with mints on the pillow?' I was a motel negotiation pro. 'No, but it has a king double. And you have to leave your bike outside.' 'In that case I won't be needing the king double.'

I switched on the TV in my room and surfed to the weather channel. A special 'breaking news' item on Hurricane Ike showed waves crashing over seafront promenades and gave evacuation warnings for low-lying coastal areas. News reports showed gridlock traffic heading out of New Orleans, but the most fascinating reports were the experts predicting the path of Ike, including pinpointing where it was going to make landfall. Their general conclusion was that, wherever landfall was going to be, you'd be best advised to be elsewhere at the time. They forecast that Ike would slam into the Gulf Coast at Texas in 36 hours and make its way inland, whacking into Dallas in three days' time. I checked my diary. Interestingly, my scheduled bike service was at Suzuki Dallas in . . . let's see . . . three days' time. Oh, goody. The same experts suggested that anyone wanting a dry holiday shouldn't be anywhere near the south coast at all, including New Orleans. This was a problem for me, as I desperately wanted to ride across Lake Pontchartrain Causeway, the longest bridge in the world over water. For a bridge-phile, the adrenaline rush of doing this would be like an astronomy student discovering a new planet.

For the rest of the evening I was racked with indecision: to get down to the Gulf coast so I could say I made it to the third side of America, to get to New Orleans to ride the causeway, to ride through the bayous to Lafayette and track up the Mississippi River into Mississippi? Or to get out of the way of the hurricane? I opened the motel door to let air in. The rain was back to horizontal status again. The sky was a deep black and the wind gusty. At that moment I knew I had to out-run the hurricane, get to Dallas a day earlier for the service, and stay ahead of trouble. I couldn't afford to sit out a storm on my schedule. I looked at my atlas. A direct route from where I was in Florida up to Dallas was a 1,200-kilometre ride through Alabama, Mississippi, Louisiana and as far into Texas as I could go before falling off. I turned off the TV, crawled into my king double and got an early night.

I woke at 5.00 a.m. and was on the bike at 6.00 a.m. The sky was the ominous clear that you associate with woodland animals twitching their whiskers and fleeing before a forest fire. I fired off down the I-10 towards Pensacola. Out to sea were the same broiling light-grey clouds, like huge balls of dirty cottonwool against a black horizon. But it was remarkably still, and I saw an exit ahead to Gulf Breeze. The temptation to get a Gulf of Mexico photo was too great, and I took the exit. I rode across a massive causeway called Garcon Point Toll Bridge and reached the shore at Pensacola Beach. The sea was smooth, and a family walked along the beach collecting driftwood. They can't have watched the weather channel the night before.

Once through Pensacola, I crossed back into Alabama and felt the wind start to stiffen. It was blowing directly up Mobile Bay, and by the time I rode across the causeway the bike was struggling to stay upright in the gusts. Just to my left I could see Battleship Memorial Park, with its several decent-sized battleships, now a tourist attraction. Ironically in 2005 the biggest ship, the USS *Alabama*, was slammed by Hurricane Katrina so that it tilted eight degrees in the water. And I, leaning over 20 degrees, thought *these* gusts were strong.

Chapter 32

Mississippi–Louisiana

Nicknames: The Magnolia State–The Bayou State

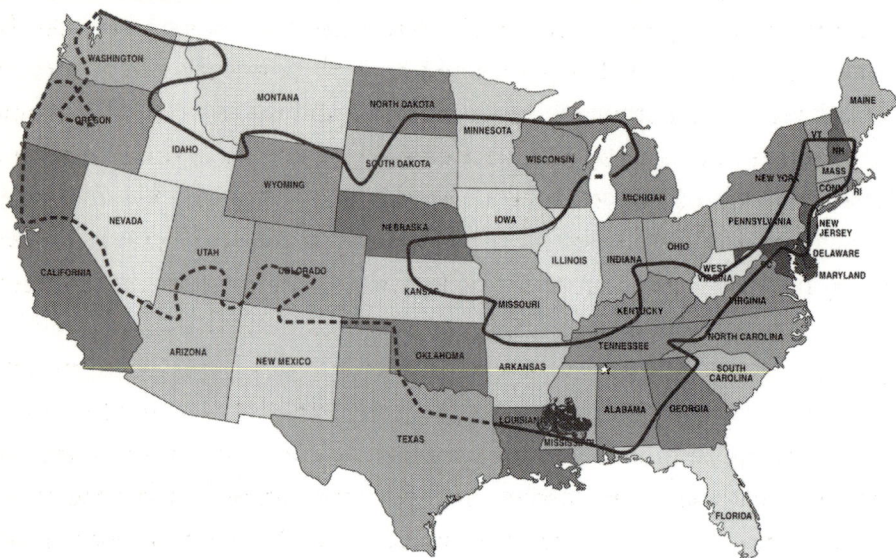

These states: 791 kilometres. Journey to date: 21,861 kilometres.

A ND SO THE 1,200-KILOMETRE DRAG north began. By the time I had cleared Mobile, Alabama, and crossed the state line into Mississippi before breakfast, there was only 1,000 kilometres to go. When I got to Hattiesburg I had to choose between the 98 to Natchez or the 49 to Jackson and then Vicksburg. I was favouring Natchez, but at the junction had to swerve right around an old lady turning left and not indicating. Thus I ended up in the Jackson lane.

In the battle of the sexes it's often the male of the species who draws the short straw. There are several examples in Nature where this is very evident. One such example was on my windscreen. I was thundering along through a wooded area called De Soto National Forest when I was spattered with insects. Several bounced off my visor, and several ended their lives on my windscreen. They had heads at both ends, and I now know they were lovebugs, common to Mississippi and Louisiana. Rather than being one bug, they were a male and a female conjoined in a permanent mating pose, except they were both facing opposite directions as if trying to get away from each other but fused at the rear end. Lovebugs spend their life in permanent copulation, hence their name, and after the male dies the female still drags around his body, even in flight. One such combination — let's refer to them as Romeo and Juliet — splattered onto my screen, and I watched with morbid fascination as the ritual of certain death played out in front of me. One of the ends, let's say Juliet, crawled slowly towards the top of the screen, dragging Romeo behind her. He may or may not have been alive. She finally reached the top edge of my screen, but her curse was that carrying her comatose mate meant she couldn't fly away. Therefore she was torn, and I hate to use that word literally, between casting off Romeo to die on my screen and escaping herself, or staying behind with him and dying together. This Shakespearean tragedy was unfolding inches in front of my face and I watched enthralled to see whether love would triumph over selfishness. Off she flew, leaving her dismembered husband behind. I washed him off at the next gas station.

Route 49 carved through the Mississippi countryside, and I watched the GPS as the kilometres ticked by. I saw signs to the villages of Hot Coffee, Shivers and Sanatorium. I pulled in at a Cracker Barrel restaurant, and tried to guess what a local would order. I chose meat loaf, mashed potato, corn kernels, gravy, a corn fritter and a biscuit.

Walking out of Cracker Barrel, warm and belly full, I was so sleepy I lay down on the grass by the bike and snoozed for half an hour. When I awoke and made to put on my helmet, there was a double-ended lovebug duo crawling about on the visor. I squashed them with my glove. Her ex hadn't been dead for two hours and already Juliet was carrying on with Brian. I did it for you, Romeo. RIP, my little friend.

I reached Jackson with 800 kilometres under my belt. I was well out of the reaches of Hurricane Ike, and a good day ahead of schedule. I phoned ahead to Dallas Suzuki to book the bike in a day earlier, and settled in for a sprint across Louisiana. The I-20 crossed the state line at Vicksburg. Just before crossing the Mississippi River, I pulled into the welcome centre. Welcome centres are located at state line crossing, because you call into welcome centres for information on the way *into* states, not just as you're leaving.

I was seconds away from riding out of Mississippi, but needed to use their toilet. The three young women behind the counter were doing nothing. At the sight of a traveller, they leapt into action and I was loaded up with brochures and recommendations for eating places in towns I'd just ridden through. The girls were pleased to have a real overseas tourist to process. I was there for 20 minutes, didn't have the heart to tell them I'd done Mississippi in four hours. And they didn't have a toilet.

Vicksburg was a shrine of sorts for me as well. This is where Coca Cola was first bottled back in 1894 by Joseph Biedenharn. His partner refused to buy shares, saying it wasn't the real thing. Biedenharn famously replied, 'Coke is it, man', and they parted company. Also here is America's reputedly most-haunted house, the McRaven House. All in all, Vicksburg has a lot going for it. If I hadn't been so warmly welcomed into Mississippi by the welcome centre I might have had time to visit these shrines. But time was pressing and I rode over into Louisiana, nostrils flared for Texas 300 kilometres away.

I blasted along the two-laned I-20 with the sun in my eyes. I had fuelled up in Rayville, and while waiting to pay had watched the TV showing Ike bashing away at the coast as it started its run towards landfall at Galveston and Houston. Several customers were standing about looking at the images. They commented to each other about battening down their homes, as Ike's edges were expected to hammer Louisiana in the east and west Texas. After a drag of 800 kilometres I'd thought I was completely out of the reach of this storm, but really had no idea of how large a front these things present. I was also heading due west, not so much out-running Ike as heading into its path. But so long as I had a day up my sleeve, I wouldn't have a problem.

I'd like to tell you more about Louisiana, but what I saw was from the interstate. After four hours of riding hard, fast and with only a minor opportunity to exercise skill in the rare need to overtake, I was pretty spent on reaching Shreveport. I stayed on the interstate, wanting to cross over that morale-boosting invisible line into Texas. If there was one regret for this trip, it would be having to out-run the hurricane. A strategically sensible decision, but the day's sprint meant the Big Easy's Mardi Gras, *haute* Creole and the Lake Pontchartrain Causeway would have to wait. It gives me an excuse to return.

Chapter 33

Texas

Nickname: The Lone Star State

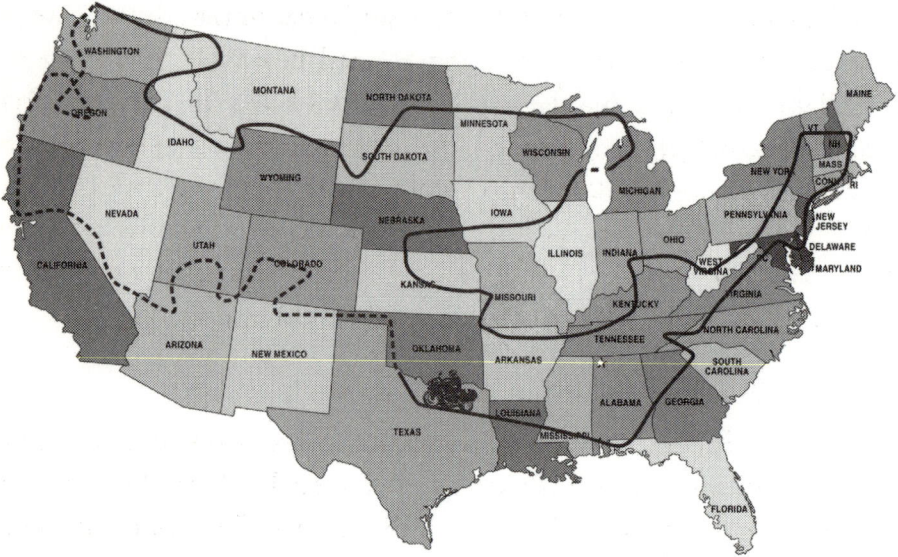

This state: 779 kilometres. Journey to date: 22,640 kilometres.

I SAW THE DISCARDED TYRE carcass about 1.9 seconds before reaching it. In that window of time, my brain engaged a gear I never knew I had. Instinct took over the controls of the bike, and I was close to an out-of-body experience watching how I took evasive action. The sun had sunk below the horizon an hour before, and I was night-riding along the busy I-20. I figured there'd be plenty of lights: everyone was travelling at the same speed and in the same direction, so what could the risk be? I wouldn't chance it on an unlit country road with deer waiting to play chicken. What I hadn't bargained on was that scourge of motorcyclists: tyre debris. Back in Louisiana, I'd noticed a gang of men spread out on the highway shoulder picking up litter, two of them carting away a whole tyre carcass. It's a problem all over the country. They're often called 'gators' as, stretched out, the tyre casings look like an alligator crawling across the road.

The gator in my lane was invisible at night until my lights picked it up at the last moment. A whole tyre tread had been ripped off a truck and flattened by subsequent vehicles. Had I run over it at 125 km/h, you would not have needed to spend money on my book. In those 1.9 seconds, my brain instructed my nervous system to take over and I threw the bike into a sort of S-swerve, missing the tyre carcass by decimal points of an inch. The human heart, at rest, beats about 70 per minute. It took me five minutes to calm down. My heart, in that period, beat 900 times. My mouth contributed several expressions I never knew I knew. I understood then that I had to call it a night. I took the near-miss as a sign to re-tyre.

The next interchange was at Lindale, where there was a collection of motels and fast-food places. I had ridden 1,200 kilometres through five states. That was enough. Lindale would be a good enough springboard to get to Dallas the following morning in time for the service.

I flicked on the weather channel. Hurricane Ike was hours away from smashing into Houston. Evacuations were gridlocking the roads. By the time I got clear of Dallas I'd be well out of it. The sprint had been worthwhile. I don't remember falling asleep, but in hindsight I wish I'd taken off my boots first.

The traffic build-up happened about 25 kilometres out of Dallas. I was heading for Plano, a city in its own right to the north of the huge, sprawling Dallas metropolitan area. This was morning commuter-time, and the freeways were jammed. But say hello to HOV lanes. High Occupancy Vehicle lanes are the answer to gridlock for bikes. They are a single, marked lane, usually on the inside of the freeway against the median barrier. You can drive in these marked car-pool lanes only if you have two or more people in your car — which counts out about 95% of American vehicles on their way to and from work. Therefore, these HOV lanes are empty, fast, and the ultimate method of travelling unrestricted in commuter traffic. A problem authorities are wrestling with is drivers having a blow-up doll in the passenger seat so they can use the HOV lane. Federal law has it that motorcycles can use the lanes, and you don't even need a doll on the back.

There's one catch, and that morning, blasting along an HOV lane scoffing at the other seven lanes of stationary traffic, I learned what it was. Once you get in the HOV lane you are in for life, as the lane is bounded by a raised median or rubber stanchions. There are a very small number of exit options, so you have to know your destination and where to exit well in advance. This presents two problems. When you do exit the HOV lane, you are in lane number six of the seven-lane freeway and have to get over six lanes of stationary or crawling traffic. The other slight issue is for tourists like me, who have a GPS snapping at them that their exit is coming up but with no way of getting out of the HOV lane. And this is precisely what my trouble was that morning in Dallas.

I set my GPS to navigate me to the Suzuki dealer. When I saw the gridlock, I slipped neatly into the HOV lane, finding myself trapped in the exit-less lane. My GPS, in its condescending, holier-than-thou voice, asked me to exit onto another freeway. I could see the looming interchange a mile ahead, but it might as well have asked me to do a wheel-stand down the median strip. I flashed through the interchange, ignoring the GPS's catcalls that I'd failed a simple navigational instruction and that it would re-calculate the route. This meant taking the very next exit, which of course I couldn't do either as I was still trapped. Each time the GPS re-calculated, I felt its pronouncements were edged with rising frustration and an unspoken 'if it's not too much trouble'.

I grabbed the chance to exit the HOV lane at whatever the next exit was. As the GPS re-calculated yet again, I was speeding around a cloverleaf interchange in traffic that didn't take too kindly to a wayward tourist dithering about with his lane selection. The whole navigation thing was a mess, and by the time I arrived at the Suzuki dealer I was an hour late, the GPS was sulking, and my whole team was in a state of nervous exhaustion. And fair enough, too. The chain and sprockets knew this was the end of their career, the tyres were saying goodbye to the rims, and I could hear strains of 'Now is the Hour' coming up from the brake pads. This was my major service that would see me through the remaining 12,000 kilometres.

The mechanic had the bike for five hours. I spent that time in a Krispy Kreme Donut shop making a cup of coffee and a Krispy Kreme Kombo spin out for five times longer than usual. In the end, the manager came out and said if I had nothing else to do, could I pop down to the bank for him. He gave me the keys to his car, a blow-up doll and said I should use the HOV lane.

I collected the bike, shook the mechanic's hand and spent a few quiet moments with the old tyres, chain, sprockets, brake pads, air and oil filters, and can of blackened oil. They wished me well for the rest of the trip and said it had been a privilege to be part of the team. Apart from the chain and sprockets, these parts had come on board in Milwaukee and were happy to be staying in America. They said they'd look after Chainey and Sprocky, who were excited to be forging a life in a new land. The mechanic said he didn't get too many customers who spoke like that to old bike parts.

I rode out of Dallas past Southfork Ranch, popped in to buy a fridge magnet, and couldn't get the theme tune to *Dallas* out of my head for the next 100 kilometres. At Denton, I got off the I-35 and headed west towards Wichita. At Jacksboro, I found a campsite at the Fort Richardson State Park, pitched camp and asked the local ranger what she'd describe as Texas's local dish. 'Own-lair wern thaing ah cain say, an thayts Tayxus berba-cue.' She pointed the way to the local BBQ diner, a local gem by the sounds of it, called Dairyland.

The smell of grilling meat hit me. The floor puddled with my saliva. I had arrived at the Pearly Gates. The waitress sat me down, immediately spotted a newbie, and pointed with her finger at what I needed to order — namely, the BBQ Platter for $11.95. 'Ah'll git the boys to pep it erp a bait.' And pep it erp a bait the boys certainly did. On the huge, oval plate were ribs in sauce, beef slices, chicken, refried beans, coleslaw, slices of toast and a jumbo coke. There was a napkin with a metal chain to go around your neck, and a dish of warm water to wash your fingers in. The diner was full. I knew they were locals, as they'd all stopped eating and were looking at me. The presence of a Crocodile Dundee accent in Jacksboro, a little off the beaten tourist path, had novelty value. I thought about play-acting to the crowd and asking the waitress for a boomerang because that's how we eat BBQ back home. But the food was sizzlingly delicious and everyone just smiled and nodded at me as I looked at them looking at me, and went back to eating. I never knew I had that much room in my stomach, but I cleaned the plate. The waitress came back. 'Mah, yew're hungrair, herny. The boysa lark t'mate yew.' I followed her out to the diner's kitchen to mate the boys. It wasn't a place for vegetarians, I'll wager.

That night, I heard far-off coyotes on the howl. A neighbouring camper had a pet raccoon, and the ranger had told me to look out for roadrunners on the road through to Crowell. I knew I'd kill an animal at some time on my trip. I just didn't think it would be an owl.

I was in a world of my own, thumping along the deserted rural Texan back road from Windthorst to Seymour. This was the Texas that you expected to see: flat, barren, a sparse landscape with the only signs of human presence being those mechanical seesaw type of pumps out in the middle of nowhere. I never knew where the owl came from, but there was a thump down around my headlight and a spray of feathers. I looked in my mirror and saw nothing on the road. Remembering the ranger's words about roadrunners, I tried to recall from those Wile E Coyote cartoons how big a roadrunner was. I pulled over. Wedged into the front forks of the bike was a massive owl. Its yellow eyes were still open, but its head was at an odd angle. I couldn't believe the sheer bad luck of hitting this magnificent-looking bird out in such an open and featureless place. And why was an owl out there anyway? There were no trees from horizon to horizon. All I can do is show remorse for ending its life by placing a picture of it in my book.

Chapter 34

Oklahoma

Nickname: The Sooner State

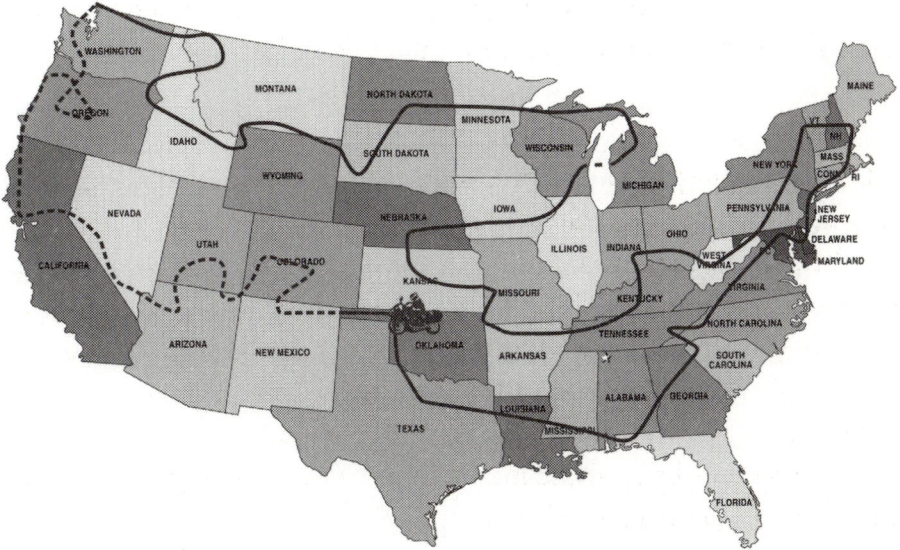

This state: 637 kilometres. Journey to date: 23,277 kilometres.

OKLAHOMA'S OFFICIAL STATE SOIL, rock and grass are, in order, port silt loam, rose rock, and indian grass that you may know better as *Sorghastrum nutans.* You may snigger, but riding north up the 283 I could easily see why Oklahoma would place a lot of importance on the ground. This was the closest I could describe to riding across Northern Queensland or parts of the Nullarbor. Yet it wasn't as harsh as Australia somehow. The open and utterly deserted landscape was a little gentler on the eye, perhaps because of the corn or the greenness. I crossed the state line over the Red River at Eldorado and plugged northwards heading for the Oklahoma panhandle, that saucepan-handle part of the state you think should belong to Texas.

The odd thing about the part of Oklahoma I was in was that the village names were mostly people's first names: Ron, Sandy, Warren,

Russell, Martha, Marty, Elmer, Madge, Carl, Blair, Greta, Louis. It was only this small area in the south-western corner. I passed through the small town of Laverne, which proudly displayed a banner across their main street saying: *Laverne: Home of Miss America 1967.*

In Sayre, a large white caravan caught my eye on the roadside. It advertised alligator-on-a-stick for $4. I pulled off the road immediately. The menu on this Oklahoman pie-cart was a cracker. What really tempted me — apart from their sausage jambalaya and shrimp gumbo, naturally — was their Small Bayou Special for $25. This is what you got: four catfish, six fried shrimp, 10 boiled shrimp, two crab cakes, two frog's legs, six boiled red potatoes, two corn-on-the-cob, Cajun sauces, and rolls. I settled on the $6 crawfish dinner, which comprised 1.5lbs of crawfish, one corn-on-the-cob, and two potatoes. Aussies know crawfish as 'yabbies', Kiwis know it as 'koura'. The unshaven guy in a dirty apron wiped his hand across his mouth and said, 'Yeah?' 'Crawfish dinner, thanks mate.' 'Got none crawfish 'day. You want shrimp'n stead?' I thought about the freshness quotient of seafood being sold from a street vendor in a small town 1,000 kilometres from the ocean, whereas I could imagine the freshwater crawfish being caught by his young sons, Billy-Bob and Jethro, down at the Sayre Creek. 'Nah, thanks. I's hopin' for the crawfish.' I rode away both hungry and wondering why I'd spoken to him in a hillbilly accent.

At Rosston, I turned left. That's more significant than you realize, because it represented the start of the long, hot ride across the Oklahoma panhandle towards New Mexico. This was the longest, straightest road I'd ridden since North Dakota. The sun was sinking low in the west and made visibility a pig. The small hamlet of Gate, population 112, advertised itself as the home of Hank the Cowdog. Mention of the word 'cowdog' reminded me of a hotdog which reminded me I hadn't eaten since the Texas barbecue in the last chapter. I plugged on westwards, my left hand off the handlebars, shielding the sun from my vision. Riding into the early evening was suddenly very taxing. My thoughts turned to camping options. From horizon to horizon was sheer flatness. Lines of telegraph poles stretched to a vanishing point. A few farms popped up with windmills and grain silos, but mostly there was just open prairie. I fuelled up in the town of Guymon, and considered asking if they had a campground. But in the air was the most unholy stink you could imagine. It was raw meat of some sort. I've since learned that it was a pork-processing plant which handles 16,000 piggy customers a day, and at which one out of five Guymon citizens works. I rode on, inwardly heaving.

The state line to New Mexico loomed large as I cantered through Boise City and onto the Rita Blanca National Grassland. The sun had dropped below the distant Sangre de Cristo Mountains of New Mexico, and I counted on the town of Clayton, just over the border, to provide a patch of grass and a toilet. It did. I finished my day's businesslike slog through Oklahoma reliving the endless days in outback Australia, and thinking how much this American ride was, apart from that day, so different.

I set up my tent under a tree, checked over the bike, and opened a can of peaches I found in my tyre kit. Having no tools to open the can, I used a screwdriver to puncture and widen a hole about the size of a 20-cent piece. Inserting the screwdriver, I mashed up the peaches. I lay back on the bike seat in the cooling night air in this small dusty town in New Mexico and slurped out the peach purée. It was heaven. Pig heaven.

Chapter 35

New Mexico

Nickname: The Land of Enchantment State

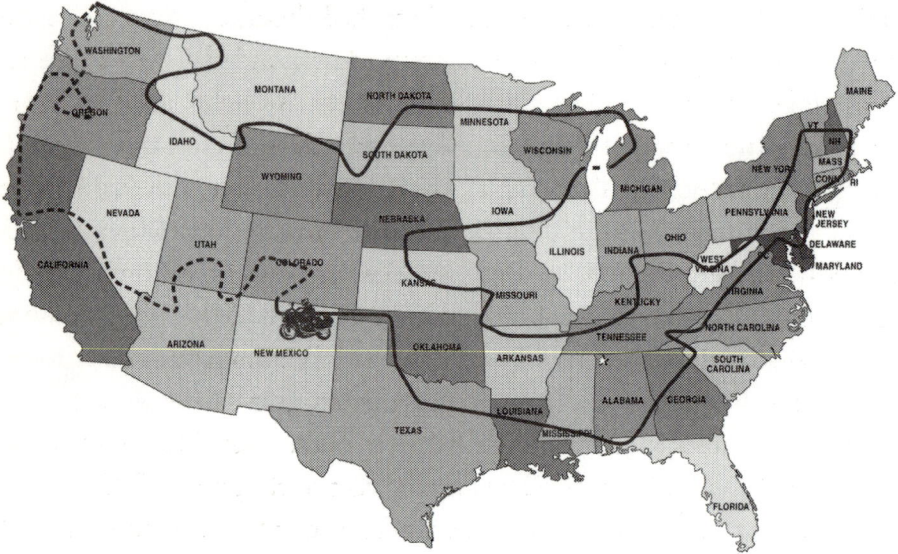

This state: 898 kilometres. Journey to date: 24,175 kilometres.

Anoche era como frío como el infierno en mi tienda de campaña. Temblé dentro de mi saco de dormir y me desperté muchas veces. Sorry, I'm lapsing into my native New Mexican tongue that you may not understand. I'll start again. The night was as cold as — how you say — Hell in my . . . my . . . *campaña*. Tent, I think you call it. I shivered inside my *saco de dormir* and was woke many of the times.

When I rode out of Clayton the next *mañana*, I noted from my GPS that elevation was 3,100 metres. No wonder I was *frío de mierda*. I'd no idea I was up that high. How could that have happened? I'd spent two days riding across flat plains. There was no hill climbing. How can you gain 3,100 metres by not ascending a mountain pass? That was the height

244

of the Blue Ridge Parkway, and I knew I'd climbed that at the time. It troubled me, the whole elevation thing, as I got closer to actual real mountains, the Sangre de Cristo.

This was a new phase right in front of me. These were the southern Rockies, and it was time for some focus. The route possibilities in New Mexico were unlimited. I'd researched the best biking roads in the Rockies, and New Mexico had some beauties. I marked them on a map and joined up as many as possible. The result was downloaded to my GPS and would take me on a looping ride into Colorado through some of the most spectacular scenery on Earth. I'd allowed two days.

I rode past the surreal Capulin volcano, a conical mountain just rising out of the plateau. Pulling in at a Denny's in Raton, my hunger, after no actual meal for 36 hours, was beyond description. There was no other option than the Heartland Blast — and I might add that the references to 'heart' and 'blast' were highly ironic. The HB included a scrambled egg and bacon mash, two pancakes, hash browns, two sausages, two bacon rashers, three cups of coffee, and some sourdough toast. This all came free with a small sprig of parsley. The parsley cost a whopping $7.95.

I rode out onto the Cimarron Plateau towards the mountains. My first open-mouthed stare was entering Cimarron Canyon. After weeks of flatness — or at the most gentle wooded hills — the towering, rocky canyon walls and outcrops were overpowering. The sky was a deep blue, and I passed over a hundred bikes on the road during the rest of the day. The road dropped down into a beautiful valley and sparkling lake at Eagles Nest in the shadow of Wheeler Peak, the highest point in New Mexico. This was ski country, but I could only guess at what it would look like snowed in. Highway 38 curved through forested canyons, over Bobcat Pass at 3,000 metres, through the villages of Red River, Questa, Arroyo Hondo and on to what is officially known as The High Road to Taos Scenic Byway. My speed slowed to a crawl as the road pootled between brick-red haciendas and Mexican-style adobe veranda-ed shops in the dusty town of Taos.

On impulse, out of Taos I turned off onto a narrower side road that looked a bit more challenging. How right I was. The road twisted and climbed through forest, opening out on the ridge top at Vadito. I could have been in Mexico. Little kids ran along beside the bike, shouting things that I couldn't catch beyond 'gringo' and 'money'. It looked like there'd been a few accidents on this tortuous road with its ravine drop-offs. Instead of simple white crosses to mark a fatality site, there were whole shrines with colourful flowers, toys and life-sized crosses. It gave the impression of being a highly religious area, but the best was yet to come. As the road wound down through Cordova, I reached a little village called Chimayó. This tiny speck in the hills is known as The Lourdes of America. Here's why.

Approximately 200 years ago, a local man was wandering through the hills of El Potrero, near to Chimayó, and saw a light springing up from the ground. He dug down with his hands to find a buried crucifix. He ran down the hill to fetch the local priest. The priest and most of the townspeople went to the site, retrieved the crucifix, and carried it down to place it on the altar of their church in the nearby village of Santa Cruz. The next morning the crucifix had disappeared. They returned to the burial site and dug. The crucifix was back. A second time they carried it down to Santa Cruz. The next morning it was back up on the hillside. The townspeople realized then that the holy icon had to stay at that spot, so they buried the crucifix again and built a small chapel over the hole. That chapel is called El Santuario de Chimayó and is a mecca for over 300,000 visitors a year who come to pray, ask for healing, and seek enlightenment.

I parked the bike outside El Santuario, removed my helmet and entered the chapel. I was after one thing: a handful of Holy Dirt. At the back of the chapel, in a small, dimly lit room with a low ceiling, is a hole in the concrete floor. That hole is directly over the spot where the crucifix lies, and the sandy dirt that you are allowed to scoop up is, by association, very holy. That dirt is the solid equivalent of the Holy Water of Lourdes, France. I lined up in a hushed queue of mostly Mexican-looking people, wizened old crones to fathers holding sniffling babies. One by one, you bent down and entered the dirt room. You were given a small plastic cup so you could reach into the hole and scoop up a tablespoon of Holy Dirt.

All around the waiting room were statues of the Holy Mary and Jesus on the cross. There were hundreds of tiny infant shoes on which names like *Esmeralda*, *José* and *Juan* were written, plus a rack of over a hundred walking sticks. Apparently, the shoes were those of sick children, and the sticks were not required by infirmed pilgrims who walked upright again after tipping the dirt on themselves.

I felt like a fraud. I had nothing wrong with me, and technically didn't need the dirt. Apart from, that is, a small infection in my thumb from when the owl's beak had pierced the skin by my thumbnail as I prised it out of my forks the week before in Texas. That would do. I waggled my thumb about in the dirt: was the healing instant, or did it need a few days and maybe some Savlon to help? I sat around in the courtyard and tried to be reverent, taking sly photos with my digital camera while looking the opposite way. I watched the procession of people filing out of El Santuario. The crones were still hunched over and the babies still crying. But then what do you expect? That an 80-year-old Mexican grandmother goes in one door, scoops up some dirt, and emerges out the other door looking like Penelope Cruz? Despite my cynicism, it was a moving experience, as it was my first time in close quarters with this sort of religious faith in shrines. But as I mounted up again, I glanced over to the commercial arm of the shrine industry. The Santuario gift shop: the stall selling Holy Chillies, plastic crucifixes and — if my luck was in — Holy Fridge Magnets.

The mountain road curved up from Chimayó and out into a valley at Totavi. I was searching for a road that would take me through the Jemez (pronounced 'Hemez', where you gob out on the 'H') Mountains through an area called Los Alamos. The road was called the Jemez Mountain Trail, and it was meant to be just (pronounced 'hust') stunning riding, justifying (pronounced 'hustifying') the detour from Totavi Junction (pronounced 'Hunc—' never mind). I found the road and immediately knew I was in for a treat. The switchbacks were electrifying and the views impossible to describe.

I saw a turn-off to Bandelier National Monument and decided to have a look. A ranger kiosk relieved me of $5, but pointed out I could camp the night in the forest if I wanted. I wanted. I rode down into the narrow Frijoles Canyon to find a visitor centre for some cave dwellings.

To kill time before pitching camp on the cliff above, I hiked to the caves and climbed into a few, using the rough log ladders supplied. A lone woman hiker said hello. When she found out I was intending to camp in Bandelier, she warned me about mountain lions, black bears, rattlesnakes, tarantulas, horned toads and bats. I said yeah but I carry with me some Holy Dirt. She asked was it the real thing or bought from the gift shop. I asked her if she meant the real gift shop or the one selling Holy Chillies. She asked if I meant red or green chillies. The word 'bat' occurred to me in another context as she listed the hazards of camping. I wondered if she owned the Los Alamos motels 20 kilometres down the road.

I found a spot in the forest and set up camp. It was the most idyllic camping site of my whole trip. When the sun set, the sky over the mountains turned an incredible purple hue. To cap it off was a full moon. As I lay back on the bike seat, my feet flopping over the windscreen and head resting on the top box, helmet perched on the mirror with Neil Diamond crooning softly from the speakers out into the moonlit desert, I wondered if solo riding could get any better than this. As if on cue, a lone coyote howled somewhere out in the inky twilight. I was wrong. This should have been shared.

I packed up my tent and gear, wondering what the paw prints in the soft sand belonged to. Perhaps the woman hiker knew her stuff after all. I rode out of Bandelier onto the Jemez Mountain Trail route. The road, dewy and partially hidden in wisps of dawn mist, skirted the Valles Caldera, officially a super-volcano at 22 kilometres across. I was riding through the Valles Grande, a vast, grassy valley in the caldera.

When I pulled over to take a photo, I switched off the bike and immediately heard a bubbling sound like boiling water. It *was* boiling water, and it was coming from my radiator. I hadn't noticed the temperature gauge max out. I put the bike on its centre stand, and over the next half-hour patiently removed the various bits of fairing to get to the radiator. I found two wires disconnected, which meant the cooling fan was not receiving the radiator switch's instruction to turn on. The mechanic in Dallas had forgotten to reconnect them after working on the bike. Due to the strain on the engine in the mountains, this was the first time the cooling fan had been required since Texas. I was very lucky I'd pulled over: had I ridden on with my radiator water turning to steam, even my Holy Dirt might not have got me out of it.

The highway continued on to the Jemez Springs *pueblo* — all adobe huts and the odd gift shop and café. The landscape was becoming dominated by brick-red escarpments and canyons. At San Ysidro I could have nipped down to Albuquerque for breakfast, but chose to wheel around north again up the magnificent Route 96. This dual-lane expressway begged to be ridden at speed. I fuelled up.

A junction called me to turn off on the next piece of motorcycling nirvana: The High Road to Chama. Chama is a little town high up on the Continental Divide, and this road was going there slowly, just how I liked it. Passing through the Santa Fe National Forest, I descended to one of the most picturesque lakes I have ever seen: Abiquiu Reservoir. A couple in a Ural sidecar motorcycle trundled up the road from the lake, and I waved. I slowed for a little village in the hills called El Rito. Three men in white singlets sat outside what might have been a café. They had massive bellies and handlebar moustaches. One man on seeing the bike approaching made a sign like he was doing a wheelie, possibly wanting me to drag down their main street in a prolonged wheel-stand. Instead, I stood up on the pegs and then knelt on the seat like a stunt-rider's granny. All three men stood up and clapped. I waved back. It was a heart-warming moment.

The High Road to Chama twisted through wooded hills, through canyons and across plateaux, all under a beautifully blue sky with towering fluffy bright-white cloud formations. The vividness of the landscape was mesmerizing, and I was enjoying the riding on a virtually deserted highway through intoxicating mountains. I reached the junction at Tres Piedras and made the decision to head north to Colorado. I could have continued looping back and forth for days, but I knew that New Mexico was really just the dress rehearsal for the main mountain-riding event — Colorado and the Rockies.

If I ever had the chance to return to America and revisit and explore an area further on a bike, this time with someone else, that area would be New Mexico. *Pero primero yo tendría que volver a El Santuario para conseguir algún Holy Dirt más.*

Chapter 36

Colorado

Nickname: The Centennial State

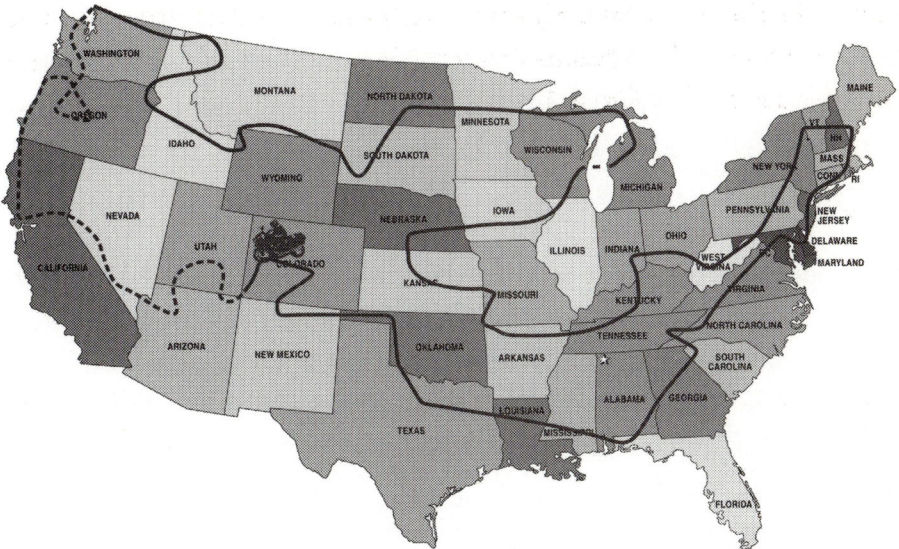

This state: 1,641 kilometres. Journey to date: 25,816 kilometres.

JUST OVER THE BORDER in Colorado, I pulled over at an enticing tourist roadside attraction. It was a ramshackle adobe house with an arched gateway over which was inscribed: *El Oratorio de Juan Diego y la Sacrada Familia.* This is Spanish for 'The Ripoff House of Juan Diego Who Is Unemployed, Sound Familiar?' Scrawled on the dried mud wall was: *Mysteries of the Rosary. Open The Public To. Not Responsible For Acident.* A skeletal dog sniffed around the bike, but no one else was around. I rode on, resigned to the fact that the rosary would have to be mysterious for a while longer.

In the distance were the towering San Juan Mountains, and beyond them the Rockies. This was what I was here for. These roadside oddities were fine in a low-key way, but you didn't come to a state like Colorado to see a two-headed calf. With some of the world's most stunning alpine scenery half a day away, seasoned travellers would not waste their time on kitsch and eccentricities. On the other hand, you can't just ride through Antonito without paying your respects at the Beer Can Castle.

Antonito is a dusty hamlet on the way to nowhere, but one of its residents with a bit of time on his hands has fashioned a two-towered castle out of junk, mainly hubcaps and beer cans. To get empty beer cans I'm assuming he wouldn't have just tipped out the beer. Which is why I found his sign ironic. It read: *Alcohol and tobacoo is kills*. You have to find your way down a dirt side road to get to the Beer Can Castle. I took a photo and returned to the main highway.

✪

An hour later, the other side of Alamosa, overlooking the Great Sand Dunes National Park in the shadow of the Sangre de Cristo Mountains, is another member of the Roadside Nutters Society. Stuck out in the middle of the desert brush is a one-storey steel platform called the UFO Watchtower. How could I not pull over? It was that sort of 'only in America' day. The lady who owns the watchtower is apparently described by locals as a harmless weirdo. She believes the area is an inter-dimensional vortex, and the platform is like a lightning rod for any alien spacecraft looking to take a break. This whole region is seemingly known for more than the usual number of UFO sightings, so maybe she's onto something. If you have either been abducted by aliens or seen a UFO, she would like to tape-record your story. In return, you can take your pick from a free frisbee, a blow-up alien doll, or a bumper sticker. I rode down the sandy, stony access road. A chain across the road near the watchtower said it was closed. That was a big disappointment, as I had my alien abduction story formulated in my mind.

✪

But it was time to stop messing about and embrace Colorado. I rode west into the San Juan Mountains, entering the Rio Grande National Forest at Del Norte. The road carved through a spectacular valley tracking alongside the sparkling Rio Grande River, bounded by green meadows covered in yellow and purple wildflowers. It was warm, the sun was at my back, and the ride was entrancing. After South Fork the highway was known as the Silver Thread, threading its way nearly 120 kilometres through Wagon Wheel Gap and over several passes to Lake City, just the other side of the Continental Divide. I didn't want this ride to end.

Although it was earlier than I'd usually be getting off the bike for the day, at 5.00 p.m. I reached the town of Creede nestled in a towering ravine, near to the headwaters of the Rio Grande and steeped in history from the silver boom of the 1890s. Creede's elevation is 2,700 metres, and once the sun went down I knew it would be a cold night camping. It was then I saw the sign for the Snow Shoe Lodge. I walked in and went straight into motel-negotiation mode, being a pro. 'Hi. Can you tell me what your cheapest room is?' '$60.' 'Has it got a bed?' 'Yes.' 'Has it got a TV?' 'Yes.' 'Is it noisy?' 'Yes.' 'Great, I'll take it.' These motel people were putty in my hands.

But here's the reason that the night in Creede was the most memorable of the whole trip. I was put in Room 102. I first noticed the John Wayne memorabilia when I popped to the toilet. There was a framed picture of the duke right above the throne. I then looked more closely at the other pictures in the room. They were all John Wayne. Sitting on the TV was a pile of John Wayne videos. I went down to the office. Behind the counter was a framed, autographed photo taken in 1972 of John Wayne outside the motel with the then owner. He had stayed in Room 102, my room, slept in 102's bed, my bed, and sat on 102's toilet, my— Well, you get the drift. Without meaning to be rude, the décor looked a bit John Wayneish, too. I tossed up whether to try to find a diner in Creede that dished up grits. True Grits.

I was all saddled up, chowed down and hitting the trail by sun-up. The early mist still hung around the Rio Grande valley, and I shivered with the cold. The sun soon peeked over the peaks and the highway started the ascent of the first pass on the Silver Thread: Spring Creek Pass at 3,300 metres. The climb up was majestic. The morning sun illuminated golden aspen trees, which in turn cast a golden hue across the meadows. I passed not one other vehicle for an hour leading up to the summit. The corners were superbly cambered, and the bike was humming, enjoying the smooth ride through this mountain wonderland.

The next summit to be crested was Slumgullion Pass at an even higher 3,500 metres. I saw patches of snow on the roadside, and the cold mountain air filtered in through my slightly open visor, chilling my face. I pulled over into a clearing at the summit of Slumgullion to take some photos. I also wanted to change my gloves from padded to very padded. My number-one pair of gloves, after 20,000 kilometres of throttle and clutch work, could have a well-earned rest. It was time to give the substitutes a run off the bench.

If you've read my Australian book, you'll know about the personal loss I suffered up in the Kakadu when a moment's inattention saw me ride off leaving behind, in the bush, my right-hand glove. Glovey was never seen again. Months later, I received an email from a couple in Darwin who'd read my book. They'd recounted the Glovey story to their young children, who were so distressed that the family drove 200 kilometres into the Kakadu to see if they could find him. They didn't, but the kids were able to sleep at night again. I say all this because it happened again, on Slumgullion Pass. I have a disastrous habit of putting things on my top box and forgetting them. Back in Illinois, I'd ridden 90 kilometres with my credit-card wallet wedged between top box and camping gear.

I started the slow and winding descent to Lake City. Halfway down, I got annoyed at the number-two gloves and decided to change back. I pulled over . . . and the realization set in. The gloves had been resting on my top box back at the summit, and I'd ridden off. Somewhere on this mountain they'd fallen off. I flew back up to the summit, looking left and right. They weren't at the clearing, and all I could do was creep back down the descent, scanning each side of the road. It was a hopeless exercise, as the speed I'd been doing on the first descent meant the gloves could have flicked off over the side of a ravine. I couldn't believe that I'd done it again. *Déjà vu* wasn't the phrase for it. These were the twin Sons of Glovey, now stranded — hopefully together — in the Colorado mountains, awaiting an unknown and frightening fate from freezing to mountain lion to eagle to forest fire. The last sound they would have heard was the bike accelerating away and then silence. I wondered if gloves whimpered.

✪

I've hardened up a lot since Australia, so I rode down the mountain into Lake City rationalizing the loss of Sons of Glovey as collateral damage. They took one for the team. There is no 'I' in glove. Alferd Packer also took one for the team. In fact, he took the actual team. In fact, he ate the actual team.

I was standing looking at the Alferd Packer Memorial rock, which marks the site where five pioneers, being guided by Packer, were found dead. It was 1874. Alferd Packer was guiding the party cross-country from Salt Lake City to Los Pinos. They got lost in a severe snowstorm and were a few weeks overdue. Then Packer arrived in Los Pinos by himself, claiming that, to survive, the living had had to eat the dead one by one as they pegged out. The townspeople started to smell a rat when Packer headed straight for Denny's and ordered ribs. Waiting for the summer thaw, they trekked to the site of the snowstorm — where I was standing now — and found five clean skeletons, some cutlery and a pile of napkins. Actually, I made that up. What they found was the macabre sight of skeletons with skulls bashed in. Packer was arrested for murder, cannibalism and littering a picnic area. He was sentenced to 40 years. Apparently, the jail where he was serving had a record mass escape in 1895. Authorities traced it back to a comment Packer was overheard making in the mess hall, saying how he was sick of prison food.

✪

I entered the Gunnison National Forest as Highway 149 continued to descend into a wide valley mostly filled with the Blue Mesa Reservoir. No sooner had I cleared the town of Gunnison, now on Route 50, than the road started to climb up into forested mountains again. This was the southern end of the Sawatch Range, and for the second time that day I crossed the invisible dotted line, the Continental Divide at the 3,450-metre Monarch Pass. The Monarch is widely accepted as one of the most scenic in Colorado, and I would be hard-pressed to disagree. The highway twisted its way down the other side in a series of wide, sweeping switchbacks, eventually reaching Salida.

In Salida, I decided to expand my repertoire of eating experiences and branch out into pastures new. The new pasture was called Arby's and I had a burger. When I got out to the car park, I couldn't find my credit-card wallet. Mentally retracing my steps, I recalled paying for the Arby's meal half an hour before. The wallet must be there somewhere. I went back in and checked on and under the table where I'd been sitting. (The diners sitting there were understanding.) I asked the girl behind the counter if it had been handed in. She said no. I was stumped. I went back out to the bike and fruitlessly searched through my luggage.

Then it dawned. I'd put the wallet on my food tray. At the end of the meal I'd thrown the napkins onto the tray, thus covering the wallet. And we all know what you do with the rubbish on your food tray in fast-food places. I went back in. By now we were on first-name terms. I asked the supervisor, Shelby, if I could rummage through the waste bin. He said why not go for the Arby's lunch combo — that was only $4.95. I said he didn't understand: I'd lost my wallet, and it was probably, as we spoke, sitting in a mess of half-eaten burgers, sauce and milkshake residue. In his eyes was sympathy, not mockery. He looked towards the waste bin and nodded. Arby's was full with lunchtime diners who, without exception, put down their newspapers and watched me burrow into the waste bin. I saw a black shape to the side. I pulled it out: it was a beef burger with a bite out of it. And then I saw the wallet. A small amount of tartare sauce was squished over my driver licence, but at least I had it. I held the wallet up for Shelby to see. He nodded and looked the other way. The diners went back to their papers. I rode away from Arby's in Salida, thinking that I've had better afternoons.

That night I was hosted by friends Heath and Cheri Herber, and their lovable dog Remy, in their palatial home in Colorado Springs. Again my boots were requested to be left down by their letterbox, but I was used to this by now. Cheri had prepared a barbecue meal that would have rivalled anything Texas BBQ or even Alferd Packer could have dreamed up. Heath — another American who needs no excuse to take a day off work and roll his BMW 1150RT out of the garage — offered to escort me out of Colorado Springs as far as Wilkerson Pass. I leapt at the chance of a riding companion for the morning.

And what a morning it was. Heath acted as guide as we toured through the surreal Garden of the Gods in Colorado Springs. After Heath turned back at Wilkerson Pass, I continued on through Buena Vista looking for the turn-off to Aspen. This put me on Route 82 and the 3,700-metre Independence Pass. The ride up to the summit was one of the best of the trip. Bright golden aspen trees bordered green meadows, bisected by twinkling streams. At the top I gazed open-mouthed at the vista below. These were the Rockies in all their breathtaking splendour. It's impossible to capture them in written word — you'll have to go there to see for yourself. The descent into Aspen was equally magnificent. I could only imagine what sort of alpine paradise this place would be in January.

At Glenwood Springs I rode up the on-ramp to the I-70 westward. I was making for the town of Fruita, just the other side of Grand Junction, my intended overnight stop. But first I had an important shrine to visit in Fruita: I refer of course to the statue of Mike the Headless Chicken. This is a good one. Back in 1945, a farmer called Lloyd Olsen was asked by his wife to prepare a chicken for their dinner the next day. Lloyd went out to the yard with his axe and selected Mike. He swung the axe and severed Mike's head. The chicken then ran off, in circles, which Lloyd put down to the usual death throes of beheaded poultry. When he went out the next day, he noted two things. Mike's head was on the ground by the chopping block, yet Mike himself was with the other chickens hopping around as if nothing had happened. Seemingly the axe had not severed the jugular vein and Mike's brain stem was intact. Lloyd then started to feed Mike grain and water with an eyedropper straight into his oesophagus. Mike the Headless Chicken became a media star and the Olsens took him on tour. He was in magazines and on TV, and was insured for $10,000. The thing is that Mike didn't realize he was missing his head. Which was lucky, because a cat had eaten it, so surgery was out of the question. One night, 18 months after the beheading, Mike choked to death on a corn kernel in a motel room in Arizona — or at least that was the official version of events. The Olsens collected big-time: $10,000 in insurance money and a delicious roast that night. The town of Fruita has a Mike the Headless Chicken Festival every May. As I parked by Mike's rusted-iron headless statue in Fruita's main street, I thought back to Andy the Footless Goose in Nebraska and realized just why I loved America so much.

I set off early from Grand Junction and did the 150-kilometre sprint along the Gunnison River to Ouray as if it was a trip down to the mall. I passed a sign that said a correctional facility was nearby and you shouldn't pick up hitchhikers. I felt it was reasonable to expect them not to be able to escape in the first place. As I approached the mountain village of Ouray, my adrenaline started coursing at the sight of the San Juan Mountains. I was about to commence an assault on the Million Dollar Highway, a stretch of about 50 kilometres between Ouray and Silverton in the San Juans.

The opening burst is through the precipitous Uncompahgre Gorge to the summit of Red Mountain Pass. If steep cliffs, frequent slips, narrow lanes, no guardrails and ravines are your thing, then the Million Dollar Highway is a must. The more adventurous types drive the MDH north to south, which puts you on the outside lane looking over the drops. That's where I was, and it was fantastic. Had I taken my eyes off the road and oncoming campervans, it might not have been. From Silverton, the San Juan Scenic Byway just goes on and on. Molas Pass, Coal Bank Pass and Durango Mountain were summits that I ascended, crested and descended, all the time riding in scenery I had hitherto only seen in Switzerland and Austria. I was almost mountained-out.

In Durango, I had to get off the bike. Perhaps it was the constant high elevation and a touch of altitude sickness, I don't know. I just had this urge to sit down, put my head back and drift off somewhere. I scolded myself for being such a wimp, and wondered if the lethargy and listlessness were just hunger pangs. It was 2.00 p.m. and I hadn't eaten since 6.00 p.m. the night before, which of course was fried chicken in Fruita. I went into a little café and ordered a Koprek sandwich. Name the three fillings in a Koprek sandwich. You have until Cortez in two paragraphs' time to come up with the answer. Whatever was in it, the sandwich was spot-on and a burst of energy spurred me back on the bike.

Out of Durango, the landscape instantly opened out onto a vast plateau with buttes in the distance that told me I was nearing Utah. This was the Mesa Verde National Park, but it was more of a tablelands vista region than a park in the traditional sense.

I pulled into a gas station in Cortez. The pump I was parked at was Number 3, but the number wasn't obvious. I went inside and queued to prepay $15. The way you do that is to say — like a pump prepay pro — '$15 prepay on 3'. They take your money and say something like 'Good to go.' So I said '$15 prepay on whatever pump the bike's on', and pointed out the window. 'Good to go,' said the young attendant, but he planted my $15 on Pump 1 not 3. Meanwhile a car pulled up at Pump 1 and started fuelling while I was wondering why no fuel was gushing out of Pump 3. I went back inside and complained about the nil fuel on 3. 'But I just got a reading of $15 on 1,' said the guy. We looked out the window to see the car drive away with my $15 worth of petrol in his tank. There was a silent stand-off in the gas station. 'You put the prepay on the wrong pump,' I opened the proceedings with a jab to the heart. 'You said Pump 1,' parried the attendant. 'I said whatever pump the bike was on,' I blocked his punch. 'I'll have to get my supervisor,' he said, handing me a points victory for round one. The supervisor came and clipped the young boy around the ear, apologized to me, put $15 on Pump 3 and wished me a nice day. *Ding!* And the winner is Twisting Throttle, pump prepay pro. The attendant wasn't happy. 'Think you know everything,' he called as I was walking out. 'Bet you don't know what's in a Koprek sandwich.' 'Ham, egg and cheese,' I called back with a wink. I believe you're also out for the count?

A sign told me I was entering the Ute Mountain Ute Indian Reservation. The border between the Ute Reservation and Navajo Nation is at a spot called Four Corners. This is also where Colorado, Arizona, New Mexico and Utah collide, the only quadripoint in the US. So, overall, this pinprick in the desert was worth getting to. The Four Corners Monument is off Route 160 towards, eventually, the Grand Canyon in Arizona.

It's the Navajo who administer Four Corners, and a Navajo lady relieved me of $3 to get through the gate, which I thought highly worthwhile. There is a concrete platform with an 'x' in the middle, signifying the actual dot where the four states intersect. The tourist photo is you straddling the 'x' or — if you are a tourist-photo pro like me — you go down on all fours as if you're playing Twister, so you've got a limb in each state. When you're a solo traveller and have to set up a tripod and wait 12 seconds for the shutter to click, it rams home the lonely nature of your chosen method of travel, especially when you're down on all fours with other people watching sympathetically. There were the usual collection of Indian stalls ringing the monument, selling Four Corners T-shirts, jars of dirt, and authentic Navajo carvings. I refuse to trivialize the spirit and history of a proud indigenous nation by fostering this sad commercialism at a sacred site. To register my silent protest, I limited my purchases to a mere six fridge magnets (that's one for each state, one for the monument and a neat one with a stylized Navajo lizard motif).

Chapter 37

Utah

Nickname: The Beehive State

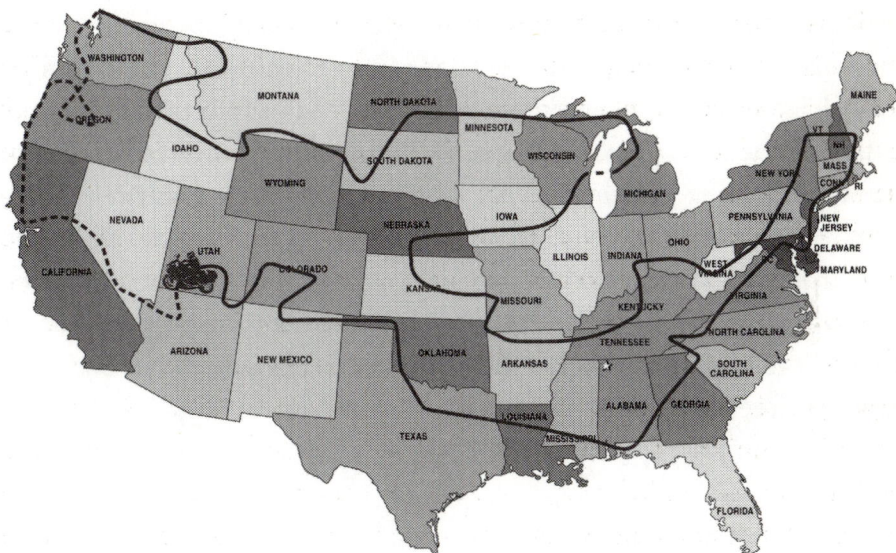

This state: 915 kilometres. Journey to date: 26,731 kilometres.

I COULD HAVE BEEN in Western Australia. The arrow-straight highway from Four Corners to Kayenta was deserted and, well, straight as an arrow. Desert stretched to the horizon on both sides of the road, the flatness broken only by distant red buttes sticking up like grasping fingers. Officially, I passed through Teec Nos Pos, Mexican Water, Tes Nez Iah and Dennehotso, but I can't remember them because they weren't there. My GPS had them on Route 160, but all I saw was a cluster of ramshackle huts off the road that must have been those communities. This was Apache County in Arizona, and I was nicking the corner of it to get to Monument Valley and the scenic overload that Utah promised to deliver.

Monument Valley is that familiar chocolate-box-lid vista of brick-red rock formations and buttes. It's part of the massive Navajo Tribal Park, but you don't have to pay a toll to drive through it. First, I had to pitch up in the small town of Kayenta, a dusty settlement at the junction of the 163 and 160. With no obvious campground, I rode past the Best Western and Holiday Inn searching for a cheap B&B.

A rickety house had a sign outside: *Roland's Navajo Tours B&B*. It had the look of a $30-a-night accommodation, so I went in. A Navajo Indian man answered the door. I took him to be Roland. 'Can I help you?' 'Just seeing if you've got any single rooms.' 'No, we're full, but you can sleep in the tepee for $100.' I looked over to his front lawn that was all sand and tussock and saw two large white tepees. '$100? That's a little off my budget radar.' By the fence was a yellow school bus painted with a sign: *Roland's Navajoland Tours Monument Valley*. 'What about I pitch my tent by the bus?' 'No problem', and with that he disappeared back inside, closing the door in my face. I stood there wondering if he was going to come back with a Visa machine to charge me whatever his camping fee was. But he didn't return, so I wheeled the bike over to the school bus and set up camp for free.

The trick with Monument Valley is getting the time of day right so the sun shines on the buttes. I'd spent a lot of time figuring this out the previous day, and by my calculations I needed to be on the road at 6.00 a.m. just as the sunrise was illuminating the desert. I also had the aid of an extra navigational technique: two German couples in campervans.

As I was fuelling up in Kayenta, I overheard the conversation.

Campervan couple 1 (whispering):	Sieh diesen Motorradfahrer dort. Wir müssen ihn nach Monument Valley schlagen.
Translation:	*See that biker there? We must get to Monument Valley before him.*
Campervan couple 2 (looking at me):	Ja, stimmen wir zu. Wir wollen diesen kerl nicht, der unsere Fotographien das zerstört, im weg seiend.
Translation:	*Ja, that's right. We don't want him getting in the way and ruining our photos.*

Campervan couple 1 (sniggering):   Er reitet einen Suzuki. Welches
                                      stück der piece of Scheiße. Wir werden ihn
                                      leicht schlagen.

Translation: *Oh look, he is riding a Suzuki. What a piece of
                                      Scheiße. We'll easily beat him.*

And so tourist wars commenced. Unfortunately for the German couples, I understood every word they said, from years of watching *Hogan's Heroes* as a kid. The race was on to get to the pull-over place in Monument Valley where the famous photo vista was. To give them their dues they drove off like madmen, and, by the time I had finished fuelling, the campervans were specks on the distant highway. I raced out onto Route 163 on my piece of *Scheiße* and soon had them in my sights. We crossed into Utah at well over the speed limit.

The trouble was there were stunning photo opportunities the moment Monument Valley started. Should I ignore my tourist rivals, stop to take lots of photos, and queue up behind them at the vista point? I kicked the bike into sixth gear and overtook them. That'll be the day Das Twisten Throttleisch yields to mobile homes. As the vista point came into view at the far end of a long straight, I looked in my mirrors to see the first campervan pull out to overtake me. I was staggered. I had no idea those things could go that fast. He lumbered past me as if I was standing still. I looked over and the woman passenger's knuckles were white. She was shouting something at her husband, which probably included the words *zu schnell*, *Dummkopf* and *Scheiße*. I slowed right down and the second camper roared past.

The vista point was a gravelled lay-by that was perhaps 50 metres long. The vans, braking hard, had ended up at the far end of it, and by the time I reached the pull-over they had their tripods out and were setting up the famous shot looking back down the highway over Monument Valley. I slewed to a halt at the start of the lay-by, kicked the side stand down, and immediately ruined their photo by placing myself in the foreground. I *scheiße* you not. They had no option but to wait for me to mess about taking my shot and leave. There is an unwritten rule among tourists that you form an orderly queue to take photos and don't place yourself in the foreground of someone else's shot. A bit like hitchhikers positioning themselves at the far end of a line-up on the roadside. But the gloves were off in Monument Valley and it was photo wars.

I rode off from the lay-by, past the fretting campervan couples, without a sideways glance. With spectacular photos, a boosted ego, and a day of desert riding ahead, this was no time to provoke international hostility. Anyway I couldn't hang around. I needed to beat them to the Mokee Dugway.

The Dugway is a tortuous gravel road which claws its way up the vertical escarpment of the Cedar Mesa, some 1,100 feet in 5 kilometres of twisting switchbacks. Signs leading up to the Dugway warn of the risks. There are no guardrails, and this is a track you want to keep your eyes on at all times, especially if you're descending and gazing out at the stupendous views over the Valley of the Gods. It was outstanding. I got to the top, pulled over and looked out over the Utah desert. It took my breath away. I could see the two campervans as dots on the horizon, making their way towards the bottom of the Mokee Dugway. I felt for the women passengers. After the driving choices exercised by their mad husbands, the brothers Schumacher, their next year's holiday is undoubtedly going to be lying by a pool in Greece.

The sun was high in the deep blue sky as I rode, a lone vehicle on an empty highway, across the Red Rock plateau. There were red, dusty tracks leading off into the desert and up into the escarpments to who knows where. I couldn't believe anyone would actually live out there, but possibly there was some mining around. There were colourful yellow wildflowers dotted in among the sagebrush, and I saw birds wheeling high above the cliff tops on thermals. Eagles perhaps, but it suited my mood better to think of them as condors. I reached the junction of Highway 95 and a minor road signposted to Lake Powell.

Decision time: introduce an element of the unknown into my trip or play it safe? To stay on the 95 and loop around to Boulder via Hanksville and Torrey, a safe, tar-sealed route with gas, places to eat, and campervans? Or head off to Lake Powell in Glen Canyon, take the hourly car ferry from Halls Crossing to Bullfrog, and tackle a gravel road called the Burr Trail, cutting through Capitol Reef National Park to Boulder? The latter option involved unknown fuel availability, unknown road conditions, unknown weather, and I assumed you didn't call it a trail if it wasn't a little demanding. No contest. I had to beat the Germans to Boulder. The Burr Trail it was.

Lake Powell was a blue gash in a red-and-brown landscape. I rode onto the small car ferry, paid my $10 and enjoyed the half-hour crossing to Bullfrog on the other side. This was Glen Canyon, the lesser-known younger-sister canyon to big brother Bryce and, further away, the mother of all canyons, Grand. The Burr Trail presented me with my first sobering obstacle only 10 kilometres in. A dry creek bed was a foot deep in soft sand. I wobbled my way across, with both feet on the ground, slightly anxious that this might be the standard of the road all the way through Capitol Reef.

My fuel was under half a tank, and thunderous black clouds scudded over the cliff tops to obliterate the blue sky in minutes. The first drops of rain spattered my visor as I rode in second gear across washboard ruts in this gravel road. I thought of my riding pals back home, the Dust Devils, and how this trail would have been heaven on their KTMs and BMW GSs. On a road bike, I was making hard work of it. The rain stopped as suddenly as it had started. The track narrowed and I struck more sand. My mind turned to fuel, but I had complete reliance on my GPS that counted down the kilometres to Boulder. The Burr Trail wound up an escarpment in a series of narrow switchbacks and popped me out on a plateau in the shadow of the Circle Cliffs. Utter solitude. A pterodactyl soaring high above the cliffs would not have turned my head. My GPS claimed I had just passed through Eggnog. The only sign of habitation was a rusting wagon-wheel in the sagebrush.

This whole area is referred to as Grand Staircase Escalante National Monument, being 7,500 square kilometres of land in southern Utah full of canyons, cliffs, desert and plateaux, a region bigger than Delaware. I started to get some idea of what the early pioneers felt like when they pushed on through this vast, somewhat bleak landscape. But they had it easy. They didn't have to worry about fuel and where there might be fried chicken for tea.

I finally got back onto tar-seal and reached the town of Boulder. Unleaded fuel gushed into my parched tank at the rate of $4.58 a gallon, the most expensive yet in the US. But I didn't care. It was a wonderful feeling to be topped up. I treated myself to a pack of 12 doughnuts. They tasted like cardboard and I gave up after the sixth. I reached the town of Escalante spent and exhilarated. It was a short-distance day at only 400 kilometres, but I felt like I had crossed the Gobi. My last thought as I sunk into a deep sleep in a cheap motel was whether my German rivals had made it to the top of the Mokee Dugway.

The next day was to be Zion National Park day. This was going to be a big one. Zion is a national park among national parks. A bit like Yosemite. I was on the road nice and early, making for Cedar City to join the I-15 for a loop around to the start of Zion. At Long Valley Junction, I turned right and wound my way up on to the Markagunt Plateau. Shortly before Cedar City, I saw a signpost to Kolob Terrace Road that pointed down a narrow, paved road winding up into the hills above Cedar. It looked enticing. I consulted the GPS and we agreed to give it a go. Some people never learn.

The GPS assured me that Kolob Road would be a shortcut to Zion, bringing me out at Virgin, just a heartbeat away from Rockville, the gateway to Zion. Just like Burr Trail, Kolob turned into a fairly taxing gravel and rutted track, taking me miles into an empty landscape. I reached a junction where the gravel road simply forked. There were no signposts, nor any indication which fork was the Kolob Road continuation. I got off the bike and considered my options. The two gravel tracks heading off in opposite directions were identical. It was simply a 50:50 decision. The GPS didn't register the existence of a fork and refused to participate. In the end I just picked the fork going downhill, rationalizing it would be easier to turn around at the bottom. It was the right way. I reached Virgin vowing to stay off these back-country tracks in future.

Zion National Park simply overloaded my senses. The smooth, heavily-trafficked road wound through Zion's red plunging cliffs and ravines. As I waited in a line of cars for the tunnel to open, high above on the sheer rock face were two specks, climbers who would probably be camping the night up there, dangling on their ropes like glow worms on a thread. Dusk was approaching as I reached Carmel Junction, but I wanted to make the North Rim of the Grand Canyon by nightfall.

As I thundered down the open Highway 89 towards Kanab and the Arizona state line, insects bouncing off my windscreen and visor in the usual evening rictus of death, I mentally rated Utah the state I'd most like to return to in the future, even surpassing New Mexico. Next time, knowing what I know now, I'd bring a KTM Adventure bike, someone else, a satellite phone and my own doughnuts. *Donuten in Utah sind Scheiße, ja?*

Chapter 38

Arizona

Nickname: The Grand Canyon State

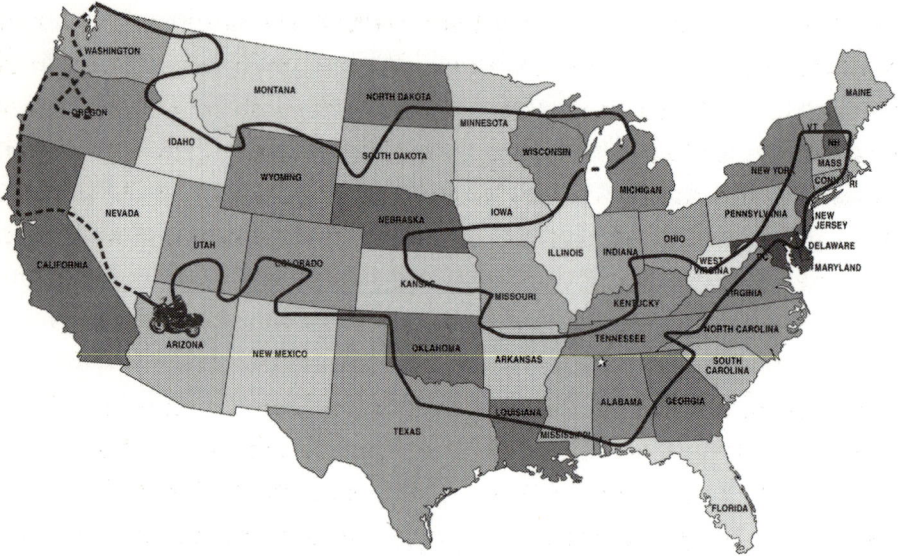

This state: 893 kilometres. Journey to date: 27,624 kilometres.

I STOOD ON THE LIP of the Grand Canyon gazing out over an abyss that was a mile deep. This was the North Rim. As the crow flies, the South Rim was a mere 17 kilometres over the other side, but to ride around there was going to take the best part of a day. That's about the time it also takes extreme rim-to-rim hikers — but let me refer to them by their technical name: nutters — to walk from the North Rim, down into the canyon, across the canyon floor and up the other side. Most normal walkers do it over three days.

While I was perched on the lookout wondering if anyone was down there, Bill Kathan was. Who, you ask? Mr Kathan, 56 years old from Vermont, decided to try for the world record rim-to-rim hike, except that he made it a fraction tough for himself by doing it walking backwards. I found out the next day that he'd made it. He reported to the local paper,

The Grand Canyon News, that it was a bit tricky, and the hardest part was keeping his head swivelled so he could see where he was going, a definite advantage when descending a narrow, rutted and loose-stoned track with precarious drop-offs into the canyon. But Mr Kathan was no novice. The previous year, he'd walked across America at the same time as driving his own support van. Here's how he did it. He would drive his van 5 kilometres along the road and park it. He would walk forwards 5 kilometres, then walk backwards 5 kilometres to his van. He would then drive 5 kilometres and do it again. In this fashion he crossed from Connecticut to Oregon. But in reality he crossed America three times in total within the same trip. Once backwards, once forwards, and once driving his van. I'll bet his daughter just can't wait for him to walk her up the aisle at her wedding.

The road to the North Rim is mirror-smooth, and I enjoyed riding it the second time as I headed back to rejoin Highway 89. The loop to get around to the South Rim means crossing the Colorado River over the Navajo Bridge at Marble Canyon. The ride was simply stunning. I slowly roasted in my helmet as the day heated up. To add to the magic of such a brilliant day I was riding with a companion, Marque 'Thumper' Nelson, a leather-clad criminal and forensic investigator from Eden Prairie, Minnesota, who had shared his campsite with me the night before at North Rim. Thumper was so-called because he was on a Harley with a side-car. We thumped past the Vermillion Cliffs, an outstanding rock formation, but the jewel in the desert crown is looking over the side of the Navajo Bridge down to the emerald-green waters of the Colorado River. Apart from a bridge at Page in Glen Canyon, the Navajo Bridge is the only roadway crossing of the Colorado and the Grand Canyon for 1,000 kilometres.

At Cameron I was faced with the agonizing decision whether to ride west to the South Rim of the Grand Canyon or continue south to Flagstaff, the direction in which Thumper was heading, and pop over to see Meteor Crater. As I was fussing about with my map book in the car park of a restaurant, a well-dressed Navajo Indian-looking man walked up.

'Hey, man, I just ran out of gas. Can you help me with a dollar?' 'Where's your car, then?' I decided to play the game. 'Over there somewhere. I got a wife and little girl in the car. Be good to get them home.' 'What good's a dollar's worth of gas going to do you?' 'Just a dollar, friend. That's all I'm asking.' 'OK. Here's $2. I'm giving it to you on the condition that you leave your wife and daughter to their own devices in your stranded car, and you take this money to buy alcohol. Deal?' All right, maybe I didn't quite say that, but I gave him two bucks for the simple reason he looked my age and simply appeared to be poor. He took the two notes and wandered off without a word of thanks. Our worlds were poles apart.

I decided to make for the South Rim, but it was a hard choice and I was enjoying riding with Thumper on his thumper. Meteor Crater was one of those places I'd have loved to visit for the sheer magnitude of what happened. Listen to this. Sometime in the Pleistocene epoch — that's before you and I were born: 50,000 years ago to be precise — a 50-metre-wide meteor hit Arizona at 46,000 km/h. The open grasslands at the time were inhabited by woolly mammoths, giant ground sloths, and camels. If you were a prehistoric animal grazing on some bushes, you suddenly heard a whooshing noise from the sky, looked up and saw a meteorite heading towards you fast, and you only had seconds to get out of the way, you probably wouldn't want to be a sloth. The resulting crater is massive and is a popular tourist attraction. Apparently a couple of guys in a Cessna decided to fly into the crater for a closer look. The downdrafts inside meant they couldn't climb out, and they simply had no choice but to circle and wait for their fuel to run out. The remains of the crashed plane are still on the floor of the crater.

The camping ground at Grand Canyon Village at South Rim was spread throughout the forest, making for a perfect site. The big tourist thing to do is watch the sun set over the Grand Canyon. It was a clear sky and the sunset promised to be a beauty. I rode to the rim lookout and into a circus. Security men in fluoro vests were there directing the zoo of cars, campervans, pedestrians and tour buses. Most people flocked to viewing points facing the west where the sun was setting. I scoffed at their naïveté and headed in the opposite direction. You wouldn't look directly into the setting sun. Canyon-watching pros, like myself, knew that you faced the east where the effects of the setting sun behind you would be the most splendorous.

And here is the odd thing about the Grand Canyon viewing areas. I was struck by the sheer lack of safety. There were no fences or guardrails. You could walk out onto a finger of rock overhanging the abyss and just lean over. A misplaced step, a lean too far, backing up to get everyone in the group photo, larking about for the camera or just looking the wrong way . . . well, your fading screams would be heard for many seconds until a distant thump and silence. I hate to dwell on this, but it intrigued me that even though there was such an obvious risk of falling off the edge there seems to be quite a low death rate since records began in the 1870s. Apparently, there have been 50 accidental falls, 47 suicides and 23 murders involving the canyon edge and oblivion. Wandering about waiting for the sun to pop below the horizon, I couldn't help thinking this would be the ultimate way of dispensing with your loved one on whose life you have just taken out an insurance policy. People were swarming like ants all over the rocky outcrops, posing for sunset photos, setting up tripods, and entwining romantically, watching the changing hues of the canyon as darkness slowly enveloped the chasm. By the time the crowds filtered away back to their hotels, it was dark. A quick push and no one would have seen you. It was almost the perfect murder.

I followed the hordes back to Canyon Village. The restaurant had wireless and Navajo tacos. Let me try to describe this dish. Take a large-size dinner plate. Imagine the plate is covered with a sweet, doughy base like a pizza. This is Navajo fry bread. Pile on the bread base ground beef, chilli, refried beans, shredded lettuce, corn, grated cheese and sliced tomatoes. Slap on some sort of guacamole-type relish and tuck in. You will never finish it. I hadn't eaten all day, and had the hunger of a man who had just pushed his loved one over the edge. The Navajo taco was outstanding.

I lay in my tent willing sleep to come, but keeping one ear tuned for some snuffling noises I'd heard earlier on. I had pitched camp some distance away from the road for security, but right outside in the dark was something that was taking an interest in my bike. I'd built up to this moment all trip, and reached for my personal weapon: a spark-plug wrench I kept under my stretcher. I exited the tent quickly and almost head-butted an elk. It was a female. I knew this as I am an elk pro, and I noted it didn't have antlers. The elk was nosing around the plastic bag that contained the uneaten Navajo taco. I had hung the bag on my handlebars following the rule that you don't keep food in your tent. The elk bolted, but it was too late for the taco.

★★★

I rode away from Grand Canyon the next morning, feeling a bit canyoned-out after the past few days. I fretted about losing my breakfast to the elk, but knew payback would be mine at lunchtime, as I was heading for Seligman, on Route 66, and the Road Kill Café. I would order anything they had so long as it was elk. I reached the Mother Road just out of Seligman after a long, hot blast down interstate I-40 from Williams.

To a motorcyclist there is something pilgrimish about riding along part of Route 66. It was established in 1926, running 4,000 kilometres from Chicago to Los Angeles. When the interstate system got up and running, US Route 66 was removed from the highway system. But those communities who enjoyed the popularity of travellers driving Route 66, and who worried that their towns would suffer from the interstate bypassing them, fostered the new Historic Route 66, linking portions of the old road, and it's now a National Scenic Byway.

Seligman is one of those towns. It has nothing going for it except all its Route 66 memorabilia. I rode up the main street of Seligman, population 500, and stopped outside the Rusty Bolt and Thunderbird Indian Store. The owner came out and started to say hello. At that moment a tour bus double-parked and out poured a horde of, I think, Dutch tourists. The owner, probably Rusty Bolt himself, left me in mid-sentence and walked quickly over to the milling crowd. It disappointed me that the Main Street of America was reduced to this. I was there because of a spirit, a passion and an awakening of a bond between rider and road. The Dutch tourists were just ticking off another sightseeing stop. I resolved not to participate in this obscene tourist industry and limited my Route 66 souvenir purchases in Mr Bolt's store to simply a key-ring, a mug, two types of fridge magnet, a model Edsel which played 'Get Your Kicks' when you pressed its bonnet, a Harley Davidson jacket badge, a shot-glass for my brother back home, a cap for Johnny the hairdresser, and an *Easy Rider* DVD. That'll be the day Twisting Throttle succumbs to the crass commercialization of a motoring icon.

Too Slow Doe. Centre Line Bovine. Rack of Raccoon. No Luck Buck. Highway Hash. The Chicken That Almost Crossed The Road. Tyre Tread Teriyaki. Rigor Mortis Tortoise. Hard Luck Duck. Long Gone Fawn. And my personal favourite: Mystery Meat, Could Be Beaks Could Be Feet. The menu in the Seligman Road Kill Café was to die for. Their motto — 'You kill it, we grill it' — told the story. It wasn't a place for vegetarians, and I was in culinary Heaven. Still smarting from the previous night's encounter, I ordered the Elk Melt and a root beer. Delicious.

But I couldn't hang around on Route 66 any longer, as I had some miles to do before sundown. And those miles would see me do a long, hot, fast sprint west on the I-40 to Kingman, turning north to the Hoover Dam, the state line with Nevada, and into Las Vegas. I couldn't wait to get there. My beautiful 19-year-old daughter, Sophie, was living there for three months, and I knew it was my duty to protect her from the ills of gambling in Sin City. I hadn't seen her in two months and we would have a lot to catch up on. Besides, I'd bought her a Route 66 inflatable petrol pump. Wouldn't she be surprised.

Chapter 39

Nevada

Nickname: The Silver State

This state: 1,357 kilometres. Journey to date: 28,981 kilometres.

L AS VEGAS, IF YOU ARE AN ASTRONAUT in orbit, is the brightest city on earth. I could believe it, driving down the Strip at night. I had a well-earned day's break lined up in Vegas with Sophie and her fiancé, Brice. He's a super heavyweight boxer on the Vegas fight circuit. Given the arm-wrestling skills I'd exhibited in Ohio I could have taken him on, but I still called him 'Sir'. Sophie, together with my wife, Sandy, would be flying back to New Zealand with me after the bike trip, with us all rendezvousing in San Francisco for a week's holiday. I was on notice from the pair: said holiday would not involve the words 'motorbike', 'Denny's' or 'tent'.

I put myself in Sophie's hands and wondered how many casinos it would be possible to visit in a day. I suggested it would add a twist to my 50-states-in-60-days journey if I could do 50-casinos-in-6-hours. 'Some questions, Dad,' she said. 'What have you got to wear? How much can you afford to lose? Haven't you got a razor?' I took her point with humility, and instead we spent the day on the bike riding to Pahrump and back via Indian Springs. We had lunch at Terribles Casino in Pahrump. Lunch cost $95. All right, if you want a breakdown: it was $15 for the actual food, and the rest was, well, collateral expenditure that the casino extracted. And here's a tip for nothing. If you're ever holidaying in Pahrump, Nevada, and you pop into Terribles, go to the Cleopatra's Treasure machine three down from the bar. Try for three camels in a row and send me $80 from your winnings, I beg you. I have a loan to repay to my daughter.

The next day was Death Valley day, and I knew I'd miscalculated my timings from the moment I left Vegas after farewelling Sophie and Brice. Here's the thing. Death Valley in the middle of summer is quite a hot place. In fact, it is the lowest, hottest, driest place in America. In 1913, the hottest temperature ever recorded in the Western Hemisphere was at Furnace Creek. It was 56°C. I was going to be in Furnace Creek for lunch, the hottest part of the day. The best time for motorcycling through Death Valley is early in the morning or in the relative cool of the evening. I turned off the main road towards Tecopa and Shoshone. As my speed decreased on the narrower side road, the temperature seemed to double, and I wasn't even near the Valley. I fuelled up in Shoshone, eager to make sure that petrol worries wouldn't add to my anxiety burden. I bought three bottles of cold water and felt like Lawrence of Arabia.

To describe the Death Valley landscape as 'bleak' is like saying the Antarctic is white. I crossed the Armagosa Range at Jubilee Pass, and immediately started the long, winding descent into Death Valley. I set my GPS to show the rapidly decreasing elevation, and it passed sea level as I was still riding downhill. The road bottomed out at the valley floor. In front of me was a bleached vista of what Hell might look like if you were a green-fields pretty-meadows type of person. It was like riding into the full force of a hair dryer.

I reached the lookout at Badwater, officially the lowest place in the US at minus 85.5 metres below sea level. I took off my helmet. The pads inside were wringing, and my hair was as if I'd just emerged from a swimming pool. I had no idea I could sweat so much. Without pausing for breath, I downed two of my three water bottles. The salt flats stretched to the far mountains.

As I messed about with my camera, a couple sat watching me from within their mobile home parked a few yards away. I heard the clink of chilled glasses and just knew they were sipping cool Chardonnays. I prayed it wasn't cold beer they were drinking, because then I'd have to kill them on the spot. The side door was open and I knew what was coming. Sure enough. 'Bit hot to be on a bike,' he called out. 'Sure is,' I looked up and invited myself over to their vehicle. I stood at the open door looking up into their palatial mobile home. They were in the middle of a light lunch. A Greek salad if I wasn't mistaken, accompanied by fresh rolls and a dry, crisp, chilled wine. A Sauvignon Blanc by the look, possibly a '97 Dry Creek from Sonoma, deft and sleek, racy and exuberant, a cheeky yet herbaceously-assertive blend that is eager to please. On the other hand, it may have been another mirage. All I got, though, was: 'You want to watch you don't dehydrate out there. It's 44°. Have a good ride. Bye for now.' And the door closed.

Within five minutes of riding off, I could feel the rivulets of sweat cascading down my chest and back. The dehydration comment festered a little, and I checked the GPS: Furnace Creek seemed close enough, so I put the whole survival thing to one side. I passed the Devil's Golf Course and turned into Furnace Creek Visitor Centre after a long, stiflingly hot 15 minutes. I bought another three water bottles and a tray of ice-cold watermelon. My accommodation budget was blown for the night, but I was living for the moment.

But here's why I feel like an old granny just talking about my trials in Death Valley. Every July the 'world's toughest foot race' is held here. The course starts at Badwater at 85.5 metres below sea level and ends 217 kilometres later at Whitney Portal at 2,500 metres. The Portal is the trailhead where you start to climb Mt Whitney, the highest summit in the contiguous US. Some ultra-runners, after finishing the Badwater marathon, run up to the 4,400-metre summit and back. This race is not for your average keep-fit sort of marathon runner. About a third of all starters do not finish. In 1994, an ultra-runner named Scott Weber ran, walked and staggered from Mt Whitney summit to Badwater, back to the summit and then back to Badwater. He did the first leg pushing a 'baby jogger' cart he'd brought from home, to keep his supplies, such as water, blister cream and Sauvignon Blanc in.

★★★

The temperature showing at Furnace Creek was 46°C. I rode out onto Route 190 back into the hair dryer. The landscape was sheer desolation, though in winter it can get very colourful with wildflowers. But here in the middle of the day in the middle of summer it was parched and colourless. I pulled over after 10 minutes and finished two bottles of water in a single session. I realized I was over Death Valley, and resolved to just get some altitude and relief from the furnace. I found a side road that looked like it headed up into the Armagosas. I reached the summit of Daylight Pass at 1,300 metres and breathed in lungfuls of cool air. Looking down at the shimmering, bleached valley far below, I saw the mobile home I'd met in Badwater, a speck on the distant highway, crawling slowly up Daylight Pass.

I turned up a gravel road signposted to Rhyolite ghost town, a collection of derelict houses and a railway station. Fifty kilometres north of Beatty, I passed the Shady Lady Ranch. On their driveway sign they'd added *A Gem in the High Desert*, which seemed odd. As I approached, a big rig turned down the driveway. I now know what Shady Lady is, and it isn't a house of repute. Their website is advertising free $50 fuel vouchers with every $300 spent. It costs $2,000 to stay there overnight. Unlike Roland's Navajo B&B back in Utah, I doubt if I could have pitched my tent on their lawn for free.

★★★

After a long, tedious drag across the desert skirting Nellis Air Force Range Complex, I arrived in Tonopah. I was strangely exhausted, probably due to the energy expended negotiating Death Valley. I saw a sign — *Motel*

Rooms From $27.95 — and almost cried with delight. To set up camp would have been beyond my abilities right then.

I parked the bike and walked into the office. A grey-haired lady came out of a side room at the sound of the opening door. 'Hi, you've got rooms advertised for $27.95?' *'From $27.95,'* she parried. 'I'll take one at the $27.95 end of the range then.' 'Got a single at $39.95. You want it?' Of course I wanted it, but I was a motel-room-negotiating pro and had work to do. 'What's a $27.95 room got less of than a $39.95 room?' 'You got no heating.' It was still over 30° outside. 'I'll take it then.' 'Take what?' 'The $27.95 room with no heating.' 'You want a bed?' 'That'd be good.' 'Then you got to take the $39.95 room. You want it or not?' She wore me down and I handed over $40 cash. 'I got no change in the office.' 'Put it towards the furniture account then,' I thought but was too frightened to say out loud. 'Here's your key and TV remote. Room 3. My rules are simple for bikers. No using towels as rags. Coffee's on in the office from 5.30 a.m., not before. If you check out early, place your key in this basket with your TV remote. And we ask that you don't park your bike in your room. Last week we had a biker who changed his oil inside.'

The motel room was in fact excellent. But I didn't hang around. I had more riding to do, and I headed back out of Tonopah towards Highway 375, also known as The Extraterrestrial Highway. This stretch of 150 kilometres or so between Warm Springs and Crystal Springs is shrouded in conspiracy theories, for it's the home of Area 51. The highway has also recorded an abnormally high number of UFO sightings. I couldn't wait to ride some of it. Towards the southern end of the 375 is a gravel road that heads off west into the vast Nellis air-force testing range. There is a dried-up lake called Groom Lake, and Area 51 is a base that is out in this wilderness but has its own runway.

It is here that J-Rod works. J-Rod is the alien that was captured alive at Roswell when the UFO crashed back in 1947. Since then, he's been working for the US government as a Team Leader at Area 51. J-Rod, or 'Jay' as his workmates call him, is an Extraterrestrial Biological Entity or EBE. Aliens like him are also referred to as Ebens. J-Rod is a diminutive grey and pale humanoid with large, black, shiny eyes, four fingers on each hand and no thumbs. There have been two other previous Ebens, but only J-Rod has survived. Not only that, he's worked his way up the corporate ladder at Area 51 and now manages over 30 scientists and staff in his top-secret lab. If you don't believe me, search the internet. It's never wrong.

There's no way you can get close to Area 51 other than look down the gravel road into the desert. The only other way is to watch a re-run of *Independence Day*, which proves the existence of live aliens once and for all. But as I rode back towards Tonopah after a 20-kilometre stretch of the Extraterrestrial Highway, continually looking up into the sky, digital camera at the ready strapped to my handlebars, I saw no UFO action. I am now a complete cynic about this sort of stuff, and as a mild form of protest at the whole UFO tourist beat-up I'm putting a picture in my book here of the very empty Extraterrestrial Highway.

The next morning, I continued my northern trek towards Lake Tahoe and Reno. Highway 95 was as straight as a die as it crossed the plateaux of western Nevada. I reached the town of Hawthorne and saw a diner called Maggie's that advertised 'free Wi-Fi'. I went in, sat down and ordered the pancake sandwich special. I switched on my laptop, but it didn't find a wireless signal. When the waitress topped up my coffee, I asked her about the lack of wireless. She said some tables were 'dead spots' and that she'd ask the chef. After a while she returned, saying I should connect to the 'linking system'. There was a Linksys network, password protected, but it wasn't connecting. 'Do you think you could reboot your router?' I asked, knowing what the answer would be. Sure enough. 'I better talk to the chef.' She came back. 'The chef says he doesn't know anything about no rat.' Customers at the next table pricked up their ears at the mention of the words 'chef' and 'rat' in the same sentence. It was time to cut my losses. The breakfast came to $9.27 and I left $10. She did try for me.

My last fling in Nevada was a detour into the hills after Silver City for some long-forgotten twisty-road riding. In Virginia City, I walked up and down the wooden boardwalks under verandas in this replica Wild

West town. The road out of Virginia City was a beauty as it wound its way down into Reno.

I was staying the night with Ken and Cynthia Kress in Sparks. Ken is a member of the Nevada Dust Devils, a sister club of the New Zealand Dust Devils, a motley bunch of adventure-bike riders back home. Fellow Nevadan Dust Devils Jeff, Dean and Scott came around to Ken's place and tried to teach me how to drink beer. They were a great mob of guys, and it occurred to me how out of practice I'd got in simply holding a conversation with anyone other than gas station attendants, diner waitresses and my imaginary pillion, Dave.

The next day was California and the Pacific Ocean. Dust Devil Scott Sibbald was going to ride with me as far as San Francisco. I should have been getting an early night. But Ken had stocked up with cold cans of beer and I was nearing the end of my trip. The re-familiarization back into mainstream society needed to commence — and the time was now.

Chapter 40

California

Nickname: The Golden State

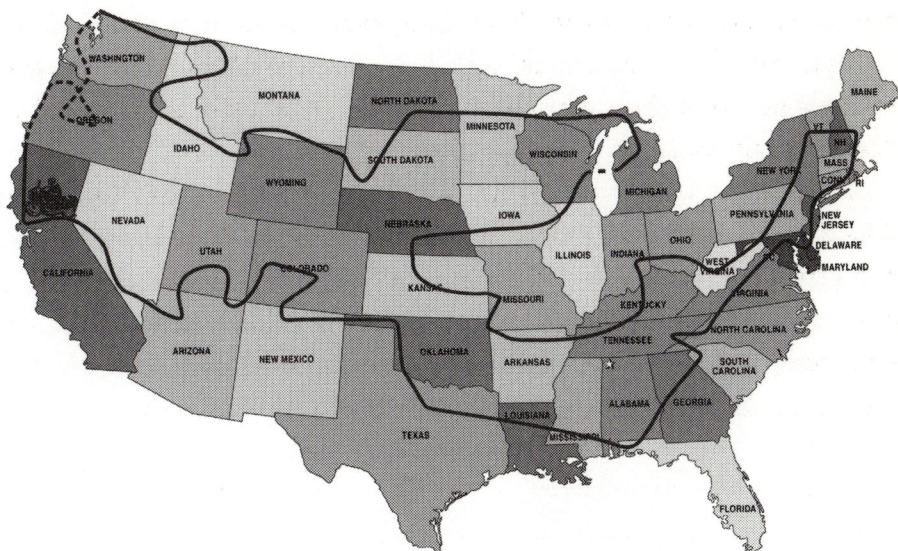

This state: 1,052 kilometres. Journey to date: 30,033 kilometres.

I'M NOT SURE how it happened, but coasting down the endless twisting descent of Mt Rose overlooking Lake Tahoe I had the sudden realization: I was on the home straight. There was something symbolic about crossing into California from Nevada. I suppose it was because California was on the Pacific and that was my last side of America reached. Never mind, I would still have 3,500 kilometres and three states to go.

Scott, who was on a KTM Adventure, needed no excuse to saddle up for a blat. At San Francisco, I would turn right for northern California and he would go left to visit relatives in Half Moon Bay. Most of our ride would be screaming along the I-50 interstate that started in Placerville, bisected Sacramento, and delivered us 150 kilometres later in Berkeley. The opening salvo was a stunningly beautiful ride along the western shore of Lake Tahoe. We must have passed over a thousand bikes coming the other way. There was a major bike rally on in Reno called the Silver Run, and it seemed as if half of California's Harleys were on their way over to it. But here's the interesting thing. California has a compulsory helmet law; Nevada doesn't. On the Nevada side of the state line, hardly any riders wore helmets; on the California side, they all had to. Therefore, I can only assume that everyone heading for Reno stopped on the state line, removed their helmet, fastened it to their luggage and took off. It seemed a bit like taking off your seatbelt in a car because you were suddenly allowed to.

At Kyburz, we started the long, slow downhill wend from the Sierra Nevada to sea level. I'd no idea we'd been up that high. I could have switched off my engine and coasted for 50 kilometres. The build-up to Frisco started as the freeway widened to four lanes at Davis. Vacaville, Fairfield and Vallejo blurred into each other as we sat on the tarmac ribbon, weaving in and out between the 18-wheelers which were weaving in and out between slow-moving cars and pick-ups, which were just weaving.

Suddenly the I-80 dipped over the brow of a slight hill, and ahead of us was the shimmering San Pablo Bay, official first sighting of the Pacific. But by my own definition it wasn't, as you couldn't gaze out to the horizon; so it wasn't technically the ocean. However, the thought that the technical ocean was just around the headland did raise some hairs on the back of my neck. Also raising hairs was my blinking fuel-warning light. We nicked off the interstate at Richmond and topped up. The attendant in the gas station was enclosed in a steel cage, and I felt I should hand him a banana through the bars, not $20. I guess they know their market.

We exited the I-80 onto the I-580 and onto the toll bridge that spans San Francisco Bay, the Richmond–San Rafael Bridge. I spent the crossing sitting in the middle lane gazing across at a huge bank of thick, white fog blanketing San Francisco. There was no sign of the city skyline, and the tips of the Golden Gate Bridge pillars peeped above the shroud of sea fog. I could just make out Alcatraz. At Sausalito we careened off to a lookout point high on the hillside, looking over the Golden Gate back towards the city. The fog was rolling in like an express train.

As I gazed down at the vague shape of the bridge in the mist, my thoughts turned to suicide. It was Scott's company and— No wait, sorry mate, that wasn't it. The Golden Gate is the most popular place in the US to end it all. The deck is 75 metres above the water, which you hit after a fall of 4 seconds doing 138 km/h. If the impact doesn't do the job, then you have the backup of hypothermia in 8°C water, ruptured spleen followed by drowning, fierce currents that will wash you out to sea, and great white sharks who have been known to mill about under the bridge. One person leaps off every 15 days, but the figures are a bit vague as many people do it at night, in fog, with no witnesses, and bodies are never recovered. A plastic-covered anti-suicide net is being built, which will extend out 6 metres each side of the bridge. It's costing $50 million. Apparently the sharks are sending a strongly worded message of protest to the mayor.

We mounted up and rode north on US101. At Manzanita, we exited onto the famous Highway 1, not to be confused with the famous Highway 1, or US1, that runs up the east coast of the US from Florida to Maine. This is California Highway 1, referred to as Highway 1 or State Route 1. When I entered in Highway 1 on my GPS, it set a course for Key West in Florida. I decided to follow Scott, who decided to follow the signs. Scott was meant to peel off south over the Golden Gate, but the prospect of trying to keep up with me on the never-ending twisting road of Highway 1 was too tempting. We rode on. Finally, rounding a bend in Mt Tamalpais State Park, there was the technical ocean — sparkling, blue, and stretching all the way to Japan. It was a wonderful moment as I looked out over the Pacific. You build up these milestones in your mind as markers to be ticked off. I wondered how I would feel switching off the bike in Vancouver in three days' time.

Highway 1 ploughed northwards. At times the road tracked right on the seashore. At other times, it curved inland. Whoever designed the road had a thing for corners. Where the road could easily have gone in a direct line between two points, the road architect simply bent it around in a series of S-bends for no apparent reason.

At Tomales we made the strategic decision to get off Highway 1. It was taking too long to get anywhere with the constant low speed, tight bends and intermittent sea mist freezing our eyelashes.

Paralleling Highway 1 inland is US101, the faster alternative for getting north. The 101 is a bit Route 66-ish. It's the longest highway in California and was one of the 'originals' formed in 1926 as part of the US Route System. Highway pros are allowed to call US Highway just 'the 101', or if you are a long-distance highway pro it's just '101'. It stretches 2,500 kilometres from Los Angeles to Olympia in Washington. The portion of 101 that we were riding is also named The Redwood Highway, and why would become obvious the next day.

First, we had a rendezvous in a town called Ukiah with another motorcycling friend, Blane Howell, who'd decided to pick up escort duties in Oregon. He'd ridden down from his home in Salem, 850 kilometres away. What is it with these American bikers? Scott would have a 500-kilometre journey home from Ukiah to Sparks the next day. As we sat in a bar in Ukiah, drinking Bud and talking nothing but motorcycle travel, we all knew the unspoken bond that existed between us . . . all three of us had the badge of honour. We were highway pros. We could call it '101'.

The last we saw of Scott on his KTM was his receding tail light as he exited 101 onto Route 20 back to Nevada. Blane, on his BMW 1150RT, sat a good distance behind me as we rode north towards Oregon. This was redwood country, and the whole of this part of northern California is known as the Redwood Empire. I think the name 'sequoia' also means 'redwood', but I'll need to consult the infallible internet to check that out. Whatever, these trees are ramrod tall, have massive trunks, and I couldn't wait to get into the forests of the series of national parks that are strung out all the way up into Oregon.

You might be misunderstanding me, though. This is the author who dwelt on murders at the Grand Canyon, suicides at the Golden Gate Bridge, and UFOs at Area 51. What do you think . . . that I'm a Greenie fascinated by tall trees? I'm sorry, but no. It's what the redwoods presented to the travelling tourist that I was here for. Listen to these. Trees of Mystery. The Chandelier Drive-Thru Tree. The Big Tree Drive Thru, The Eternal Tree, Klamath Tour-Thru Tree, Step-Thru Stump, The Upside Down Root, The Immortal Tree, The Living Chimney Tree, the famous One Log House. It was going to be a long day.

If you're short on time, the one way to get your redwood fix over and done with is to — and I'm sorry about this — 'branch' off the 101 onto The Avenue of the Giants. This is a 50-kilometre road in the Humboldt Redwoods State Park which meanders through groves of mighty redwoods. It was fun. The redwoods were there long before the road, and the redwoods weren't moving. Therefore, the road had to be put in around the massive trees and simply winds its way around their trunks. We rode through stands of redwoods, and it was impossible to see their tops. They stood like sentinels right by the road. If you were gazing around not watching you'd just hit a tree at the next bend, because that's why the bend was there: to go around that tree you were now embedded in. Sunlight filtered through the canopy and created a stripy psychedelic effect on the roadway. We stopped at The Immortal Tree. It is 75 metres tall and 950 years old. It used to be 90 metres tall until a lightning strike topped it. The Chandelier Drive-Thru Tree was like a drive-through ATM. The trunk is so wide you can get a car through it. The top box on my bike was groaning with the weight of all the fridge magnets I was buying at these iconic tourist attractions. But the big one was still to come. And I refer to the Trees of Mystery at a place called Klamath, just near the state line with Oregon.

We pulled into the T of M car park, which was in a grove of redwoods. This is the sort of crass touristy place I love, making money out of basically nothing. Shroud the trees in self-appointed mystery, and use words like 'supernatural', 'not of this world' and 'tree-mendous', add a café, a gift shop, a Native American museum and a craft shop, toilets, and a giant statue of Paul Bunyan and — voilà — you can charge $14. I dug out my wallet.

You're meant to walk along the forest tracks — sorry, Kingdom of Trees Pathways — look up into the branches of the trees, and experience something unnatural and a bit 'out of body'. I felt I could have done that back home in my own garden. But the best feature was the 15-metre statue of Paul Bunyan leaning on his axe with his sidekick, Babe the Blue Ox. Apparently the year before Babe's head had fallen off, narrowly missing a visitor. A little boy, about six years old, stood gazing up at the statue. Out of Paul Bunyan's mouth came 'Hi there, little boy.' The young fella ran back to his mother a bit shocked. His mom said, 'What's up Toby?' Then the statue boomed down: 'Yeah, Toby, what's up? Come on, Toby, come back here. Don't you know I'm just a big ole friendly guy? Don't be scared.' And no matter where Toby and his mother went, the witty statue called out after them. It was brilliant. I scanned the car park for the operator. Presumably he had a microphone headset. I never did see him. Another mystery? As we went back to our bikes, the statue called out: 'Have a good ride, fellas.' We called back, 'Thanks, Paul.' 'Sure, fellas. No problem.'

We passed through yet another redwoods grove, called Del Norte Redwoods Park. Nestled in a clearing was a gift shop dedicated to Bigfoot. Much to Blane's amusement, I braked to a halt and climbed off. This was becoming a day of discovery and educational enlightenment. Bigfoot, also known as Sasquatch, is a big, hairy, human-like ape figure that surfaces every now and then when someone is short of money and attention. Two months earlier, two men had claimed they had a frozen Bigfoot body in a freezer and would only release it to the official organization searching for Bigfoot, called Searching For Bigfoot Inc. SFBI paid up. When they thawed the block of ice, they found a hollow head, human hair and rubber feet. Suspecting a hoax they cancelled their cheque, but it was too late. My favourite Bigfoot story is the 1958 one where a bulldozer crew working in a remote area in the hills found some massive footprints like those of an oversized ape. They took a cast and sold it to a newspaper. The bulldozer driver was a Mr Wallace. After Mr Wallace's death some years later, his children found in his attic a pair of 41-centimetre wooden feet on sticks covered in dried mud. I had to have a Bigfoot fridge magnet.

At Smith River the 101 hit the coast, where it would stay right up into the guts of Oregon. We crossed the state line at Brookings, and got off the bikes at Gold Beach, finding a Motel 6 for $46 a night and a foot-long sub for only $5. This was no place for camping. After dark, you needed to be inside behind a locked door, TV turned up loud, and the bike chained to a fence railing outside. First, there were the surrounding trees cloaked in mystery and supernaturalness. Then there were those enormous footprints I saw as we parked the bikes. Huddled in my motel room, I sifted through the day's fridge-magnet purchases. I looked at the Paul Bunyan magnet. That was strange. How mysterious. Babe the Ox's head was missing.

Chapter 41

Oregon–Washington

Nicknames: The Beaver State–The Evergreen State

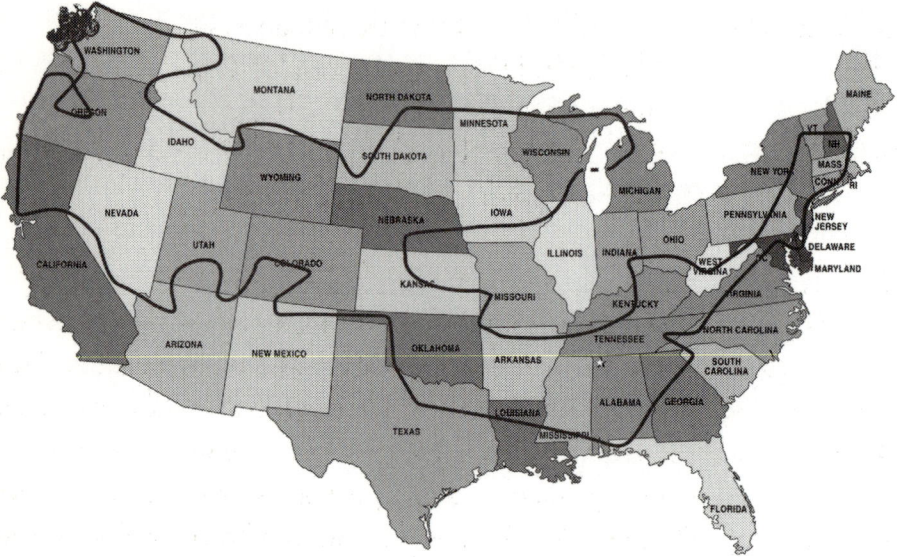

These states: 2,216 kilometres. Journey to date: 32,249 kilometres.

IT WAS A STRANGE FEELING riding out of Gold Beach back onto the 101 north. Oregon was my 50th and final state. To get back to Vancouver I had to cross Washington again, but that was already ticked off the list as state #3. The finishing line was 2,000 kilometres away, but it seemed like I was just hopping on the bike for a ride to the shops for a pint of milk. This was the first time I'd the sensation of wanting to just carry on around for a second lap. It wasn't to be the last.

Sea Lion man:	That'll be $10. That includes entry to the Sea Lion Cave, and a guided tour.
Me:	Can we just go down to the lookout on the cliff without going into the cave or taking the tour?
Sea Lion man:	Yes.

Me:	How much then?
Sea Lion man:	$10.
Me:	Is the cave worth it?
Sea Lion man:	Yes, it is. It is the world's largest sea cave and is normally full of sea lions.
Me:	Normally?
Sea Lion man:	Yes. All the sea lions are out at sea right now.
Me:	And it's still the full price of $10? To see a sea lion cave minus actual sea lions?
Sea Lion man:	You think that's a tourist rip-off? You should go to my other business The Trees of Mystery.

This exchange took place at a cliff-top visitor centre signposted as The World's Largest Sea Cave, near the town of Florence on the spectacular Oregon Coast. We wanted to get a photo of the nearby Heceta Head Lighthouse, but baulked at paying the $10 to get to the lookout when for the same price you could take a guided tour of an empty sea lion cave. I bought a sea-lion fridge magnet and a postcard of the lighthouse from their gift shop. They cost $9.65. That'll be the day Twisting Throttle gets scammed like some deadhead tourist.

The 101 ploughed northwards along the coast. On our right was Siuslaw National Forest; on our left, waves crashing on the rocky shore. At Newport we met up with Terry Boehm, another Oregonian who needed little excuse for a ride on his Harley. And that day's excuse was to escort Blane, who was escorting me, to their hometown of Salem. It was a wonderful ride, as Highway 20 — sorry, 'the 20' — twisted its way through beautiful meadows and gentle, wooded hills away from the coast. That night we enjoyed a barbecue at the home of Terry and his wife, Linda. They, together with daughter Courtney and her husband Evan, made me very welcome, and in return I paid them the ultimate courtesy of leaving my boots outside without being asked. Several streets away, in fact. It had been a long trip and my clothing was, in general, at the end of its useful sanitary life. I wondered if there would be any value on eBay and scoured my bug-covered jacket for any sign of the Virgin Mary.

✪

Over the next two days, I rode with Blane on a loop through central Oregon which saw us cross the lower Cascades, the Deschutes National Forest, across what is known as the Oregon Outback, partially circumnavigate Crater Lake, the deepest lake in America, and return to Eugene, with the smoke from nearby forest fires creating a haze that at times turned the sky a shade of ochre I'd never seen before.

My last night camping was at Odell Lake, an idyllic spot that we had to ourselves. As the sun set blood-red in the forest-fire haze, at the far end of the still lake I reflected, in a rare moment of nostalgia, how this would be the last time I clipped together my tent poles, rolled out my sleeping bag, pegged out my tent fly, and wished my bike a safe night. It is therefore fitting that I acknowledge, in this the final chapter of my book, the role that my B-team support gear played. As I flip back through the pages of the book, I see that the primary support team — namely: bike, helmet and GPS — gets most of the limelight. But the unsung heroes of the Twisting Throttle expedition have to be the B-team gear. Please stand as you continue reading, or if you can't do that at least place a closed fist across your heart and join with me to the tune of 'Now is the Hour':

> *New was the gear, when we rode 'round Hawaii*
> *Soon you'll be sailing, far across the sea*
> *Your job is now done, it's time to set you free*
> *Aussie, now America, you've earned yourselves a beer.*
>
> *Nigh is the hour, for tent, poles, pegs and fly*
> *Day in, day out, pack up, pack down; in wind and dirt and rain*
> *All them nights of camping, not once did you complain*
> *Thank you, boys, I'll clean you good; as befits top gear.*
>
> *Near is the hour, when we must say goodbye*
> *Tank, chain and sprockets; tyres, clutch and screen*

290

Thanks to you all, what great support you've been
When you get through Customs, you'll find me waiting here.

My last night in Oregon was spent at the home of Scott and Madelyn Russell, and son Kendrick, owners of the BMW dealerships in Eugene and Tigard, Portland. In Eugene, I spent the afternoon in a whirlwind of admin. I found a car-wash where you could pour quarters into a water-blasting machine, and for half an hour I drenched the bike, cleaning off two months of bugs, grime and dust. Out from the nooks and crannies sluiced grasshoppers from South Dakota, wasps from Michigan, and dried mud from the bike's lie-down in Connecticut. I emptied two cans of engine degreaser all over the motor. I'd forgotten how shiny the cylinder heads could be with the proper care and attention. At a suburban laundrette, I chose the largest washing machine on offer, and sat in shorts and T-shirt reading a celebrity gossip magazine while my tent, fly, clothes and helmet pads turned the water grey.

I rode out of Eugene towards Portland on a misty, dull morning, my penultimate day of the American ride. Blane was leaving me in Cascade Locks, a bridge away from Washington. I'd enjoyed his company. We had a farewell meal at McDonald's in Troutdale, and once again I had a lump in my throat. This time it was the Sausage McGriddle, not nostalgia. I'm not that sentimental. We rode along the Columbia Gorge Historic Highway, high up on an escarpment looking down on the wide Columbia River. I waved to Blane as he carried on to Hood River, while I paid the $2 toll and crossed the Bridge of the Gods spanning the Columbia. I entered Washington.

Within 10 minutes, I felt like the only human on earth. The road curved up into dense forest, where there was nothing to suggest any sort of human civilization. These were the lower slopes of Mt St Helens. Had I been riding here in May 1980, I wouldn't have even been human, full-stop. This was when Mt St Helens erupted in the deadliest volcanic explosion in America's recorded history. 600 square kilometres of forest were mown down, and 57 people were killed or just never found. A volcanologist who was stationed on a ridge monitoring the mountain saw the hot ash cloud coming and uttered his famous last words into his radio: 'Vancouver. Vancouver. This is it!' Now, virtually 30 years later, I saw signs of the eruption in parts of the forest where petrified tree trunks were lying on the ground.

I reached Randle, a small settlement at the junction of Route 12. As I crossed the bridge into town, a helmeted motorcyclist ran out into the road and snapped off a picture. This was Keith Evans, and I was expecting him. Remember my escorts out of Vancouver back in Chapter 3? Keith and Pat had ridden 400 kilometres to meet me here at Randle and escort me on the last hurrah back to the finishing line the next day. It was great to see them. As we celebrated the rendezvous in a diner, Keith asked, 'So what've you been doing since we last saw you?' I told him I'd spent the past two months since Kettle Falls trying to work out the punch line of his John Wayne toilet-paper joke.

And then commenced one of the most stunning pieces of riding on the whole trip: a loop through Mt Rainier National Park. To try to capture in print the magnificence of the scenery on this tortuously-winding route up and down the slopes of Mt Rainier, the highest mountain in Washington, is impossible. There is an area with a visitor centre at the top of the road called Paradise, and it has been classed as the snowiest place on earth. Mt Rainier is a strato-volcano. That's a volcano that actually looks like a volcano should look: namely, like Mt Fuji — conical, snow-topped, and looking like it will blow any second. I lost count of the number of times I pulled over to click off photos. In the background was the majestic Mt Rainier. In the foreground were bright green alpine meadows ablaze with wildflowers, twinkling mountain streams and grazing deer. No wonder they named it Paradise.

After an overnight stop in Shelton, at the base of the Olympic Peninsula, we rode in a light but cold rain shower up the 101 alongside the Hood Canal to avoid having to negotiate Seattle. At Port Townsend we caught the car ferry over to Whidbey Island, and by now I had the tingling feeling that the end was in sight. At Bellingham, I got out my passport and carnet in anticipation of the border crossing up ahead into Canada. In theory it would be a straightforward exit from the US. It wasn't. Here's what happened.

The main US–Canada border crossing is at Peace Arch at Blaine, Washington. Remember I had my bike's carnet stamped into the US by Officer Cooper when I crossed two months before at Midway? That meant I was forced to, here at Peace Arch, get US Customs to stamp it out. Keith and Pat, who live 5 kilometres over the border, said they'd meet me at home and would put the jug on. They rode into the border post, flicked the guard a fiver and were through.

I parked the bike in no-man's land and walked into the US Customs building. I queued up inside along with a ragtag mob of applicants who were trying to get visas into — or perhaps out of — the US. I was waved up to the counter. 'Yeah?' 'I need my carnet stamped out of the US.' 'Why?' 'Because I'm riding into Canada on my bike.' 'You mean you're exporting your motorcycle to Canada?' 'Yes, I suppose so.' 'Then you're in the wrong place. You need to be at Truck Crossing. Go back half a mile and take D Street to the 543. Next.' I returned to the bike and rode back the way I'd come, but technically I had to re-enter the US out of no man's land. A border guard stopped me. 'Passport.' 'OK, I've just been in to see Customs to get my carnet stamped. I have to go to Truck Crossing.' 'Why?' 'The guy inside told me that's where they do the carnets.' 'Where are you coming from in Canada and what's the purpose of your visit to the US?' 'I haven't come from Canada. I've just ridden here from the US around the other side of this building. I'm trying to get *into* Canada.' 'Then why are you entering the US?' 'Like I say, I haven't actually been in Canada.' I pointed through the window into the Customs office. 'See that officer in there. Mr Rodriguez. He's directed me to Truck Crossing.' The cars were building up behind me. 'OK, off you go.'

I rode back into the US and found my way over to Truck Crossing, which appeared to be a border crossing point devoted to big rigs. I rode down an entrance ramp and had no idea whatsoever where to go. There were buildings everywhere, and I just idled around looking for some sort of sign that might help. Two border guards, who were inspecting a truck, looked up at the sound of the bike and didn't appear to like what they saw. 'Over here.' I rode over. 'What are you doing here?' 'I was over at Peace Arch trying to get my bike's carnet stamped out. They told me to come to Truck Crossing.' 'This is Truck Crossing.' 'Yes, I know. But where's the office for carnets?' 'Right here. But it's closed. Closes at 3.00 p.m. Come back at 8.30 a.m. tomorrow morning.' 'You sure there's nowhere else that can do carnets?' It seemed odd that a Customs office would close so early. 'What's a carnet? Who are you anyway? What's the purpose of your visit to the US?' I felt the atmosphere ratchet up a notch. 'I'm riding back to Canada. I've got a carnet for the bike, that's like a vehicle passport. It has to be stamped as evidence of exiting the US.' 'So you're exporting a vehicle? That process takes three days and you can't leave the US in the interim.' 'No, it's just a stamp. It took three minutes coming in, and all I'm doing is leaving.' 'Understand me, sir. Exporting a vehicle takes three days. This is the office here. It opens at 8.30 a.m. You cannot leave the US until you have the correct documentation. Show me your passport.' I handed it over together with the carnet. 'What's this?' 'It's the carnet.' 'You don't need this.' 'Yes, I do. If it's stamped *into* a country, it has to be stamped *out*. Otherwise the bike hasn't officially left the US, and it will cause problems on the Canadian side who'll probably send me back here.' 'Just park your bike over there and bring all your papers with you.' This was spiralling downwards fast. The two guards were distracted by the driver of the truck coming back. I rode over to where they indicated, but just carried on out of the car park and back up the entry ramp onto D Street.

I found a gas station and fuelled up, thinking hard about my situation. I had a cup of tea in Canada getting cold. I nosed back to the top of the sloping ramp that was three lanes wide. An 18-wheeler turned onto the ramp. I slowly rode down the ramp in the shadow of the truck, positioning the bike as close to the double-axled wheels as possible, on the side away from the border guards. Like a sucker fish I stuck to the truck as it cruised through the US border post, into no-man's land and stopped 500 metres further on at the Canadian border kiosk. I quickly peeled off and parked up at the Canadian Customs building all the time looking over my shoulder.

The vexatious question was all about the absence of a US exit stamp in my carnet. I delved into my tool kit and got out a screwdriver. I levered up the staples on the carnet and ripped out the US page. I carefully re-inserted the staples and folded them down with the screwdriver. A perfect piece of forgery. 'Hello, sir. What's your business today?' The Canadian Customs officer was a friendly guy. 'I'm entering Canada and this is the carnet for my bike. I need to have it stamped in.' He leafed through it. 'That's good you didn't get it stamped into the US. They can be sons of bitches about exports on these things,' he said sympathetically as he stamped my carnet. I have never heard a sweeter sound than that rubbery thud. 'You have a good day, sir. Welcome to BC and safe riding.' Had he asked me to quickly polish the boots of his staff, I would have gladly obliged.

And so it was with sweaty palms and several years added to my life that I crossed the finishing line. I was back in British Columbia. Just over 32,000 kilometres through all 50 states, a few more than once. I'd left from this point an American novice and returned a pro — specifically, a diner pro, a bridge pro, a motel-negotiating pro, a camping pro, a toll-plaza pro, a waving pro and, just lately, a border-crossing pro. I parked by the *Welcome to BC* sign and took some photos, arms raised in a mixture of triumph and relief that it had all been trouble-free. Several passing trucks tooted as they observed the odd sight of this self-congratulation. I basked in their acknowledgement and thought about the ride. The distance hardly registered. In fact had I ridden on for another 10 days it would have equated to circumnavigating the Earth around the equator as the crow flies. It just didn't seem that far.

I liked America and had only scratched the surface of this huge and diverse place. You could spend years on a motorcycle, never cover the same route, and still not come close to seeing it all. But, just like finishing the lap of Australia, my thoughts instantly turned to 'What's next?' As this midlife crisis shows no sign of abating, I'm working my way through the alphabet of continents. Both Australia and America start with 'A' and end with 'A'. As for the other 'A's? I don't want to ride around Africa, as my cooling fan might play up again. I don't want to ride around Asia, as I don't like rice. Antarctica, well it's not overly suited to camping. It was time to move on to 'E'. But standing there on the side of the road, I couldn't think of any continent or collection of countries in the world that started with 'E' and ended with 'E'. If you think of one and can guarantee it has driving on the right, bottomless coffee in their diners, seamless border crossings, and people who don't start their sentences with 'y'all', I'd be interested. In the meantime I have to get the bike crated and on the ship bound for New Zealand. I have a loving family back home who are waiting for their fridge magnets.

See y'all.

Acknowledgements

I may have been on the bike alone, but there were plenty of supporters who will hopefully help me again next time if I mention their names in print. I couldn't have done this ride, or produced this book, without them. These are who they are.

Corporate sponsors who provided me with bike, support 4WD vehicle, spare parts, tools, hotel accommodation, a film crew, a doctor, a fixer, global DVD rights, and swags of cash are listed below:

1.
2.
3.
4.
5.
6.

That's right, there weren't any. Fine then, you missed out on a unique global marketing opportunity this time, but I'm still prepared to prostitute my helmet and fuel-tank advertising space in return for lots of euros on the next trip.

My technical and mechanical support people at Twisting Throttle HQ. He's called Gavin Sargent, and I renewed his contract after Australia. What little he doesn't know about bikes he will make up, and I have no option but to believe him like Grasshopper. He rides a KTM LC8, is undisputed leader of the Dust Devils, and we're all waiting for him, digital cameras at the ready, to fall off crossing a ford. After some unflattering comments I made about him in *Twisting Throttle Australia*, he told me by email when I was in Alaska that he'd installed a radio-activated kill switch on my bike that would cut out the engine whenever he felt like it. Twice when I stalled the bike on mountain passes in the Rockies I almost rang him to say sorry and could he turn it on again. That's how much I depend on his technical expertise. For the record, I have yet to encounter a more skilled motorcycle rider, on-road *and* off-road.

The Dust Devils motorcycle club threw an American-themed farewell party at which Red Leader and Dusty organized a local constable to burst in and take me away handcuffed and in an orange Guantanamo Bay jumpsuit. Thanks, team, you're right: it *was* good practice for border crossings. The Devils and Devilettes were at the airport at both ends of my trip. To be a Dust Devil you have to be over 40, ride an adventure bike, have prostate trouble, and get a knee, shoulder or hip operation at least annually.

In Vancouver, I had the invaluable ground support of Keith and Pat Evans, friends who paved the way with the freight company and acted as crate transporters and hosts at the start and finish. I enjoyed their company immensely, including that of their delightful granddaughter Ally of White Rock, but felt I put a lot back into the relationship by pretending to understand Keith's jokes. They ride BMWs, but I still like them a lot.

I enjoyed the riding company of several Yankee bikers who didn't appear to need any excuse to saddle up and tuck in behind me, giving me both the lead and company for the day or days. Blane Howell and Terry Boehm in Oregon, Curtis Crowdson in Idaho, Scott Sibbald in California, Heath Herber in Colorado, Rikki Homchick in Alaska, Marque Nelson in Arizona, and Keith and Pat Evans in Washington.

Back home I enjoyed the moral support from friends and family. The staff at the Antarctic Centre in Christchurch where I work; in particular, Denise, Gill, Nana Bev, and of course Tim who once again provided me with an MP3 player full of songs. Employers, but more so friends, Richard and Tina Benton paid for a night of my choosing in a swanky motel and lent me a laptop. Richard rides a Harley, but in all other respects he's a great guy and a close mate.

At HarperCollins the editorial team there, Lorain, Kate and Tracey, continue to proof my work in their very professional manner, although I felt they went a little overboard spell-checking the shipping label on the side of the bike crate. Kate Stone, motorcycle chick wannabe, is my actual editor. After *Twisting Throttle Australia*, she wouldn't let me forget the whole N-is-for-nectarine debacle. I asked for a new editor. They said N-is-also-for-no.

But the real support behind my perpetual midlife crisis on two wheels is my family in Christchurch.

My son, Robert, created the maps in this book, designed and applied the graphics to the bike, and made me a Twisting Throttle logo complete with number-plate surround, T-shirts and branded panniers. I felt like Ewan McGregor. Together we enjoy nothing more than a boys' outing on our dirt bikes in the back-country of New Zealand's South Island. His lovely partner, Elyse, just rolls her eyes and refuses to have his boots in the house. That's my son. Learning his father's ways. My dream trip would be to return to the US with Robert and ride/camp the forest trails in Montana and Idaho on a couple of 650s. Look out for my next book: *Twisting Throttle & Son*.

My daughter, Sophie, opened the door when I called in on her in Las Vegas. Most daughters would have thrown their arms around the father they hadn't seen for two months. Sophie screamed and covered her mouth when she saw what I looked like after six weeks on the road. Still, she spent the day on the back of the bike as we toured the desert around Las Vegas. It was one of the best days of the trip. One day, Sophie will be the general manager of a six-star international hotel somewhere in the world. That's where her career is heading, and we are as proud of her achievements as parents can be. I may just follow her around and crate the bike from country to country.

But the real star in my life is my lovely wife, Sandy. I wrote in my last book that she revelled in the swag of fridge magnets I came back from Australia with . . . or that was the impression I had on the way back from the airport. This time, I returned with a Mike The Headless Chicken T-shirt, a loyalty card from Denny's, and 114 fridge magnets from America, expecting these to similarly buy me permission for another trip in two years' time. I seem to have pushed my luck too far. Sandy is an exceptional person and I am very lucky to have her support for my long-distance riding. But the magnets are on the door of the beer fridge out in the garage and we're going to salsa classes.

Finally, my grateful thanks to you, the reader, for actually buying my book. If you borrowed this book from a library: *how could you?* Many of you will be repeat Twisting Throttle followers who emailed me as you followed my website. Let me tell you that I thoroughly appreciated those messages, more so than you might have thought, and I'm sorry you only got one-liners in reply. It was all I could do to tap out quick misspelt lines of text in often non-existent light in my tent. I receive a royalty for every book sold, and I have an overdraft that thanks you. Even a budget trip rips a hole in your finances. Your kind purchase of this — and, if you truly have a heart, *Twisting Throttle Australia* — goes a long way to helping the ignition key turn on future rides.

Best wishes to you all—

Mike Hyde
www.twistingthrottle.com

Logistics

This appendix is for fellow motorcycle tourers who, after I wrote *Twisting Throttle Australia*, said they'd like some 'how I did it' information often referred to in corporate-speak as 'house-keeping'. Go on then: bleed me dry. Here goes.

Amounts quoted below are NZ dollars.

Shipping the Bike

I used a Christchurch-based company called SB Global Logistics (www. sbinfo.co.nz). I sourced a giveaway steel-based cardboard-covered Harley crate from a dealer, made some bracing, and the freight company did the rest. In the crate was the bike, all of the camping gear, the panniers and the top box, filled with everything I didn't need on the flight — tools, riding gear, and heavily-padded electronics, such as laptop, GPS, SPOT and camera. I drained the bike of fuel, isolated the battery terminals, cleaned it to within an inch of its life, and took off the mirrors, screen, hand-guards and indicators. The bike went by sea. I was without it for six weeks before I left Christchurch, and it took six weeks to get the bike back. Mysteriously, the clutch and brake levers were broken off. Otherwise the condition was fine. SB Global used a Vancouver freight-forwarder agent, who in turn used a local freight yard where I collected the bike from. Had I wanted to store the crate at this freight yard for 60 days, it would have cost $200. Having a contact person who lives in the start/finish city is invaluable. It means you can pack in and out in comfort, rather than among forklifts in a freight yard. The total cost of shipping — including all fees, freight, transit insurance and carnet — was $4,600.

Bike Set-up

Here are the non-standard features of my bike set up for long-distance touring:

- reinforced steel bash plate
- oil cooler protector

- radiator guard
- Givi crash bars
- MRA Vario-Touring tinted windscreen
- Oxford heated grips
- Baehr Verso comms unit hard-wired under seat, managing audio outputs for radar detector (not taken to US), GPS, music and navigational instructions
- handlebar-mounted, hard-wired Garmin Zumo 550 GPS, incorporating MP3 player, with City Navigator North America mapping software
- handlebar-mounted SPOT tracking unit
- Scottoiler chain lubrication with long-distance sleeve reservoir
- digital camera battery-charger mounted on shelf under screen, powered by accessory socket
- Olympus SP570US 10-megapixel camera with 12-second shutter delay (all images in this book were taken on my own, using this camera: many were multi-attempts — I have thousands of 'out-takes') in a bag cable-tied on a shelf under screen
- additional power socket installed in rear fairing for laptop charging
- my preferred tyres are Continental TrailAttacks

Gear

After Australia, where I over-packed and ended up sending silly things home in Darwin, America was load-minimalist.

Left pannier
- Dell Inspiron laptop used for photo storage, Wi-Fi for website maintenance, mapping software with related GPS uploading, email, internet browsing for weather, accommodation and ferry bookings on the run, etc
- associated chargers, optical mouse, and USB cables
- portable hard-disk drive for backup
- road atlas
- spare oil for Scottoiler
- fridge magnets
- first-aid kit

Right pannier
- two T-shirts, two pairs of undies, two pairs of riding sox, Draggin Traffic jeans, pair of sneakers, hot-weather gloves, toiletry kit, quick-dry towel which doubled as a rag

Top box
- puncture-plugging and tube-installing tools, sufficient to repair roadside punctures, including wheel removal and breaking beads, on both wheels
- spare indicator assembly, spare bulbs, fuses, oil filter, air filter, front sprocket, cable ties
- basic toolkit sufficient for effecting minor 'easy' repairs roadside
- bike lock
- tripod

Tank bag
- credit card and cash in travel wallet
- sunglasses
- cellphone, that ended up being useless thanks to lack of Telecom roaming

Strapped to back seat
- Mutha Hubba three-man tent
- army camp stretcher
- roll bag, containing sleeping bag, travel pillow, tent footprint sheet

Hidden inside fairing (in case of luggage loss)
- US$1,000 cash

Riding Gear
- Olympia AST padded jacket with detachable inner jacket liner
- Spool padded riding trousers with detachable liners
- Caberg Justissimo two-visor helmet
- BMW boots
- Orina Gore-Tex padded gloves

- scanned copies of passport and driver license
- spare bike keys
- spare credit card

Servicing
Milwaukee @ 11,000 km, $850
- Tyres, oil change, oil filter, lube pivot points, check cush drive, bearings and brake pads, install toggle switch for cooling fan, adjust throttle cable

Dallas @ 12,000km, $2,200
- Tyres, oil change, oil filter, air filter, chain, sprockets, brake pads, spark plugs, lube pivot points, check cush drive, bearings and brake pads, adjust throttle cable

Finances
- My daily running costs were budgeted at $160 per day, broken down as $60 fuel, $40 accommodation, $30 food, $30 other bits, including park entry fees, magnets and ferries
- Here is a summary of trip costs:
  - Bike shipping $4,600
  - Bike rental, Hawaii $350
  - Bike rental, Alaska $700
  - Flights $4,200
  - SPOT subscription $200
  - Bike insurance $950
  - Personal insurance $450
  - Fuel 1,900 litres @ $2 ave/litre $3,800
  - Motels and camping fees $2,600
  - Food $1,800
  - Ferries, park fees, magnets, misc $1,500
  - Cooling fan $800
  - Services $3,050
  - **TOTAL TRIP COST**   **$25,000**